UNKN?WN
MARKET
WIZARDS

UNKN?WN MARKET WIZARDS

The best traders you've never heard of

JACK D. SCHWAGER

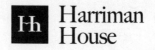

HARRIMAN HOUSE LTD
3 Viceroy Court
Bedford Road
Petersfield
Hampshire
GU32 3LJ
GREAT BRITAIN
Tel: +44 (0)1730 233870

Email: enquiries@harriman-house.com
Website: harriman-house

First published in 2020.
Copyright © Jack D. Schwager

Hardback ISBN: 978-0-85719-869-3
eBook ISBN: 978-0-85719-870-9

British Library Cataloguing in Publication Data
A CIP catalogue record for this book can be obtained from the British Library.

Printed in Canada.

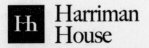

To Aspen

The Next Generation

*May you have the charm, beauty,
and sense of humor of both your parents
and the spending sense of neither.*

⚡

There is no such thing as being right or beating the market. If you make money, it is because you understood the same thing as the market did. If you lose money, it is simply because you got it wrong. There is no other way of looking at it.

—Musawer Mansoor Ijaz

⚡

Every decade has its characteristic folly, but the basic cause is the same: people persist in believing that what has happened in the recent past will go on happening into the indefinite future, even while the ground is shifting under their feet.

—George J. Church

⚡

We have two classes of forecasters: those who don't know— and those who don't know that they don't know.

—John Kenneth Galbraith

CONTENTS

PREFACE

THE premise I had when I set out to write *Unknown Market Wizards* was that there were solo traders, operating in complete obscurity, who were achieving performance results that far surpassed the vast majority of professional asset managers. I found these traders and proved my premise. But I also found something else that amazed me.

I never thought I would again find traders whose records matched those of some of the traders in the first *Market Wizards* book. I assumed the extraordinary performance achieved by some of those traders, while a testament to their exceptional trading skill, was partially made possible by the unique markets of the inflationary 1970s. Moreover, the ensuing decades witnessed enormous growth in the application of quantitative power to trading and investing, with professional managers accounting for an ever-increasing percentage of all trading—trends that suggested it would be far more difficult for traders to excel by wide margins in today's markets.

To my great surprise, some of the traders I found in writing *Unknown Market Wizards* may well have the best performance records I have ever encountered.

The opening sentence of the preface to the first *Market Wizards* book, written over 30 years ago—"There are some amazing stories here"—seems entirely appropriate to this volume as well. Here are the remarkable traders you will meet in *Unknown Market Wizards*:

⚡ A college graduate who started with a $2,500 account and in the course of the next 17 years pulled $50 million of profits out of the market.

⚡ An ex-advertising executive who in a 27-year career as a futures trader achieved an average annual return of 58%.

⚡ A stock trader who developed a unique trading approach that utilizes neither fundamental nor technical analysis and turned his original $83,000 stake into $21 million.

⚡ A futures trader who over a 13-year career has averaged 337% per year without any drawdowns exceeding 10% after his first trading year.

⚡ A bellhop in the Czech Republic whose day trading strategy for buying stocks has provided return/risk performance that far surpassed over 99% of both long-only funds and hedge funds.

⚡ A futures trader who made and lost over one-half million dollars twice before developing a contrarian methodology that led to a 20-year career of consistent trading success.

⚡ A former US marine who designed proprietary software to automatically trade market events and has a 10-year record of outstanding return/risk performance.

⚡ A futures trader who has averaged a return of 280% per year with an end-of-month maximum drawdown of only 11%.

⚡ A music major who used his self-taught programming skills to design stock trading systems that delivered an average return of 20% during the past 20 years, well over triple the S&P 500 return during the same period.

⚡ A one-time professional tennis aspirant who achieved a remarkable average annual return of 298% over a near-decade as a futures trader.

⚡ An equity trader who by combining long investment positions with short-term event trading has tripled the S&P 500 performance in both return and return/risk terms.

If you are expecting to find step-by-step instructions on how to make 100% a year in the markets with only two hours of work a week, quick, put this book down—you've got the wrong book!

If, however, you are looking to learn from some of the world's best traders— how they think about markets; what they have learned about trading; how they have improved; what mistakes they have learned to avoid; what advice they have for other traders—you will find much here that is instructive.

ACKNOWLEDGMENTS

The first step in writing a *Market Wizards* book is identifying exceptional traders. In this regard, two individuals were extremely helpful. Steve Goldstein, Managing Director of Alpha R Cubed, a London-based coaching firm, was the source for two of the traders included in this book and several others who might appear in a follow-up volume (if there is one). Mark Ritchie, an excellent trader in his own right, recommended two other of the included traders. Ironically, I had intended to interview Mark himself, but the text I completed reached book-length before I scheduled the trip. Perhaps he will appear in a future volume. Posthumous thanks go to Bill Dodge, who brought Jason Shapiro to my attention.

FundSeeder.com (a website created by FundSeeder Technologies, a company I am affiliated with) was the source of three of the traders in this volume. I also used FundSeeder.com analytics to calculate all the performance statistics referenced in this book.

I am grateful to my wife, Jo Ann, who, as in all previous *Market Wizards* books, provided an invaluable sounding board and offered constructive criticism where appropriate—advice that I always followed.

Of course, there would be no book without the willingness of the traders interviewed to participate and openly share their experience, wisdom, and insights. They provided me with great material to work with.

Acknowledgments

Thanks to Marc Niaufre, who proofed all the chapters and managed to find typos that had eluded me despite multiple readings.

Finally, I would like to thank my editor at Harriman House, Craig Pearce, who made the final step of bringing my manuscript into polished form a pleasure rather than a chore. He struck the perfect balance between offering revisions that improved the text and avoiding unnecessary changes.

PART I

FUTURES
TRADERS

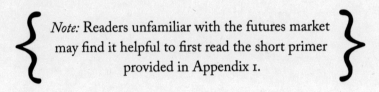

Note: Readers unfamiliar with the futures market may find it helpful to first read the short primer provided in Appendix 1.

PETER BRANDT

Strong Opinions, Weakly Held

I T is remarkable how many of the Market Wizards that I have interviewed failed in their initial trading endeavor—some multiple times. In this respect, Peter Brandt fits the bill. What is unusual about Brandt, though, is that after well over a decade of spectacular success following his initial failed attempts, he lost his edge, went cold turkey on trading for 11 years, and then resumed trading for a second lengthy span of outstanding performance.

Brandt is definitely old school. His trading is based on classical chart analysis that traces its origins to Richard Schabacker's book, *Technical Analysis and Stock Market Profits*, published in 1932, and later popularized by Edwards and Magee's, *Technical Analysis of Stock Trends*, published in 1948.

He started his financial career as a commodities broker in the early 1970s, just when spiking inflation and soaring commodity prices transformed commodities from a financial backwater to the hot new market. Back then, the futures markets were called *commodities* because all the futures markets were indeed just commodities. This period was the threshold of the introduction of financial futures in currencies, interest rates, and stock indexes, which would become the dominant futures markets, making commodities a misnomer for this market sector. Brandt started his trading career in the commodity trading pits in the quaint old days when futures market transactions were executed in the bedlam of a ring of screaming brokers, in stark contrast to the quiet efficiency of current-day electronic trading.

Brandt's trading career encompasses 27 years—an initial 14-year span and the current ongoing 13-year span—with the two trading segments separated by an 11-year hiatus. The reasons for this lengthy interruption in his trading career are discussed in the interview. Brandt does not have his performance records prior to late 1981. Over the entire 27 years he traded since then, Brandt achieved an impressive average annual compounded return of 58%. Brandt, though, is quick to explain that this return is inflated because he traded his account very aggressively—a point borne out by his very high average annualized volatility (53%).

Brandt provides the perfect example of a trader for whom the ubiquitous Sharpe ratio greatly understates the quality of the performance. One major flaw inherent in the Sharpe ratio is that the risk component of the measure (volatility) does not distinguish between upside and downside volatility. In regards to the risk measure, large gains are viewed as equally bad as large losses, a characteristic that completely contradicts most people's intuitive notion of risk. A trader such as Brandt, who experiences sporadic large gains, is penalized by the Sharpe ratio, even though his losses are well contained.

The *adjusted* Sortino ratio is an alternative return/risk metric that utilizes losses instead of volatility as the risk measure, thereby eliminating penalization for large gains. The adjusted Sortino ratio is directly comparable to the Sharpe ratio (the same is not true for the conventionally calculated Sortino ratio).* A higher adjusted Sortino ratio (as compared with the Sharpe ratio) implies that the distribution of returns is *positively skewed* (a greater tendency for large gains than large losses). And, similarly, a lower adjusted Sortino ratio implies returns are *negatively skewed* (a greater propensity for large losses than large gains). For most traders, the

---

* See Appendix 2, Performance Metrics, for an explanation of the adjusted Sortino ratio and how it differs from the conventionally calculated Sortino ratio.

Sharpe ratio and the adjusted Sortino ratio will be roughly in the same general vicinity. In Brandt's case, however, because his largest gains are much greater than his largest losses, his adjusted Sortino ratio (3.00) is nearly triple his Sharpe ratio (1.11)! As another reflection of the strength of Brandt's return/risk performance, his monthly Gain to Pain ratio* is very high at 2.81—a particularly impressive level in light of the length of his track record.

Brandt is the one trader in this book for whom the title adjective "unknown" is not entirely apropos. Although through the vast majority of his career he was indeed unknown, and he is still not widely known in the broader financial community, in recent years, through his *Factor* market letter and a rapidly growing Twitter following, he has gained recognition and respect from a segment of the trader community. Indeed, several of the traders I interviewed for this book cited Brandt as an important influence. But I had strong motivations for including Brandt in this book that overrode my preference for maintaining the purity of the title.

In a way, Brandt was the catalyst for moving me from writing this book "someday" to beginning the preliminary steps for the project. I knew that if I wrote another *Market Wizards* book, I wanted Brandt to be in it. Brandt and I are friends. I was familiar with his views about trading, which I thought were spot on, and I felt I would always regret it if I failed to capture his perspective in a book. At the time, Brandt lived in Colorado Springs and mentioned to me that he was moving to Arizona in a few months. Since I lived only about 100 miles away in Boulder, Colorado, I thought it would be more efficient to interview him before he moved and that doing so would provide the ancillary benefit of getting the book started. Ironically, by the time I got around to scheduling the interview, Brandt had already moved to Tucson.

When I arrived at the airport, Brandt was waiting for me at the bottom of the exit escalator. I was glad to see him again. Although it had only been a little over a year since we last met, his walking posture had noticeably changed, with his back bent slightly forward. Thirty-five years earlier,

---

* See Appendix 2 for an explanation of this performance metric.

Brandt suffered a terrible accident. He had gotten up in the middle of the night to go to the bathroom. He recalls wondering in annoyance, "Who left this chair in the middle of the hall?" Brandt was sleepwalking. The "chair" was actually the railing of the upper deck. He clambered past the obstacle, and the next thing he knew, he was flat on his back, unable to move. Brandt had fallen nearly twenty feet. He suddenly realized what had happened. So did his wife, Mona, who, upon hearing the crash of the fall, immediately dialed 911.

Brandt spent over 40 days in the hospital, wearing a body cast and sandwiched between two mattresses that could be rotated regularly to change his position. Since the accident, Brandt has had a half-dozen surgeries on his back, and now with age, his back is visibly bothering him more. He lives with constant pain—something I know only because I have asked him about it. He is a bit of a stoic and never complains about the pain, nor does he take any pain medication because he doesn't like how it makes him feel.

Brandt drove me to his home, which is situated in a gated community on the outskirts of Tucson. We conducted the interview sitting in Brandt's backyard patio overlooking the Sonora desert, which is surprisingly verdant, having more plant species than any other desert in the world, some of which grow nowhere else, such as the iconic saguaro cactus. A double-peaked mountain loomed over the distant horizon. It was a beautiful spring day. The steady breeze generated a constant clattering of wind chimes. "Are those going to be a problem for your recorder?" Brandt asked. "No, it will be fine," I assured him. Little did I think about the many hours I would spend playing and replaying the recordings having to listen to those damn wind chimes.

When you were young, did you have any idea what you wanted to do with your life?

I grew up dirt poor, raised by a single mom. It was really up to me to make my own money. Even back then, I was extremely entrepreneurial. I had two large paper routes. I'd wake up 5 a.m. on Sunday to deliver 150 newspapers on my wagon or my sled if there was snow. I collected bottles. I'd hand out shopper bills for the local grocery store.

How old were you then?

Oh, I started working when I was about 10.

What was your major in college?

I majored in advertising, and I really loved it.

How did you go from advertising to trading?

Two things introduced me to the idea of trading. I had a brother who was buying bags of silver coins. Back then, in the late 1960s and early 1970s, US citizens were not allowed to own gold, but you could own silver coins. At that time, my brother was buying these bags of silver coins at a premium of 20% over face value. It was a perfect example of an asymmetric risk trade: you could lose a maximum of 20%, but if metal prices went higher, the upside was unlimited.

Did you buy silver coins yourself as well?

No, I couldn't. I had no money. But I was intrigued. I bought *The Wall Street Journal* to follow the price of silver. My brother had started buying silver coins when the price of silver was $1.50 per ounce. By 1974, the price of silver had more than tripled, soaring above $4.50. My brother was driving around in a Mercedes-Benz.

You said two things influenced you to get into trading. What was the second one?

At the time, I was living in Chicago, and I met a fellow who traded in the soybean pits. Both of our sons played hockey, and I got to know him pretty well. He said, "Peter, come on down and see what I do. I'll buy you lunch." So I met my friend for lunch at the Board of Trade. The restaurant had these huge windows overlooking the pits. As I watched the traders below, my reaction was, "Whoa!" I was fascinated. It sparked something inside of me that said, "I want to do this." I peppered my friend with questions about being a trader. I picked up all the brochures at the Board of Trade.

Were you working in advertising at the time?

I was.

Were you satisfied with your job?

I was on a fast track with the fifth largest advertising agency in the world. I had lots of responsibility, and my accounts included Campbell and McDonald's.

Were you involved in any of the commercials?

Yes, the McDonald's grab-a-bucket-and-mop commercial. You can check it out on YouTube. I also was there when they created Ronald McDonald.

So you liked what you were doing?

I liked what I was doing. The only thing I didn't like was the politics in the corporate world. Also, there was something about what the guys on the floor were doing that captivated me. I liked the idea that they knew how they did at the end of each day. And they only worked from 9:30 to 1:15! Also, part of the attraction was that I found out what these guys were making.

That's because you didn't know about the 95% plus of people who try to become traders and go broke. You had what the statisticians call a biased sample.

Oh, I found that out later. But, at the time, what I noticed was that the parking lot next to the Board of Trade was filled with Mercedes and Porsches.

Having grown up poor, was the wealth angle a significant part of your attraction to trading?

Yes, that was a big thing.

How did you go from that desire to actually getting involved in trading?

I came to the decision that I wanted to be in this business. Even then, the price of floor membership was very high. There was no way I could afford it. Around this time, my brother introduced me to the broker he was using to buy silver coins. His broker was in Minneapolis and worked for Continental Grain, which at the time was the second most prominent name on the Chicago Board of Trade, next to Cargill. My brother's broker told me Continental Grain was hiring people.

Before 1972, there was very little public speculation in the grain markets, but that changed with the big bull market in commodities during the early 1970s. Continental was the first mainline Board of Trade firm to put a major effort into bringing in hedging and speculative clients. They set up Conti Commodities as a subsidiary to do brokerage business.

Didn't you have any apprehension about taking a job as a broker, which is essentially a sales job?

No, because it was a way into the business. I was in Conti's first training program for commodity brokers. They accepted eight people into the program, which lasted three months.

Did you get any salary, or were you totally dependent on commissions?

They gave you a draw for six months. I don't remember the exact amount, but it was approximately $1,300 a month, give or take. I do remember that my salary at the advertising firm was $28,000 per year when I left. So I was definitely taking a pay cut.

Once you finished the training program and started your job as a broker, how did you get clients?

The first thing I did was to head back to New Jersey to visit Campbell and then out to Oak Brook to visit McDonald's.

Oh, because you had the connections through your advertising job.

Yes, I had the connections, and they were high-level connections. They knew me well, and it so happened that all these major food processors had not hedged during the big bull market in commodities we had just seen.

They got caught with their pants down. They were hurt real bad as all their ingredients—meats, soybean oil, sugar, cocoa, etc.—shot up, and they were unhedged. Back then, the IRS didn't even know how to handle hedging profits and losses.

This is late 1974, right after the bull markets in 1973 and 1974. I'm in the business one to two years after the start of the modern futures industry, as we know it today. The deal I offered Campbell was that if they sent out one of their purchasing agents to Chicago for two months, I would make sure he got trained in futures. The person they sent out ended up becoming the senior purchasing agent for Campbell, and I had that account. I also got the McDonald's account and some other hedgers. So I was doing pretty well for a young broker.

Were you allowed to trade your own speculative account?

Oh, totally.

So when did you start trading?

I started trading around 1976, by which time I had saved a little money. I knew that what I really wanted to do was trade.

Do you remember your first trade?

[He thinks a while and then remembers.] It was actually a little bit earlier—around late 1975. I was doing enough brokerage business so that Conti assigned me a badge so I could go down on the trading floor. My friend, John, who had gotten me interested in trading, was a soybean trader. One day I see him, and he tells me, "Peter, I'm really bullish the soybean market." So I bought a contract. I had no idea what I was doing. The market went up five or six cents and then came right down. I ended up getting out with about a 12-cent loss [a $600 loss for a one-contract position]. I remember seeing John shortly afterward, and he greets me by saying, "Wasn't that a fabulous price move!" What I subsequently found out was that for John, who traded against order flow in the pit, a 1- to 2-cent gain was a really good trade, and a six-cent gain was a "fabulous" trade. The big lesson for me was that the terms "bullish" or "bearish" don't mean anything. What is the person's time horizon? What kind of move are they looking for? What price or events would tell them that they were wrong?

Where did your trading career go from there?

I blew out three or four accounts over the next three years. The old joke was that you knew your account was in trouble when you are trading oats. [Oats are typically a low volatility market, and the contract size is small (in dollar value terms), so the margins are lower than they are for other grain markets.]

How did you make your trading decisions?

At first, I would listen to the Conti fundamental guys who'd come on the firm's speaker system every morning before the markets would open and talk about what they were seeing. They would talk about stuff like grain shipments, planting progress, and so on. They would also give their trading recommendations. The first account I blew out was following their recommendations. There was also a technical analyst in the Conti Memphis office that would come on the broadcast every morning. He used point-and-figure charting [a style of price charting where intervals depend on price moves rather than time]. He made a great call in the soybean market in 1976. So I bought a book on point-and-figure charting and started playing around with that approach. There went the second account. Then I took a fling using seasonal patterns. After that, I tried spread trading [trading the price difference between two futures contracts in the same market by buying a contract expiring in one month and selling a contract expiring in another month].

You were trying to find a methodology that worked for you.

I was trying to find something, and I was getting frustrated. But, at the same time, I consider myself lucky. I look at guys today who start trading something like crypto, max out their student loan money, and end up living in their mom's basement. I had an income source to fall back on. It wasn't killing me that I was losing. I wanted to learn how to trade and become a profitable trader.

What finally broke the cycle of opening an account, trying some different methodology, losing your money over time, stopping trading, and then repeating the process all over again?

There were probably two things that turned the process around. First, I learned that you have to use stops because you can't afford to take significant losses. Second, one day, a colleague who was a chartist came over to my desk and said, "Come with me." We went downstairs, walked across the street and into the bookstore. He bought me the Edwards and Magee book [*Technical Analysis of Stock Trends*]. I just gobbled this book up. Now, someone else might read Edwards and Magee and not get anything out of it. But for me, it put a lot of square pegs in square holes and round pegs in round holes. It gave me a framework for understanding price. It gave me an idea of where to get into a market. Before I read Edwards and Magee, I had no idea what I was doing. Where do you get into a trade? I didn't have a clue. It also gave me a way to establish where to protect myself on a trade and an idea of where the market might go. That book is what brought me into charting. I saw the light at the end of the tunnel. I saw there was a chance that I could develop myself as a trader, and the account I opened to trade charts did well.

So was that the point of demarcation between trading failure and trading success?

Yes. In 1979 I had an account that was gaining traction. When I look back now, the account had a lot more volatility than it should have. I still hadn't worked out proper position sizing, but for the first time since I started trading, my account was moving steadily north.

Was the broker who bought you the book a successful trader?

He never gained success. He is a dear friend, but he never made it as a trader.

It's ironic that he was instrumental in your trading success, but was never successful himself. I guess that the book he bought you was the best present you ever got.

Oh yes! Let me show you something. [He leaves and comes back a minute later with a book.] I was looking for a first edition of Edwards and Magee for years and had queries out to several rare book dealers. I finally found a copy that Magee himself had inscribed and given to a friend in Boston.

I assume you were still managing your commercial hedging accounts at the time. When did you make the transition from broker to full-time trader?

About a year later.

Couldn't you continue to broker those accounts and still trade your own account?

I could have, but I didn't want to.

Why not?

I just wanted to trade.

But weren't you walking away from a large amount of brokerage income by giving up those accounts?

I would have, but I sold the accounts.

I didn't know you could do that.

You could; I received a trail of the commissions on the accounts I turned over.

Since these were prize commercial accounts, how did you pick the broker you could entrust the accounts to?

I gave it to a guy who was my biggest mentor. His name was Dan Markey, and he was probably one of the best traders I ever met.

How did he trade?

He used to say, "I look at the markets through the lens of History 101, Economics 101, and Psychology 101." He was a boy wonder at Conti. He was a real position trader who would hold big grain positions for months at a time. He had a great sense of when markets were at a major turning point. He would say, "Corn is bottoming right now. This is the season low." And he would be right.

Was that just intuitive?

Yes, intuitive. He couldn't tell you why.

So he was actually going short into strength and long into weakness.

He was.

So, ironically, he was doing exactly the opposite of what you were doing.

Yes, the total opposite.

But you said he was a mentor. So what did you learn from him?

Risk management. While he was buying into weakness, he wouldn't just put on a full position and hold it. He would probe the market for a low. He would get out of any trade that had a loss at the end of the week and then try again the next time he thought the timing was right. He kept probing, probing, probing.

That's interesting because one of the things I've heard you say is that anytime you have a loss in a trade at the end of the week, you get out. I take it that watching Dan trade 40 years ago is where this idea comes from. So you've used this idea for virtually all of your trading life.

Oh, I have. Dan used to say, "There are two parts to a trade: direction and timing. And, if you're wrong about either one, you're wrong on the trade."

Anything else that you learned from Dan?

Yes, I saw that he took much smaller positions than he could. The lesson I learned from Dan was that if you could protect your capital, you would always have another shot. But you had to protect your pile of chips.

And you had lost your pile of chips several times.

I had. I had.

It's interesting that all of Dan's advice deals with risk management, and none of it has anything to do with trade entry, which is what most people want to focus on. Were there any other significant mentors?

Dan was by far the most significant. The most crucial other advice I had was from a trader who was a chartist. He said, "Peter, you have to have an edge to make money, and a chart pattern does not give you an edge." That was a sobering comment at the time, and it didn't make complete sense to me then, but it did about five years later.

I guess what he was saying is that anyone else can see the same chart patterns.

Yes, and also chart patterns are subject to failure. I know that one thing both you and I agree on is that when a chart pattern fails, that is a more reliable signal than the chart pattern itself. [I not only agree, but I titled the chapter in my book on futures market analysis discussing this exact concept, "The Most Important Rule in Chart Analysis."*] Also, chart patterns morph. You think you have a handle on the chart pattern, and then it changes into another pattern. A morphing chart is nothing more than a bunch of patterns that fail and don't do what they're supposed to do.

So what happened after you turned over your accounts to Dan to focus solely on trading?

In 1980, I incorporated Factor Research and Trading and rented an office.

Why did you pick the name *Factor*?

That was my own inside joke. From 1975 through 1978, I did a really good job providing Campbell with fundamental information and helping them with their hedging decisions. By 1979, I had gotten the hang of chart analysis, and I started seeing some significant potential price movements in the grain markets. I couldn't exactly go to Campbell and tell them that I thought they should be hedging because I saw a *head-and-shoulders* bottom forming in the market. So, I would go to Dan Markey or some of the other fundamental guys when soybeans were at $6, and say, "I think soybeans are going to $9. What do you see in the markets?" And they would give me some sort of fundamental narrative of how such a move could happen.

The guys at the CBOT would hear me talking to Campbell and saying stuff like, "We could be seeing some anchovy problems off the coast." [Anchovies are used to produce fishmeal, which is a substitute for soybean meal.] I was really speaking my charts, but I was giving them my opinion in terms of fundamentals. So they started calling it the "Brandt bullshit factor."

---

* Jack D. Schwager, *A Complete Guide to the Futures Market* (New Jersey, John Wiley and Sons, Inc., 2017), 205–231.

What were you planning to do with the company? Were you planning to manage money?

No, just trade my own account.

But you didn't need to have a company to trade your account.

I know, but I just liked the feel of having my own trading company.

Has your methodology changed from what you were doing when you started as a full-time trader?

There are some substantial differences.

What are they?

Back then, I would have popcorn trades.

Popcorn trades?

You know how a kernel of corn pops, goes up to the top of the canister, and then falls all way back down to the bottom? A popcorn trade is what I call a trade that you have a profit on and then ride it all way back down to where you got in. I try to avoid popcorn trades now.

What else has changed?

The charts have become much less reliable. It was much easier to trade on charts in the 1970s and 1980s. The patterns were nice and neat. There were fewer *whipsaw* markets. [A *whipsaw* market is a market in which prices swing widely back and forth, causing trend-following traders to be positioned wrong right before the market abruptly reverses direction.] Back then, if you saw a chart pattern, you could take the money to the bank. The patterns were so dependable.

I have my own theory why that may be the case. How do you explain it?

I think high-frequency trading operations have created volatility around chart *breakout* points. [A *breakout* is a price movement above or below a prior *trading range* (sideways movement in prices) or consolidation pattern (e.g., triangle, flag, etc.). The underlying concept is that the ability of prices to move beyond a prior trading range or consolidation pattern indicates a potential trend in the direction of the breakout.]

But they trade so short term. Why would they impact volatility?

Because they create volatility *at* the breakout points. It is very short-term volatility, but it can knock a trader like me out of a position. I also think that the markets are more mature now with bigger players. What's your view about why the markets have changed?

My perception is that once too many people are doing the same thing, by definition, it becomes impossible for that technique to continue working as before.

I think that's true. Back then, there weren't a lot of people looking at charts.

What else has changed in your approach from the early days?

I used to trade one- to four-week patterns, now I trade 8- to 26-week patterns.

Because they are more reliable?

Yes.

Any other changes in the types of signals you take?

I used to trade any pattern I could see. I would trade 30 to 35 patterns a month. Now, I am much more selective. I used to trade patterns like symmetrical triangles and trendlines, which I no longer do. I only trade patterns where the breakout is through a horizontal boundary.

Why is that?

With horizontal boundaries, you can find out much more quickly whether you are right or wrong.

Was there a catalyst for that change?

No, it was just a gradual process of realizing that I was getting my best results trading rectangles, ascending triangles, and descending triangles. Give me a 10-week rectangle with a well-defined boundary that ends with a wide daily bar breakout out of that pattern, and now we're cooking.

But you still have to deal with the issue of the market dipping back even on valid breakouts. What happens if you buy a breakout, and the market reacts enough to trigger your stop but then holds, and the longer-term pattern still looks good?

I will take a second chance but never more than a second chance. And I won't take the second chance on the same day. I remember guys on the Board of Trade complaining, "I've lost 30 cents in a 10-cent range." I don't want to lose 30 cents in a ten-cent range, and I know it's possible to do.

If you get stopped out a second time, and that pattern ends up being a major price base before a long-term trend, does that mean you miss the entire move?

Not necessarily. I might still get back in if the market forms a continuation pattern [a consolidation within the trend]. But I would look at it as an entirely new trade.

So it wouldn't bother you going long at $1.50 after getting stopped out twice at $1.20?

No, that has never bothered me. I think that type of thinking is a trap that people fall into. I trade price change; I don't trade price level.

Is there anything else that you have changed over the years?

Yes, the risk I take on a trade is much lower now. Whenever I take a trade, I limit my risk to about 1/2% of my equity from the point of entry. I want to have my stops at breakeven or better within two or three days of entry. My average loss last year was 23 basis points.

Protective stops are integral to your trading methodology. I'm curious, do you leave stops in place during the overnight session? [With the advent of electronic trading, futures markets trade through the night. The inherent dilemma is that if a protective stop order is not left in place for the night session, a large overnight price move could result in a trade losing significantly more than intended by the stop-risk point. On the other hand, leaving a stop in place for the night session runs the risk of the stop being activated by a meaningless price move on thin volume.]

It depends on the market. I wouldn't use an overnight stop for the Mexican peso, but I would use one for the euro because it is so liquid. Similarly, I wouldn't use an overnight stop in copper, but I would in gold.

What was the first bad year you had as a full-time trader?

1988.

So you had nine good years before that losing year. What went wrong in 1988?

I got sloppy. I would enter chart patterns too early. I would chase markets. I didn't have orders in when I should have.

Why, to use your own term, did your trading get "sloppy" in 1988?

I think because 1987 was such a good year. I was up 600% in 1987. It was my best year ever. I'll never be there again. I think I came out of that year a bit complacent.

How much did you lose in 1988?

Oh, about 5%.

When did you get back on track?

1989. Having a losing year made me realize that I had to get back to the basics.

What do you know now that you wish you knew when you started out as a trader?

I think the big one is to forgive myself. I am going to make mistakes.

What else?

I have learned that you can believe you know where the market is going, but you really don't have a clue. I now know that I am my own worst enemy and that my natural instincts will often lead me astray. I am an impulsive person. If I didn't have a process and instead just looked at my screen for where to enter orders, I would self-destruct. It's only when I override my instincts through the process of disciplined order entry that I put myself in the position where what I do with charts can work for me. I have to be so intentional in the way I trade. My edge comes from the process. I am a glorified order enterer; I am not a trader. Some of the orders I place go against my natural inclination in a market. They are hard orders to enter.

Why?

Copper has been in a 40-cent trading range for nearly a year, and just today, I bought copper near a new recent high. That's hard to do. [As it turned out, Brandt had bought copper on the high day of the upmove and was stopped out the next day. This trade was actually quite typical for Brandt. The majority of his trades will result in a quick loss. He succeeds, nonetheless, because his average gain is much larger than his average loss.]

I think that most of my big profits have come from trades that were counterintuitive. How I feel about a trade is not a good indicator of how the trade will end up. I think that if I made my biggest bets on those trades I felt best about, it would substantially degrade my performance. A current example is that I've wanted to be a bull on grains for a year now.

Why?

Because grains are at very low price levels. They are scraping at the bottom. I think my first trade in corn, which was over 40 years ago, was at a higher price than we are at right now.

So given the inflation we have had since then, prices are extraordinarily low.

Yes, and I have tried buying grains multiple times this year with these trades resulting in a net loss. My best trade in grains this year was actually on the short side of Kansas City wheat. In fact, it was my third best trade of the year. And I made that trade only because I couldn't deny the chart. I felt that if I was not going to short Kansas City wheat on *that* chart pattern, why was I even bothering to look at the chart? I had to go against my instincts that grains were forming a major bottom.

So, ironically, your best trade in that sector during the year was precisely opposite to what you were expecting. It's like you have to bring yourself to bet against the team you're rooting for.

You do.

Has that been true over the years—that is, have your best trades tended to be the ones you least expected to work?

I think that's true. If anything, I think there may be an inverse correlation between how I feel about a trade and how it turns out.

Why do you think that is?

Because it is easy to believe in a trade that conforms to conventional wisdom. It used to bother me to be wrong on a trade. I would take it personally. Whereas now, I take pride in the fact that I can be wrong 10 times in a row. I understand that my edge comes from the fact that I have become so good at taking losses.

So instead of being bothered by losing on a trade, you're proud that you can take these small losses that prevent a large loss from accumulating. In that light, taking a loss on a trade is not a sign of a defect but rather a reflection of a personal strength that explains why you have been successful in the long run.

A trader's job is to take losses. A losing trade doesn't imply you did anything wrong. The hard part about trading is that you can do the right thing and still lose money. There is not a direct feedback loop that tells you, "good job." I only have control over the orders I place. I don't have control over the outcome of trades. Whenever I place a trade, I think, "A year from now when I look back at the chart, will I be able to see in the chart the day and the price at which I took a position?" If the answer is yes, then it is a good trade, regardless of whether it wins or loses.

What else would have been helpful to know when you started out as a trader?

Actually, if I had been as risk-averse in my early years as I am now, I would never have had that string of giant winning years in the 1980s.

What level of risk were you taking?

Oh, I could take as much as a 10% risk on a single trade. Not every trade, of course, but it would sometimes be that high.

So as much as twentyfold the risk you take per trade now!

Yes.

Ironically, it sounds like the fact that you were operating under misconceptions of appropriate risk in those earlier years was beneficial to you. I have always believed that successful people may be successful because of some innate skill, talent or drive, but that there is also usually some significant luck involved. You can have people with all the potential in the world, and nothing ever happens. Your story is an illustration of that. You did the wrong thing in the beginning by trading much too large, but it all worked out exceptionally well. You could just as easily have blown out your account again.

Oh, Jack, totally. It's only been in the last 10 years that I have reflected on the fact that my success as a trader is mainly due to what I am going to call "cosmic sovereignty." I started in the business when I did. I had certain people that mentored me when they did. I was with the right firm when I started out. I had the right accounts because of my previous job in advertising. I started trading at a time when the markets were perfectly attuned to my style of chart trading. I bet 10%–15% of my account on long Swiss franc and Deutsche mark positions, and it turned into a giant profit instead of killing me. I can't take credit for any of that. None of that is due to my own intelligence or abilities. None of that is due to who I am. That's cosmic sovereignty.

How did you get to manage money for Commodities Corporation? [Commodities Corporation was a proprietary trading firm in Princeton, New Jersey. The firm gained legendary status because some of the traders it seeded would go on to become among the world's best traders, probably first and foremost being Michael Marcus and Bruce Kovner who were featured in the original *Market Wizards* book.*]

I don't recall how it started, but they reached out to me. I think somebody at the Board of Trade may have recommended me. I flew down to Newark for the interview and was picked up by a limousine that drove me to the *castle*. [Commodities Corporation was not literally in a castle, but Brandt is using the term "castle" to emphasize how elaborate the firm's offices were.]

---

*   Jack D. Schwager, *Market Wizards* (New Jersey, John Wiley and Sons, Inc., 2012), 9–82.

Yes, their offices were really attractive; it was like walking through a beautiful gallery. [I worked for Commodities Corporation as a research analyst.]

Oh, it was fabulous!

Do you remember anything about the interview process?

The traders were all quirky. They were academic types—a big contrast from the kinds of traders I was used to on the Board of Trade.

How much money did they give you to manage?

They gave me $100,000 to start, but they raised it to $1 million and eventually to more than $5 million.

What was your experience trading for Commodities Corporation?

My major problem was that I was never very good at trading size. It made me nervous to trade more than 100 bonds at a time. I remember the first time I entered a 100-contract order. I was shaking. It freaked me out. I don't think I ever got over that.

How many years into managing the Commodities Corporation account was it before you started trading position sizes as large as 100 bonds?

About three years.

Did trading larger size impact your performance?

It did.

In what way?

It made me more timid. If you have a 100-contract position, and the market goes against you by a full point, that's $100,000. I started thinking in terms of dollars. I stopped trading the market and started trading my equity. It had a definite impact on my trading, and my performance drastically deteriorated, beginning around 1991. I see this all so much more clearly today. I don't think I was as aware of what was happening at the time, but when I look back at it today, I understand what happened.

How did the Commodities Corporation relationship end?

By 1992, my trading was trailing off, and I was not meeting their benchmarks.

But hadn't you done very well for Commodities Corporation overall?

I had. And it wasn't like I had any substantial losses. It was more a matter of my performance dropping to near breakeven, give or take a few percent. I also had cut down my trading size, and I wasn't using most of my allocation. Their attitude was, "What, you have a $10 million account, and you're trading only 20-lot positions?"

Did Commodities Corporation terminate your trading account, or did you leave on your own volition?

It was more of a mutual decision. I didn't have the sharp edge I had in previous years.

Did you still continue trading your account?

Yes, for another two years.

Did you feel better once you didn't have the burden of managing the Commodities Corporation account?

No, I wasn't feeling good about myself as a trader. The fun of trading had left me at that point. Trading had become drudgery. I was feeling the discrepancy between how I was performing and how I knew I could perform. That gap was emotionally difficult for me to live with.

Why was that gap there?

Oh, I think it was because I had become gun-shy. I felt like I had lost my edge, and I didn't know how to get it back.

But wasn't there some sense of relief in not having to trade the Commodities Corporation account?

The more significant relief was in not having to trade my own account.

Besides relief, how did you feel the day you closed your own account?

There were lots of feelings. Part of it was, "Thank God this is done." Part of it was, "I'm admitting failure." At the end of the day, I was tapping out. How was I different from any other guy tapping out on the Board of Trade?

When did you get back into trading?

Eleven years later, in 2006. I remember the exact time and place. I was sitting at my desk, my wife, Mona, was standing on my left side, and the thought of trading fluttered back into my mind. I turned to Mona and said, "What do you think about me getting back into commodity trading?" She did not like the idea.

I guess because the last few years of trading had been so miserable for you.

She remembered those years. She said, "Really, you want to do that again?" I said, "I have to do it." I opened an account shortly afterward.

You stopped trading in 1995 and restarted in 2006. In all those intervening years, did you pay any attention to the markets?

I didn't have a futures account.

You didn't even look at a chart?

I didn't even have any charting software.

So for 11 years, you didn't even look at a chart. Then you abruptly decided to start trading again. Was there a catalyst?

I think I missed it. Also, part of it was that trading had ended badly. The way it ended started to stick in my craw. I thought, "Peter, you can't let the way it ended be the last word."

What happened after you started trading again?

I had been away from trading so long, I wasn't aware that the world had transitioned to electronic trading. I even remember getting my time stamp machine out of the closet and printing a bunch of order tickets. [He laughs at how archaic these actions were.] I didn't know whether what I used to do, chart analysis, was even going to work anymore. I had a few good trades when I started trading, and it seemed that the charts were still working. I liked that. I had two really, really good years.

Psychologically, were you back to where you were?

Yes, I was really enjoying it.

Your second trading career has gone very well, but you had one losing year, which stands in extreme contrast to all the other years since you resumed trading. [In 2013, Brandt was down 13% compared with an average annual return of 49% in the other years during the 2007–2019 period. His second-worst year during this period was a gain of 16%.] Was there something different about 2013?

Yes, there was. There were two factors that reinforced each other. First, it is probably no coincidence that 2013 was the year I decided to accept other people's money.

After so many years trading just your own account, what prompted you to expand to accept investor money as well?

People I knew kept asking me to manage their money. I was reluctant to do it, but, after a while, the multiple requests wore me down, and I thought, "Yeah, I'll give it a try." I look back at that decision today and wonder, "Why in the world did I do that?" There was no reason for me to do it.

Why did managing other people's money cause you to have your only losing year since you resumed trading in 2007, as well as your worst drawdown since then?

The drawdown would have happened anyway, but I don't think it would have been as deep, nor lasted as long. The perspective I have on it now is that when I was trading my own account, it was like trading monopoly money. My trading capital was just something I kept score with. I detached myself emotionally from it.

For most people, the money in their account is very real; it certainly is not like monopoly money. How long have you been able to have a detached view regarding the money in your account?

Oh, I think that was something I was able to develop within my first few years of trading—sometime back in the 1980s.

I take it that your perspective on trading capital changed when you were managing other people's money?

It absolutely did. Once I found myself trading money for friends, all of a sudden, it was real money. It messed with my head.

How long did you manage investor money?

I started trading the first client account in January 2013, and by June 2014, I had returned all the investor money.

How close was June 2014 to the bottom of your drawdown?

It *was* the bottom of my drawdown. And I don't believe that was coincidental. I think it was the bottom because I gave all the investor money back.

That seems to imply that you wouldn't have experienced the subsequent large rebound in your own account if you hadn't given the money back.

I think it more than implies that; I think it's true. I believe if I hadn't returned investor money, I would have just dug the hole deeper.

What was the trigger for your finally deciding to return investor money?

I am fortunate that I have trading peers I can speak to who will be honest with me. They knew what I was going through, and they understood that managing other people's money was messing up my trading. Their advice was that I needed to return investor money and go back to trading just my own account the way I used to.

By that point, weren't you already aware that managing other people's money was messing with your mental trading state?

On some level, I knew what the problem was, but I had trouble admitting it to myself. I was avoiding having to go back to investors when their accounts were down and tell them that I was returning their money because I couldn't make money for them.

What was the percentage loss in your investor accounts by the time they closed?

I think the worst account loss was around 10%.

But your own percentage loss during that period was larger.

That was because I traded my own account more aggressively than the investor accounts.

Earlier, you said two factors were different in 2013. Managing investor money was the first. What was the second?

I tend to be rule-based once I get into a trade, but my trade entry decisions are discretionary. There are periods when there are lots of false breakouts and whipsaw price moves, and the markets don't care what the charts say. That is an example of my approach being out of sync with the markets. But there can also be periods where I am out of sync with my approach. I am not being disciplined. I'm not being patient. I'm jumping the gun on trades. I'm taking positions before the market confirms them. I'm taking trades on inferior patterns. And, of course, you can have periods where both conditions exist: My methodology is out of sync with the markets, and I am out of sync with my methodology. That was 2013 through mid-2014.

At the time, CTAs were all tanking. [CTAs stand for Commodity Trading Advisors, the legal term for registered managers in the futures markets.*] There was lots of talk suggesting market behavior had changed and that to survive as a trader, you had to change. And I drank the Kool-Aid. I started tweaking what I do.

In what way?

I added indicators. I tried mean reversion trades. [Mean reversion trades are trades in which you sell on strength and buy on weakness.]

But mean reversion is the exact opposite of what you do.

Exactly. [He says this in a drawn-out singsong fashion.] Out of desperation, because nothing was working, I kept on trying different things. It became a vicious cycle. So what might have been a standard three- or four-month drawdown with a loss of 5% turned into an 18-month drawdown of 17%. The losing period lasted much longer than it should have because I went down the rabbit trail.

Would you have started changing the way you trade if you hadn't been managing investor money during this drawdown?

Not a chance.

---

* This three-word designation is a misnomer in at least two ways. First, the bulk of futures trading is in financial instruments (e.g., interest rate markets, currencies, and stock indexes), not commodities. Second, CTAs manage assets rather than give advice, as the name suggests.

We talked about your account rebounding after you returned investor money. Was there anything else behind this performance turnaround?

I had bought into the lie that I had to change because the old ways no longer worked. I finally realized I had to get back to basics. My thought process went something like this: "I'm jumping from one approach to another. I'm grasping at straws. I don't even know where I am. If I'm going down, I'm going down doing what I know how to do."

What happened after you went back to trading your standard methodology?

I had a great year, but I had favorable markets.

Did the 2013–14 drawdown experience change anything for you besides knowing you never wanted to manage outside money and cementing your conviction to sticking with your methodology?

After the 2013–14 drawdown, I started looking at my equity in a different way. Before then, I looked at the total equity in my account, including open trades. That is the conventional way of looking at equity and, of course, the way the IRS looks at equity. But now, I don't want to know my open trade equity. So I graph my equity based on closed trades only.

What difference does that make to you psychologically?

In reality, open trade profits aren't mine. They don't belong to me. So it doesn't matter if I lose it. Therefore, it makes it easier for me to allow a market to come back against me somewhat.

So even though your initial stop points are very close, once you are ahead, you give the market more latitude.

Much more latitude. Also, once the profits of the trade equal 1% of my equity, I take half the position off. Then I can give the other half much more room.

Will you still raise the stop on the remaining half of the position?

I will, but much less aggressively. However, once I get to more than 70% of my target objective, I will jam my stop. That part of my trading methodology goes back to my days of popcorn trades. If I have an open profit of $1800 per contract on a trade with a target of $2000, why would I risk giving it all back to make the extra $200? So when the trade gets close to the target, I will raise the stop.

When you get to within 30% of your target, how do you decide where to raise the stop to?

Once it gets to that point, I will use a mechanical three-day stop rule.

Exactly what is that rule?

Assuming a long position, the first day would be the high day of the move. The second day would be the day the market closed below the low of the high day. The third day would be the day the market closed below the low of the second day. I would get out on the close of the third day.

I assume those three days would not have to be consecutive.

That's correct. The third day could be two weeks after the first day. I developed the three-day stop rule not because I thought it was the best rule—in fact, I'm sure it's not—but rather because, as a discretionary trader, I hate indecision. I hate regret. I hate second-guessing. So I wanted to develop a rule that was automatic and would protect against my giving back most of my open profits.

Your initial risk on the trade is about 1/2% of your equity. How far away is your target?

A point equivalent to about 2% of my equity.

And if it reaches that point, will you just take profits on the entire position?

Usually, I will just take the profits. There may be occasional exceptions where I will use a very close stop instead, especially for short positions, because markets can collapse much more quickly than they rise.

At what point would you look to re-enter the trade after you take profits?

I don't look to re-enter. It has to be a brand-new trade.

What about markets that just keep on trending?

I will miss most of those trends. I feel more comfortable playing between the 30-yard lines than trying to run a kickoff from the 10-yard line to the end zone. I will miss some huge moves.

Well, your methodology precludes you from remotely catching the major portion of those trends.

It does.

Do you trade stocks the same way you trade futures?

I trade them exactly the same.

Don't you think there is any difference between the chart behavior of stocks and futures?

No.

I'm surprised because my impression has always been that stocks are subject to much more erratic price behavior than futures.

I think that's true, but when stocks get on a run, they act the same.

I have seen you refer to an "ice line" in one of your letters. What exactly is an ice line?

When I lived in Minnesota, we lived on a lake, and the lake would freeze over. The ice would support you, but if you ever fell through, the ice would act as resistance. The analogy for price charts is that the ice line is that price area that is difficult to get through, but once you do, it should provide support. If I can find a market with a price breakout where at least half of that day's range is below the ice line, then that low can serve as a significant risk point.

What if less than half of the day's price range is below the ice line—could you use the low of the previous day?

That's what I do.

It seems like it would be so common for the low of the entry day price bar to be taken out without any consequence on the long-term chart picture. I totally get the concept that keeping your risk very low is an essential component of your success, but have you ever done the research to see whether your risk is actually too low? For example, might you be better off risking the low of a few bars rather than just a single one?

Yes, I have done that research. I found that if I gave the market a little more breathing room in the early days of a trade, over time, I would make more profits. So, if my goal were to make the highest return, I would use a wider stop. However, my goal is not to maximize my return but rather to maximize my profit factor. [The profit factor is a return/risk measure that is defined as the sum of all winning trades divided by the sum of all losing trades.]

Do you ever use a trailing stop? [A trailing stop is an order to exit the position whenever the market moves a fixed amount below the high of a price upmove (or above the low of a price downmove).]

Never. When I hear people say something like, "I'm going to use a $500 trailing stop," I think, "What sense does that make! You mean you want to be selling when you should be buying more?" That never made any sense to me. Nor does it make any sense to me that some people use their open profits on the trade to add more contracts. That, to me, is the most asinine trading idea I ever heard. If you do that, you can be right on the trade and still lose money. In my own trading, my positions only get smaller. My biggest position is the day I put a trade on.

What is the weekend rule I've seen you refer to?

The weekend rule goes back to Richard Donchian in the 1970s and basically says that if the market closes in new high or low ground on a Friday, then it is likely to extend that move on Monday and early Tuesday. The significance for me is that if a market breaks out on a Friday, then I have a completed pattern and the Donchian rule working in favor of the trade.

Have you ever checked out the validity of the weekend rule?

I have never statistically analyzed it, but I can tell you that many of my most profitable trades came from Friday breakouts, especially if it is a three-day weekend. I can also tell you that the trades that I stayed in despite showing a net loss as of the Friday close probably cost me more money than any other type of trade. I have learned that it is best to liquidate any trade that shows an open loss as of the Friday close.

Why do you think that rule works?

The Friday close is the most critical price of the week because it is the price at which people commit to accepting the risk of holding a position over the weekend.

Do you now unfailingly adhere to the Friday rule?

I sometimes violate it, but when I do, the market usually slaps me in the face. The one thing I regret is not keeping data on different types of trading decisions.

The way you trade with such tight risk control from the point of entry seems like you wouldn't be exposed to any substantial losing trades, but were there any particularly painful trades in your career?

Oh yeah. I was long crude oil in January 1991 when the US began its attack against Iraq in the First Gulf War. Before the news of the attack came out, crude oil closed around $29 in New York. Although this was before 24-hour markets, crude did trade on the Kerb [an after-hours market in London] and was trading about $2–$3 higher that night. So I went to sleep thinking, "Boy, tomorrow is really going to be something." Well, it was, but not the way I thought. The next day, crude oil opened $7 below the New York close—a $10 swing from its nighttime levels. That was by far the largest loss on a trade I ever experienced. [Another account of a trading experience related to this same stunning market reversal came up in my interview with Tom Basso in *The New Market Wizards*.*]

With the market gapping so much lower on the open, did you still get out at the open, or did you wait before liquidating your position?

I don't sit and speculate with a loss. I learned a long time ago that if you speculate with a loss to get less of a loss, you end up with more of a loss. [Notwithstanding the massive decline on that day, the crude oil market moved significantly lower the next day and didn't reach a low until about a month later.] The same trading discipline applies to an error. I have never speculated with an error.

How much did you lose on that single trade?

About 14% of my equity.

Do you remember your emotional response?

Shock. I was numb.

---

*   Jack D. Schwager, *The New Market Wizards* (New York, HarperBusiness, 1992), 286–288.

What is your motivation for writing a weekly market letter? It seems like a lot of work.

Quite frankly, the *Factor* is written for an audience of one. I write the *Factor* for me. It is my way of preaching to myself all the things I need to be continually reminded of.

Don't you have any concern that by publicizing your trades, there may be too many trades put in at the same price points, thereby adversely affecting the trade?

Nah, I don't think it has any effect.

I know you do almost all your chart analysis and trading decisions for the coming week after the Friday close and up through the Sunday night opening. Do you make any new trading decisions during the week?

By the end of the weekend, I have my list of markets to monitor for a trade. On rare occasions, I may add a market during the week, but I try to minimize such trades. If it's not on my weekend list of markets to monitor for the week for a potential trade, then I don't like to take it as a trade. This is another example of a category of trades that I wished I had kept data on. I bet if you counted up all the trades I ever did that were not on my weekend list of potential trades, they would be net losers.

Do you trade intraday at all?

For the first two or three days after I put on a trade, I am alert for an opportunity to tighten my stop, even intraday. But with that one exception, I don't trade intraday. If I sit and watch the computer screen all day, I will sabotage myself. Inevitably, I will make the wrong decisions. I will get out of winning trades. I'll second-guess an order that I placed when the markets weren't open, and I made a decision based strictly on the charts rather than being mesmerized by blinking prices on the screen. For me, what works is a disciplined approach: Make a decision, write the order, place the order, and live with it.

Your comments about how making decisions during market hours tends to mess up your trading reminds me of an interchange I had with Ed Seykota. I remarked, "I noticed there is no quote machine on your desk." He replied,

"Having a quote machine is like having a slot machine on your desk—you end up feeding it all day long."*

———————

The next morning, we continued the interview over breakfast at a place called the *Black Watch*. (Excellent breakfast spot; check it out if you are ever in Tucson.) Brandt began the conversation by saying that although he had done all right, he was not in the same league as some of the great traders in the other *Market Wizards* books. He started rattling off a string of names to make his point. Brandt concluded by saying that if I decided not to include him in the book, he would fully understand, and it would be OK with him. Brandt is a sincere person, so he was not speaking out of false modesty—although it was certainly misplaced modesty. I told Brandt there was no chance that I would exclude him from the book. I explained that he not only had a long track record with superb performance, but he also had a lot of valuable insights about trading that I thought were important to share with readers. Brandt had brought some charts along to illustrate certain of his past trades, which is where our conversation continued.

———————

This was my most profitable trade ever. It broke out, and never looked back. [Brandt hands me a chart of the New York Stock Exchange Composite Index, pointing to his long side entry in early 1987 on a breakout above an extended, horizontal consolidation—a breakout that led to an immediate and virtually unbroken upside move.]

Here is a big trade I had in 2008 when the pound crashed from $2.00 to $1.40 in a matter of months. Again, the market broke out and never looked back. [In the chart he hands me, the downside breakout of a head-and-shoulders consolidation formed at the highs leads to a sudden, huge decline, interrupted only briefly by a minor rebound after the initial downswing. He comments on that minor rebound.] What I have found is

---

* Jack D. Schwager, *Market Wizards* (New Jersey, John Wiley and Sons, Inc., 2012), 171.

that when you have a big move down, the first rally never holds. If there is ever a case where I want to sell into strength, it would be the first rally after a straight-line drop. Often the rally will last for only two days after the reversal day. [He shows me some other similar charts of breakouts from long-term consolidations leading to major price moves.]

In all these examples, you are buying or selling after breakouts from long-term consolidations. Do you ever enter trades after breakouts from pennants or flags? [Pennants and flags are narrow, short-term (generally under two weeks) consolidations that form after price swings.]

I will if they form during a big price move that has a much further objective based on the completion of a pattern on the weekly chart. But if they just happen on any chart, the answer would be no.

I remember once retweeting one of your market observations and receiving a comment along the lines: "Why would you pay any attention to someone like Brandt who recommended going short the S&P 5,000 points lower?" What is your reaction to that type of comment?

My philosophy is strong opinions, weakly held. The minute a trade reaches into my pocket, it becomes a weakly held position, and I'll drop it like a hot potato. I can go from a strong opinion to being out of the market in one day. But in the Twitter world, all they remember is the strong opinion. It's like whatever you say, it represents your opinion for the rest of your life. They remember the recommendation, but they forget that I was out a day or two later with a 50-basis point loss or, for that matter, a 50-basis point gain. In the Twitter world, there is a tendency to respond negatively if you were bullish and now switch to bearish or vice versa. Whereas, I think that the flexibility to change your mind is actually a strong attribute for a trader.

The markets have seen such enormous changes during your trading career. We've gone from a time when you needed a mainframe the size of a room to develop and test simple trading systems to current enormous computing power and easy access to trading software. We have gone from virtually no computerized trading to vast amounts of computerized trading. We have seen the advent of trading based on artificial intelligence and high-frequency trading. We have gone from a time when technical analysis was considered an arcane backwater in market analysis to a time when technical-based trading—both chart analysis of the type you do

and computerized technical systems—is widespread. Despite all these changes, you are using the same techniques you did at the beginning of your trading career based on chart patterns described in detail nearly 90 years ago in Schabacker's book. Do you think these techniques still work, despite all these changes?

No, they do not. They absolutely do not.

How then have you been able to continue to be successful using methodologies that come from such a different time?

I have thought a lot about that question. If I were to take trades at every chart pattern entry point Schabacker would have labeled, it would be extremely difficult to make money because markets no longer obey all of the patterns. There was a time when you could just trade the chart patterns, and you would make money. I believe that edge is gone.

So, you believe that classical chart analysis on its own no longer works.

Yes, I believe that is true. Large long-term patterns no longer work. Trendlines no longer work. Channels no longer work. Symmetrical triangles no longer work.

So what, if anything, does still work?

The only thing I have found that still works are patterns that tend to be shorter-term—less than a year and preferably less than 26 weeks—that have a horizontal boundary. Such patterns could include head-and-shoulder formations, ascending and descending triangles, and rectangular consolidations.

Is it that the patterns you are naming are not so much patterns that work, but instead are patterns that allow you to select entry points that have well-defined, reasonably close, meaningful stop-risk points?

Yes, charts will give you the idea of the path of least resistance, but charts do not forecast. There is a danger when people start thinking of charts in terms of forecasting. Charts are wonderful in finding specific spots for asymmetric risk/reward trades. That's it. I am focused on the probability of being able to get out of the trade at breakeven or better rather than on the probability of getting an anticipated price move. For example, I'm short gold now. I'm looking for the possibility of a $60 to $70 decline in gold. If someone were to ask me, "How confident are you about getting a $60 to $70 decline in gold?" that would be the wrong question. The right question would be, "How confident are you that you will be able to get out of the trade not much worse than breakeven?"

You are using a trade signaling methodology that you acknowledge doesn't have much of an edge. So what is your edge?

It isn't the charts that give me my edge; it's risk management. I get an edge from discipline, patience, and order execution. A reader of my *Factor* weekly letter said, "Peter, you get your edge because you are willing to watch a market for weeks before entering and then be out by the end of the day because the market didn't act right." And I thought, "My God, someone here gets me." All that charts do is give me a point at which I'm willing to take a bet. They give me a point at which I can say, "The market should trend from this exact price." Another way to look at it is: Can I find a bar on the price chart where there is a pretty good chance that the low of that bar will not be taken out?

So, it isn't that you figured out where to enter trades so much as you figured out where you can place asymmetrical trades that have a near-50-50 chance of working.

I think that's a good description. All my profits come from 10%–15% of my trades; all the other trades are throwaways. The same pattern seems to hold consistently year in and year out. The problem, of course, is that I never know which trades are going to be in that 10%–15%.

I know your trading falls entirely in the camp of technical analysis, but do you think there is any value in fundamental analysis, even if it's not the right approach for you?

Dan Markey, my mentor, had an interesting philosophy about fundamentals. He thought most fundamental news was nonsense. Dan had what he called the dominant fundamental factor theory, which postulated that, over an extended period, one to five years, there was one underlying fundamental factor that was the driver of the market. All the other news merely caused gyrations around the trend driven by the dominant fundamental factor, and, more often than not, conventional wisdom didn't have a clue about what the relevant fundamental factor was. You could watch CNBC for a week, and they would never mention the dominant fundamental factor. In fact, if people were aware of the dominant factor at all, in most instances, they were trying to fade it. I think a great example of this tendency was quantitative easing, which was implemented in the aftermath of the Great Recession and was the great driver of the ensuing bull market in stocks. People were saying, "The central banks can't keep doing this. It's causing too much debt. You have to short this market."

Do you use Dan's concept at all?

I don't, but I often wonder what Dan, who died in 1998, would have thought was driving a given market.

What advice would you give to someone who wanted to pursue a trading career?

The first thing I would ask them is, "If you lost everything you put in, would it meaningfully change your lifestyle?" If it would, don't trade. If you're not a good problem solver, don't trade. If you feel you need to have trading profits accrue on some regular schedule, don't trade. The markets are not an annuity. I would tell would-be traders to expect it to take at least three years to get even a clue of how they should trade and five years to reach some level of competency. And if you don't have the three to five years to achieve trading competency, you probably shouldn't trade. People totally underestimate how long it takes to become a profitable trader. Don't look to become a trader because you want to make money. I would say that if your goal is to earn a living as a trader, the probability of success is probably only about 1%.

Do you realize when I asked you what advice you would give to someone who wanted to be a trader, you just gave me a bunch of reasons why someone shouldn't be a trader?

Oh yeah.

If despite all that advice, someone said, "I got you, but I still want to give it a try," what advice would you give them?

Learn not to take a loss personally. The markets don't care about who you are.

What else?

You have to find your own way. If you think you can copy somebody else's trading style, it will never work for you.

That is one of the main messages I try to convey to traders myself, but tell me in your own words why you think that is true.

One of the main dangers for traders who try to mirror themselves after other traders is that sooner or later, every trader will go through a significant drawdown. When I go through a challenging period, I understand it. If I have 10 losing trades in a row, I can understand that I didn't do anything wrong as long as I followed my plan. Someone else trying to copy my methodology wouldn't have that conviction. If, as is inevitable, the approach went through a difficult period at some point, they wouldn't be able to last through it. That's why traders need to know exactly why they are taking a trade. That is the only way they will survive through challenging periods.

That raises the question of what do you do during those periods where everything you do seems to be wrong, and you are just out of sync with the markets?

I just cut size. In the past, during such times, I would ask, "What do I need to change in my trading?" That type of response typically ended up leading me down a rabbit trail that didn't end well. Optimizing your trading approach for the last series of trades is not a solution, and it will only lead you astray. I try to keep trading the same way. That's the only way I'll come out of a drawdown and get back on track.

What other advice would you give to someone seeking a trading career?

You have to learn to wait for the right pitch. The hardest thing for me early on was figuring out the answer to the question: What is my pitch? What is the pitch that I'm willing to swing on? I think something that every trader has to come to terms with is answering that question. Can you define with high specificity what trade you're willing to take a swing at? Only when a trader can answer that question is he or she ready to deal with other critical issues such as sizing, leverage, scaling, and trade management.

Before you said, make sure your motivation for becoming a trader is not to make money. What is a good motivation?

The markets are such a neat challenge. You have to enjoy the process of problem-solving. I think there is great satisfaction if, at the end of it, you can say, "I have found a way to do it, and I am satisfied with the outcome."

What is your advice on missed trades?

Live with it. I call these could've-would've-should've trades. I typically am going to have about two pretty significant could've-would've-should've trades in an average year. And I just have to accept the fact that it's going to happen.

Are those trades more painful than losses?

They used to be. They used to drive me crazy. [He says this drawing out the "a" in crazy.]

How did you get past that?

I reduced the number of missed trades by planning and having orders in place rather than waiting for a breakout and then figuring out what I was going to do. Also, with experience, I have learned there's always another trade that will come along. One of the things that I find amazing is that if I wait long enough, there's always another great trade that will set up. I am more concerned about the mistakes I make than the markets that I miss.

Contrast the characteristics of winning traders and losing traders.

I think there are things that the winners have in common. They respect risk. They limit their risk on a trade. They don't automatically assume they will be right on a trade. If anything, they assume they will be wrong. They don't get too excited about a winning trade or too bummed out about a losing trade.

And the losers?

They risk way too much. They don't have a methodology. They chase markets. They have a fear of missing out. They can't keep their emotions in check; they have wild swings between excitement and depression.

It is ironic that what most people think is most important to becoming a successful trader—the methodology for entering trades—is actually one of the least important elements for Brandt. In fact, Brandt acknowledges that classical chart analysis has lost virtually its entire edge. What is critical is risk management. In fact, the methodology—chart analysis—is merely a tool to identify points in time that are amenable to the execution of Brandt's risk management approach. Brandt places his stops to assure that he never takes a large loss on any trade, barring those rare circumstances where his stop is executed far below the intended level, as occurred in his First Gulf War trade—the only such trade in his career.

The essence of Brandt's strategy is to risk very little on any given trade and to restrict trades to those he believes offer a reasonable potential for an objective that is three to four times the magnitude of his risk. He essentially uses charts to identify points at which it is possible to define a close protective stop that is also meaningful—points at which a relatively small price move would be sufficient to trigger a meaningful signal that the trade is wrong.

An example of such a trade would be going long on a day on which the market closes strong after a major upside breakout, and the low of that day lies well below the "ice line" to use Brandt's terminology. Brandt's trading approach is yet another example of a common trait I have observed among great traders: They have a methodology based on identifying asymmetric trade opportunities—trades where the perceived upside potential significantly exceeds the required risk.

Some readers may find it puzzling that Brandt chooses to use a protective stop strategy that he acknowledges is so tight that it reduces his overall returns. Why not use an approach that maximizes return? The answer is that an approach that increases return but also increases risk *by a greater amount* is suboptimal. The reason is that, mathematically, by increasing position size, a method with higher return-to-risk can always be made to yield a higher return at the same risk level than a lower return-to-risk method (even if its return is higher).

To be successful as a trader, you have to develop your own trading style. Notably, while Brandt's primary mentor relied on fundamental analysis and took very long-term trades, Brandt developed a trading methodology that was based strictly on technical analysis, taking trades of much shorter duration, particularly in the case of losing trades. Brandt learned the importance of money management from his mentor, but the trading methodology he developed was strictly his own.

Brandt has been quite disciplined about trading his own methodology throughout his career with one major exception. In 2013, after several months of net losses when his trading approach seemed to be out of sync with the markets, Brandt let himself become influenced by general talk among technical traders that the markets had changed. In a moment of weakness, Brandt abandoned the approach that had served him so well for so many years and started experimenting with trading methods that were not his own. All of these dalliances with different approaches merely extended and increased his losses. As a result, Brandt ended up with his only losing year since he resumed trading in late 2006 and, by his own admission, turned what should have been a 5% drawdown into a 17% drawdown.

A corollary of trading your own methodology is the principle: Don't trade based on someone else's recommendations. In Brandt's first trade, he followed the trade recommendation of the floor broker who had influenced him to pursue a trading career. Even though the trade proved profitable for the broker, Brandt ended up losing money because he didn't realize the broker's time frame for a trade was much shorter than his own. It is uncanny how often following other people's advice or recommendations will turn out badly. You can learn sound principles from other successful traders, but putting on trades based on someone else's recommendation instead of your own methodology will usually be a losing proposition. Remember, the next time you lose money on a trading tip: I told you so.

When asked what he wished he knew when he started trading, Brandt said, "I am my own worst enemy." Brandt is not alone. Human emotions and impulses will often lead traders to do the wrong thing. Brandt explained that he is an impulsive person and that if he simply watched the screen and followed his instincts to enter trades, he would self-destruct. Brandt believes that his success is possible only because he employs a precise process in placing trades, one that excludes his emotional responses. In Brandt's words, "Have a process: Make a decision, write the order, place the order, live with it." Brandt avoids watching the screen and largely restricts his new trading positions to those identified by his exhaustive chart analysis and trade planning conducted each week between the Friday close and Sunday evening opening, a period when the markets are closed.

Brandt's comments on the adverse impact of human emotions on trading reminded me of William Eckhardt's observation in *The New Market Wizards*: "If you're playing for emotional satisfaction, you're bound to lose, because what feels good is often the wrong thing to do."* Indeed, the best trades may be the most counterintuitive or most difficult to take. One of Brandt's best trades in 2019 was a short grain position, which was opposite to the direction he wanted to trade the grain markets.

Having a specific process is essential not only to avoid emotional trading decisions, which are usually detrimental, but also as a prerequisite for trading success. Every successful trader I have ever interviewed had a specific methodology; good trading is the antithesis of a shoot-from-the-hip approach. Brandt selects trades that meet specific criteria, and the timing of those trades is well-defined down to the entry day. Once he is in a trade, Brandt has a predetermined point at which he will exit the trade if it is losing money and a plan for taking profits if the trade is successful.

Many, if not most, traders, particularly novice traders, fail to comprehend the critical distinction between bad trades and losing trades—the two are definitely not the same. Brandt says that if he can look at a chart a year after a trade and be able to see the day and price at which he took a position, then it was a good trade, regardless of whether it won or lost. In effect, Brandt is saying that the determinant of a good trade is whether you followed your methodology, not whether the trade made money. (Of course, the implicit assumption in this perspective is that you are using a methodology that is profitable with acceptable risk over the long run.) The reality is that some percentage of trades in any methodology will lose

---

* Jack D. Schwager, *The New Market Wizards* (New York, HarperBusiness, 1992), 132.

money, no matter how good the approach is, and there is no way to know a priori which will be the winning trades.

Many traders will have a comfort level regarding trading size. They may do well trading smaller position sizes but then see a significant deterioration in their performance at larger position sizes, *even if the markets they are trading are still very liquid at the larger position size levels*. Brandt had this experience when Commodities Corporation raised his allocation to the point that he was trading 100-lot orders in T-bonds instead of his prior maximum order size of 20 contracts. Even though his percent risk per trade was unchanged, he found himself thinking about losses in dollar terms rather than percent of equity terms. Now, it may not make sense that trading size should make any difference if the percent risk per trade is unchanged and the market is still fully liquid at the larger order size, but human emotions and their impact on trading are not subject to logic. The lesson here is that traders should caution against any abrupt, large increases in their trading level. Instead, increases in account equity should be gradual to make sure that the trader is comfortable with the increased trading size.

Success in trading one's own account will not necessarily translate to success in managing money. Some traders may be comfortable and do well trading their own money but may see their performance fall apart when trading other people's money. This phenomenon can occur because, for some traders, a sense of guilt in losing other people's money may impair their normal trading decision process. It is not a coincidence that the period when Brandt managed other people's money coincided with his worst drawdown since he returned to a trading career in late 2006. Interestingly, the month Brandt returned all investor money was the low point of his drawdown and was followed by 20 consecutive winning months. Traders who make the transition from trading their own account to managing money should be closely attuned to whether managing other people's assets impacts their mental comfort level in making trading decisions.

Brandt improved his performance by eliminating what he calls "popcorn trades"—trades that have a significant profit but are then held until the entire profit is surrendered or, even worse, until the profit turns into a net loss. The negative experience of these trades early in his career prompted Brandt to institute rules to avoid such outcomes:

1. Once he has a net profit on a trade equal to 1% of his total equity, Brandt will take partial profits.

2. Once a trade gets within 30% of his profit target, Brandt will employ much closer stop protection.

Another of Brandt's trading rules is: If an open trade shows a net loss as of a Friday close, get out. Part of the reasoning here is that carrying a position over the weekend embeds more risk than holding the position overnight on a weekday. And since the assumption is that the position is at a net loss as of the Friday close, for a trader with a low risk threshold, such as Brandt, liquidating the position in this scenario is prudent risk management. However, the primary reason for the Friday close liquidation advice is that Brandt views the Friday close as particularly meaningful, a perspective that implies that a strong or weak close on Friday is more likely than not to see follow-through price action at the beginning of the following week. Insofar as this premise is true, even if the trade ultimately proves correct, there is a good chance there will be an opportunity to re-enter the trade at a better price in the following week.

One dilemma faced by all traders is: What should you do when your trading approach is out of sync with the market? Brandt would advise that the one thing you should not do is switch from a methodology that has worked well to some other approach. Now, there may be times when such a radical change is warranted, but only after substantial research and analysis confirm such action. A style transformation should never be undertaken lightly simply because a trader is experiencing an adverse streak in the market. So what is the appropriate action in those times when everything a trader does seems wrong? Brandt's response would be: Cut your trading size, substantially if necessary, until you are once again in sync with the markets.

It is noteworthy that Brandt's first losing year after becoming a full-time trader occurred immediately following his best trading year ever. I am reminded of Marty Schwartz's comment in *Market Wizards*: "My biggest losses have always followed my biggest profits."* The worst drawdowns often follow periods when everything seems to be working perfectly. Why is there a tendency for the worst losses to follow the best performance? One possible explanation is that winning streaks lead to complacency, and complacency leads to sloppy trading. In the strongly winning periods, the trader is least likely to consider what might go wrong, especially worst-case scenarios. An additional explanation is that periods of excellent performance are also likely to be times of high exposure. The moral is: If your portfolio is sailing to new highs almost daily and virtually all your trades are working, watch out! These are the times to guard against complacency and to be extra vigilant.

Regardless of your trading methodology, how do you know which types of trades work and don't work over the long run, and which circumstances are favorable or unfavorable? Systematic traders can answer these types of questions by testing each classification of trades. Discretionary traders, however, cannot test different alternatives because, by definition, discretionary traders can't algorithmically define what their past trades would have been. For discretionary traders, the only way to determine what types of trades work best and worst is to classify and record their trade results in real time. Over time, this manual process would yield the requisite data and the resulting trading insights. One thing Brandt regrets is that he failed to keep such a log. For example, he believes that trades that were not on his monitor list after his weekend analysis (that is, trades that were formulated as a response to *intraweek* price action) are subpar performers and could even be net losers. He believes this hypothesis, but he really doesn't know if it is true. He wishes he had kept category-delineated track records so he could answer such questions. The lesson here is that discretionary traders should categorize their trades and monitor trade outcomes for each category, so they will have the hard data to know what does and doesn't work.

Patience is a common trait among successful traders but not necessarily an innate one. In Brandt's case, his natural instincts lean closer to impatience than patience, but he has the self-discipline to enforce patience. For Brandt,

---

* Jack D. Schwager, *Market Wizards* (New Jersey, John Wiley and Sons, Inc., 2012), 275.

patience is an essential component of trade entry—"waiting for the right pitch," as he expresses it. He avoids the temptation of taking every trade idea and instead waits for the compelling trade—one where the upside potential appears three to four times greater than the required risk with near-equal perceived probability. In my interview with Joel Greenblatt, the founder of Gotham Capital, he made a similar point. Referencing Warren Buffett's comment, "There are no called strikes on Wall Street," Greenblatt said, "You can watch as many pitches as you want and only swing when everything sets up your way."*

Brandt's largest loss by an enormous margin was his long crude oil position at the start of the First Gulf War. Crude oil prices dropped by about 25% overnight. Brandt just liquidated his position on the opening at prices far below his intended stop. He did not consider waiting for a possible rebound to provide a better exit point. Speculating with the loss in this way would just have made the loss even worse, as crude oil prices continued to sink lower in the following weeks. Although a sample size of one doesn't prove anything, the implied lesson of "don't speculate with a trading loss," is sound advice. A similar rule would apply to trading errors. In both cases, traders should just liquidate the position rather than gamble with the loss.

Trading for a living, as Brandt does, may seem like an appealing lifestyle prospect to many, but it is a far more difficult goal to achieve than most people realize. Most aspiring traders are undercapitalized and underestimate the time it takes to develop a profitable methodology (three to five years by Brandt's estimate). Brandt advises against trading if losing your trading stake will meaningfully alter your lifestyle. It is also virtually impossible to succeed at trading if you are dependent on trading profits to pay your living expenses. As Brandt notes, "the markets are not an annuity"—you can't reasonably expect a steady income flow from trading.

Brandt's motto is: Strong opinions, weakly held. Have a strong reason for taking a trade, but once you are in a trade, be quick to exit if it doesn't behave as expected. There is nothing wrong with being dead wrong on a market if you exit the trade with only a small loss. And don't be concerned

---

* Jack D. Schwager, *Hedge Fund Market Wizards* (New Jersey, John Wiley & Sons, Inc., 2012), 476.

that changing your opinion will make you look foolish. Completely reversing your opinion on a market reflects flexibility, which is an attribute for a trader, not a weakness.

One of the essential characteristics of successful traders is that they love to trade. This perspective was true of Brandt in his first decade-plus of trading. You can hear it in his description of his early days when he had a virtual compulsion to trade. But by the early-to-mid 1990s, the fun had gone out of trading for Brandt. Trading, in his words, had become a "drudgery." This radical shift over time from loving trading to dreading it meant that Brandt has lost perhaps the most essential ingredient for trading success, and the wheels came off his performance. Over a decade later, Brandt's desire to trade re-emerged, and he once again was very successful.

The moral is: Be sure you really want to trade. And don't confuse wanting to be rich with wanting to trade. Unless you love the endeavor, you are unlikely to succeed.

JASON SHAPIRO

The Contrarian

The following individual names in this chapter are pseudonyms: David Reed, Walter Garrison, James Vandell, and Adam Wang. The following company names are pseudonyms: Cranmore Capital, Walter Garrison and Associates, The Henton Group, and Bryson Securities.

JASON Shapiro achieved consistent success as a trader by learning to do virtually the exact opposite of what he did instinctively in his first decade of trading. Shapiro's trading career spans over 30 years, running the gamut from trading his own account, trading portfolios for various asset management firms, and managing investor accounts through several iterations of his own CTA. Shapiro has managed assets from as little as several million dollars to as much as $600 million. At this stage of his life, he is quite content running his current CTA as a one-man shop and is not planning to expand beyond that simple operation.

Shapiro's track record dates back to 2001 and encompasses money managed at several different firms. His returns during any period were dependent on the target volatility level defined by the allocator, which varied. To allow for a consistent track record, I adjusted his returns to a single target volatility level for the entire period. At a 20% target volatility, his average annual compounded return is 34.0%, and his maximum drawdown is less than half of his average annual return at 16.1%. Because Shapiro's volatility is inflated by numerous large monthly gains, his volatility level overstates the implied risk, as demonstrated by the relatively constrained maximum drawdown, even at a 20% volatility level. Shapiro's return/risk numbers are extremely strong, with an *adjusted* Sortino ratio of 2.83 and a monthly Gain to Pain ratio of 2.45 (see Appendix 2 for the definitions and explanations of these metrics). Since he resumed trading in 2016 after a hiatus (discussed in the interview), all his performance statistics have surpassed the corresponding full-track-record numbers. One unusual characteristic of Shapiro's track record is that his returns are negatively correlated to stock, hedge fund, and CTA indexes.

I found Shapiro through an email I received, which read: "You absolutely must talk to Jason Shapiro. His track record is awesome, and his approach to the market very unique and thought-provoking." The message was sufficiently intriguing for me to follow up. I sent Shapiro the following email: "I am working on a new *Market Wizards* book, and Bill Dodge suggested you would be a perfect candidate for inclusion. Let me know if you are interested in participating."

Shapiro replied: "I'm hesitant to be in print, but I have to say the first two *Market Wizards* books set me on my life path, so I would be happy to speak and see where it goes if that sounds good to you."

I replied to Shapiro, requesting his return data to make sure he was a good fit for the book before committing to a trip to do an interview. I mentioned that I lived in Boulder and that I might have a trip to New York, which I could combine with a side trip to his home in Rhode Island. Shapiro replied, mentioning that he would be attending a wedding in Boulder the following week, suggesting we might get together for lunch. I replied, "That's super convenient!"

In our subsequent correspondence to arrange a meeting, I received the following email from Shapiro: "In the interest of not wanting to waste your time, I want you to know after thinking a lot about this over the weekend I've decided I really don't want to be in a book at this point in my life. I have a lot of respect for the work you have done, and it has had a major positive influence in my life, so I would still love to meet with you and talk markets and life, etc., but it has to be with the understanding of the above."

I was disappointed, but at least there was no travel involved. I agreed to meet Shapiro at my home office. I was tempted to ask Shapiro whether it would be OK to turn the tape recorder on while we talked, just in case he had a change of heart. But, he had been definitive about not wanting to appear in a book—even mine—so I didn't ask. In the next two hours, Shapiro told me his story. Not only was it a compelling narrative, but Shapiro also had a unique perspective on trading and offered eminently quotable insights and advice.

After our meeting, I regretted not having taken a shot at asking for permission to record our conversation. I sent Shapiro the following email: "Glad we connected while you were in Boulder. I have plenty of interview material to keep me busy until spring. Hopefully, with time to mull it over, you will reconsider participating with a guarantee of your right to review and approve the chapter I write. I think you've got a great story, and I'd love to save it for posterity. I'll check back in the spring to see where you are in terms of possible participation."

Four months later, I sent Shapiro the following email: "I hope all is well in this crazy time. As I mentioned to you before, I think your story would be a great addition to the *Market Wizards* book I am working on—lots of interesting material and good lessons. As I also indicated, I always let interview subjects review the final chapter copy and provide corrections and suggest (mutually agreeable) revisions before anything gets published. The bottom line is that you would have to approve the final product before I used it. So there is no risk in participating. Before, interviewing you would have required my scheduling a trip to Rhode Island. The virus has made things easy for me. The few remaining interviews I will do for the book will be conducted via Zoom. So would you be willing to give it a go?"

Shapiro replied that he would be willing to do the interview as long as he reserved the right to withhold approval for its inclusion in the book. Concerned about doing a ton of work for nothing, I replied, "Yes, that's the deal. But you should know that 98% of the work is turning the interview into a chapter (2% is the interview). If you felt there was a significant chance you might decide against approval regardless of whether or not you like the chapter I write, you should let me know. If, however, it's simply a matter of your not approving if you don't like the finished product, I am not concerned about that."

An hour later, Shapiro replied, "I'm pretty sure I would not like to be in the end product, Jack. It's just a strange personality thing. So I don't want you to waste your time, honestly." One minute later, I received the following email: "Ah, screw it, let's do it."

Did you have any particular career aspirations as a teenager?

No, I was a terror show as a teenager. I didn't go to school, and when I did go, I didn't pay attention. I got kicked out of three high schools.

Why did you get kicked out?

I didn't do any work because I wasn't interested in anything. And when I got into trouble, I didn't listen to anybody.

Was there any particular reason you had that chip-on-the-shoulder attitude?

I don't know. I thought kids were supposed to hate school, so I did. I thought kids were supposed to rebel against teachers, so I did.

How did your parents react to your getting kicked out of school multiple times?

My father pretty much backed out of it by the time I was 15 or 16 because he couldn't deal with it. My mother was a child psychologist, oddly enough, and her attitude was—and I thank her to this day for it—let him be, and eventually, he'll grow up and find himself.

Given that you had no interest in school and presumably had poor grades, did you even bother applying to any colleges?

I grew up in an upper-middle-class suburb. I don't think I even knew anybody who didn't go to college. My GPA when I graduated high school was 1.7.

What kind of college were you able to get into with those grades?

I went to the University of South Florida. USF is no Harvard. They had an admission policy that if your SAT and two achievement tests added up to some score, you automatically got in, regardless of your high school grades. I was always a good tester. I did well enough to get in. When they received my final high school grades, they placed me on academic probation.

What did you major in?

Finance.

Did you change your attitude in college versus what it was in high school?

Not in the first year. Sometime in my sophomore year, a friend and I got arrested for drunken stupidity. We spent the night in a holding pen in downtown Tampa. I came out of that experience and thought, "This is not what I want to be doing with my life." From that point on, I got straight A's.

What happened after you graduated?

In college, I took a liking to economics. It just made sense to me. In my last two years of college, I was reading a new economics or business book virtually every few days. In my senior year, I was also working almost a full-time job in real estate. I was getting really serious, and I thought I could get into one of the top MBA schools. I took the GMAT and received almost a perfect score; I got only one question wrong. I thought I might be able to get into Harvard, Chicago, or Wharton. But, of course, none of them let me in. They all wanted several years of work experience.

I knew I wasn't going to be getting a job at Goldman Sachs with a degree from USF, and I wasn't quite sure what to do. I graduated in 1988 when Japan was booming. I had taken Japanese in college, and someone told me about Japan needing English teachers. I went to Japan with my girlfriend and taught English there for about a year. While I was in Japan, I applied for a job at HSBC. I went to Hong Kong to interview for their executive development program, and I got the job. It was a five-year program where they rotated you to different departments.

I told HSBC that I wanted to be in the Treasury Department because I had found out that was where all the trading was done. That, however, was not what this program was about. The program was intended to develop generalist bankers who could become senior managers within the firm. I lasted about a year before they fired me. They hated me from the beginning. I was a wiseass, know-it-all Jewish kid from New Jersey working in a Scottish-origin institution that had been doing things the same way for 125 years and wasn't looking to change. It really wasn't a match.

Why did you get fired?

For the same reason the high schools had kicked me out: complete insubordination.

How did you get involved in trading?

While I was still at HSBC at the Hong Kong posting, I began trading Hang Seng futures. I played on an American softball team. One of the guys was a broker, and he introduced me to futures trading. I bought one Hang Seng futures contract, but I didn't know anything. I had been an avid reader since college, so my first thought was I better go out and buy a book, to get some idea of what I am doing. I still remember going out at lunch to the bookstore across the street from our office and looking for a trading book. I found this one book with a wizard on the cover that was about interviews with traders. I thought that sounded good.

So the first book you read on trading was mine?

I had read lots of books on finance and economics, but this was the first trading book I read. I bought the book at lunch, started reading at the office, and finished it before I went to sleep. I woke up the next morning and thought, "I know what I want to do with my life now. This makes perfect sense to me."

What made perfect sense?

These guys work on their own time. They were super contrarians. It didn't matter what other people thought. Politics didn't matter. I said to myself, "That is what I want to do."

Did any of the traders interviewed resonate particularly with you?

The ones that influenced me to this day were the Commodities Corporation traders, particularly Jones, Kovner, and Marcus.

What happened to your trading after you bought the Hang Seng index?

I think the Hang Seng index was about 4,000 when I bought it, and within six months, it was at 7,000. A great time to be a young, ignorant, and stupid trader is when there is a runaway bull market. I was like the 22-year-old kid buying NASDAQ stocks in 1999—you couldn't lose as long as you didn't go short.

What did you do after you got fired from HSBC?

I stayed in Hong Kong and worked for some local brokerage firms. I stayed up at night, called US accounts, and tried to convince them to trade through me. I got some orders, but the truth is I was just trading all the time.

I sat next to a smart, Chinese-Malaysian woman named Jacqui Chan who traded her own account and had previously traded for Morgan Stanley. She funded my futures account with $100,000. It was still a bull market, and once I was sufficiently ahead, Jackie took her $100,000 back out. I ran the account up to $700,000. I bought a Porsche, and I was planning how I would live like a billionaire.

Then the bull market ended. Within six months, I blew out the entire account. All I had left was the Porsche. I switched jobs, going to another brokerage firm. Eventually, I started trading my account again. I made a lot of money when Nick Leeson blew out.

[Nick Leeson was a trader for Barings Bank who was able to successfully hide a string of mounting losses. By the time his deception was uncovered, he had lost $1.4 billion, causing the collapse of Barings Bank.]

How did you make money off of that event?

Leeson had a massive short option position in the Nikkei stock index futures when he was found out. The Singapore government announced they were going to liquidate the entire position that day. Nikkei futures traded at a 15% to 20% discount to cash all day. I went long futures and short cash. The next day, cash and futures came back in line. I made almost 20% on that trade in one day.

By that time, I had grown tired of living in Hong Kong. I attended a luncheon presentation on the London Business School Masters in Finance program. It sounded interesting to me. I applied and was accepted. I had about half a year until the program started. I quit my job and took the next five months to travel through Asia, including Singapore, Malaysia, Thailand, Burma, China, and India.

I spent nine months in London, which was the length of the program. I spent 10% of my time on schoolwork and 90% of my time trading Hang Seng and S&P futures. It was during that period of trading that I learned a valuable lesson. The internet existed, but it was in its early days. Remember, it could take five minutes to load a page. So, I had my broker fax me charts every day. I was trading in and out and making some money.

At one point, I was super bullish on the Hang Seng index and had a large position. I was scheduled to go on vacation to Africa with a friend of mine during the holiday season break. I was going to be away for about a month with no way to get communication about the markets. I didn't want to get out of the Hang Seng position, but I had no way of following it. So, I told my broker to sell half my position if the Hang Seng went down to a specific price and to sell the remaining half if it got down to a specified lower price.

I left and traveled around Africa. Three weeks later, I called my broker and found out that the Hang Seng was 15% higher. I made over $300,000 while traveling. Here I was going through all the trouble of getting charts faxed every day and trading every day, and then I make far more money because I am away in Africa and can't see or do anything. That experience had a significant effect on me. It was like Jesse Livermore used to say, "You make your money in the sitting."

[Shapiro was referring to a quote in the book *Reminiscences of a Stock Operator* by Edwin Lefevre, whose unnamed protagonist is widely assumed to be based on Jesse Livermore. The specific quote is: "After spending many years in Wall Street and after making and losing millions of dollars, I want to tell you this: it never was my thinking that made the big money for me. It was always my sitting. Got that? My sitting tight!"]

Was there anything instructive about the London Business School Masters in Finance program itself?

The program gave me a solid grounding in financial theory. It was where I first learned about the concepts and math behind value at risk and other risk metrics. But there was another memorable and impactful experience that occurred because I was in that program. A professor at my business school was married to the head of global fixed income for Salomon Brothers. At my request, she was generous enough to set me up with a meeting with him. He was a very friendly and personable guy. He asked me how I approached the markets. I told him, "I try to find out what everyone is doing, and I do the opposite because when everyone is in the same trade, they lose money."

He smiled at what he perceived my naïveté and said, "Well, there are times when everyone can make money. Take the European interest rate convergence trade right now. Everyone is putting it on, and as long as the euro comes into existence, everyone will make money."

His reasoning was straightforward: If the euro came into existence, which seemed a very high probability, European interest rates had to converge. It was a mathematical certainty. The implied trade was to buy the bonds of high-yielding countries, such as Italy, and sell the bonds of low-yielding countries, such as Germany. Because this convergence trade seemed like such a sure thing, all the smart guys on Wall Street, including Long-Term Capital Management (LTCM) and Salomon Brothers, put the trade on in as much size as they possibly could.

Another trade that LTCM and other hedge funds had sizable positions in at the time was long Russian bonds because of their extremely high interest rates. In August 1998 Russia defaulted on its bonds. To help cover the margin calls on this trade gone very wrong, the holders of these positions had to sell other positions they held, which were primarily their European interest rate convergence trades. When they all tried to liquidate this trade at the same time, they found there were no buyers because anyone who wanted the position already had it on. This trade ended up blowing up LTCM and Salomon Brothers.

The fascinating thing about this whole episode is that the convergence trade ultimately worked. The euro did come into existence, and European interest rates did converge. But because the participation in this trade was so extensive, most of the people who had the trade on lost money, and in some cases, the loss was significant enough to sink their firms.

What happened after you finished the program at the London Business School?

I passed all my classes, but I never handed in the final paper because I just didn't want to do the work. I was sitting on over $500,000, and I thought I was king of the world. I was 27 years old, had plenty of money, and thought I could do anything I wanted. I knew I didn't want to look for another job. I had a girlfriend in Thailand, so I moved there. I rented a house in Phuket on the beach, brought in a satellite dish, and then proceeded to blow myself up. It took about eight months for me to lose all the money in my account.

How did you lose the money?

The answer to that question brings up another important lesson I learned that had a lasting effect on me. Now I see people make the same mistake all the time, and I recognize in them what I did then. At the time, the US stock market had been going straight up, and therefore I was going to be bearish, so I could be the hero. I kept shorting it and getting stopped out, over and over again, all the way up. I remember the market selling off after Greenspan made his "irrational exuberance" speech and thinking, "Look at how smart I am. Greenspan and I are the only ones who get it." That same day, the S&P rallied back and finished the day higher. I remember looking at my girlfriend and saying, "I'm fucking dead."

So, you did recognize the importance of the market initially selling off on bearish news and then closing higher.

I recognized it, but I had been shorting all along, and I fell into this psychological trap of thinking, "What, *now* I'm going to go long after being short all this time and losing all this money?" It was a fear of missing out on the short move when it finally happened. I don't ever think like that anymore, but I see other people fall into the same trap all the time.

After I lost all my money, I still felt, "I can do this." I sat down and wrote out pages and pages of what worked and what didn't work.

What was the essence of what you wrote down?

Don't have an opinion. We used to have a saying in Hong Kong, "Should've been up, but it's down, so short it; should've been down, but it's up, so long it." That trading philosophy became the basis of what I wanted to do: When the tape is telling you something, don't fight it; go with it.

What happened after you blew out your account?

I moved to Hawaii to be a partner in a new CTA. I had gotten married to my girlfriend in the interim, and she wasn't too thrilled to move to the US.

At this point, you had made money and blew out the account, and then made money again and blew out the account. What gave you the confidence that you could manage other people's money?

It wasn't a matter of confidence; it was what I was going to do. There were no two ways about it. I was going to figure it out. We opened a futures account with the other partner's money, which I traded. I did pretty well, and we used the track record to raise about a half-million dollars. I ran this account for about 18 months or so. Although I was doing OK, especially in terms of return to risk, this period coincided with the 1998–1999 bull market in NASDAQ stocks. I would tell potential investors, "We made 12% this year." They were clearly unimpressed and would say, "Yeah, so what, I made 12% this week." I went to some of the CTA conferences to try to raise money, and they looked at me like I was crazy. "What, we're going to give you money, so you can go back to Hawaii? Get the hell out of here." So, we never really got anywhere with the CTA, and it was clear that we weren't ever going to get anywhere. At the beginning of 2000, I moved to Chicago to take a job as a prop trader with the Gelber Group. I traded for them for about a year.

Why did you leave after a year?

I had a job offer from a hedge fund in New York. But before we discuss that, I want to go back to the CTA because I skipped over a pivotal part of the story. It was while I was running the CTA that I discovered the COT (Commitment of Traders) report. I was being a contrarian trying to short the stock market during the second half of 1999 because it had all the typical signs you see in a market bubble—the proverbial shoeshine-boy-giving-you-stock-tips euphoria. I knew it was a short, but the NASDAQ went up another 50% between August and January. I did a good job with risk management because, even though I was shorting stock futures, I didn't lose any money since I was making money elsewhere, and I was cutting my losses quickly. So when the market was making new highs, I wasn't staying short. I had at least learned those lessons. Later on, when I was at Gelber, I did catch the top and made money riding it down. Looking at the COT reports, I saw that the data never provided a sell signal until January 2000. I thought, "That is powerful data."

[The Commitment of Traders is a weekly report issued by the Commodity Futures Trading Commission (CFTC) that shows the breakdown of futures positions held by speculators and commercials (industry participants). The report also provides more granular breakdowns. For example, for physical commodity futures, the Disaggregated COT Report shows four categories: Producer/Merchant/Processor/User, Swap Dealers, Managed Money, and Other Reportables.

Since, by definition, there will always be an equal number of long and short positions in each futures contract, the commercial and speculator positions will move inversely to each other. The underlying premise of traders, such as Jason Shapiro, who use the report as a market indicator, is that commercials will tend to be right (because they are better informed) and, by implication, speculators will tend to be wrong. There is no consensus as to what particular readings (levels, change, or duration) constitute a bull or bear signal. Roughly speaking, though, a relatively high commercial long position (relative to historical levels and seasonal tendencies, if any) or, equivalently, a relatively large speculator short position, would be considered bullish, and the reverse configuration would be considered bearish.]

So, you might think that people are long, but are they actually long? While the small guys may have been buying stocks and making money in late 1999, the large speculators knew it was a bubble and were short. The bull market didn't end until they got squeezed out. Once they all got squeezed out, the market topped because there was no one left to buy. The COT report picked up that information. That is why I started to look very closely at the COT reports ever since that time.

So, did your approach change to not looking for a market top until the COT data told you that the environment was ripe for a potential top— namely, that the commercials were heavily short?

That's exactly right. I started using the data from that point on.

Aren't there times when the commercials are short for a very long time, and the market keeps going up, or the commercials are long for a very long time, and the market keeps going down?

Sure, but I don't just trade on the COT numbers. First of all, I need price action confirmation, and second, I have tight stops. For example, I got long heating oil about a month or two ago, which meant the commercials were very long, and the speculators were very short. I got stopped out. I put the position on again, and I got stopped out a second time. Then, all of a sudden, the positioning entirely changed—the commercials were no longer long—which meant that I could no longer buy that market. That is when the market really started to go down. So it is true that a couple of months ago, the COT suggested being long the market. But within a few weeks, it had turned neutral again, and that is when the price collapse really got going.

In the COT reports, are you looking just at position levels, or do you also use the weekly change in positions?

I just use the position levels.

There are some markets, such as gold and crude oil, where the commercials are almost always short. I assume you must be looking at *relative* as opposed to *absolute* levels. Is it correct to say that in these types of markets, a buy area for the COT would be when commercials are short, but the short position is relatively small compared with the historical range?

That's correct. I look at relative levels.

What happened with the hedge fund in New York that you joined?

It turned out that it wasn't as much a hedge fund as a bunch of thieves and incompetent traders in a room. At that point, I started using the COT numbers, not in any systematic way, but just looking at the report. It didn't really matter. The other guys in the firm were such amateurs that all I had to do was listen to what they were doing and do the opposite. In the year I was there, I made really good returns, while they all lost money. At the end of the year, they kicked me out.

Why would they kick you out when you were the only one who made money?

Those guys hated me. I was essentially fading them, making money, while they were losing money.

Who fired you?

This guy named Leno, who managed the firm.

What reason did he give you?

He told me they weren't going to be trading futures anymore.

Why did you say they were a bunch of thieves?

A few years after I left, the FBI busted Leno for insider trading.

What did you do after you left the hedge fund?

I had no job, and I had a wife who was telling me I was a loser. My wife hated me, and she wanted a divorce. At the time, I was living in Princeton. I went to see a lawyer, and he asked me what I did. When I told him I was a trader, he asked me if I had ever heard of Helmut Weymar. I told him that I knew who he was because I had read *Market Wizards*. [Helmut Weymar was a cofounder of Commodities Corporation, the firm that had hired some of the great traders interviewed in *Market Wizards*, as well as Peter Brandt (see Chapter 1).] The lawyer told me that his wife and Helmut's wife were best friends. I told him that if he wanted to be my divorce lawyer, he had to get his wife to introduce me to Helmut.

Two days later, I was sitting in front of Helmut in his large office with the fireplace. Although Helmut had just sold the firm to Goldman Sachs, he still had his office in the Commodities Corporation building. I told Helmut about how I was a contrarian trader and used the COT reports as a guide for market positioning. Helmut backed me, giving me $2 million to manage. He also brought me in front of the new management of Commodities Corporation, and they gave me another $2 million. I started a small CTA with $4 million. I did well for them, making 22% in my first year managing the account. I was expecting that they would give me more money to manage, but it never happened. I think it was a political thing where the new Goldman Sachs people didn't want to be told what to do by Helmut, who was supposed to be leaving the firm.

At the time, I got a job offer from David Reed, who ran Cranmore Capital Management to trade an account for them. Knowing David the way I do now, but I didn't know then, he hired me for one reason: He figured that if Helmut wanted me, then he wanted me. He offered me a bonus to join the firm. So I closed my CTA and moved up to Connecticut to work for Reed.

How much money did he give you to manage?

He gave me a $5 million account to manage to start, which was still more than I was managing for Helmut and Commodities Corporation, and I knew they had the assets to build the account to much larger levels if I did well.

So how did that work out?

It was a nightmare. As much as Reed told me that he got everything I was saying when he recruited me, once I was there, he didn't get it at all. During the six months I was there, trend following went through a great period.

I was about to ask you about that. I know that Reed's firm—at least in those days—was entirely focused on trend-following strategies. Your approach—contrarian trading—was virtually the exact opposite.

It should have been complementary, though, because my approach would be negatively correlated to their trend-following strategies. After I had been there for a half year, Reed called me into his office. I was down maybe

1% or 2% at the most, but during the same time, trend following had a great run. He said, "I don't understand how your strategies will work. I'm going to make money 70% of the time. That means that you're going to lose money 70% of the time."

I said, "We talked about this for a month while you were recruiting me. I told you why that wasn't the case, and you agreed it wasn't the case." Variations of this conversation went on for a month or so, and I was getting increasingly frustrated. During that time, the firm moved into new offices, and Reed gave a speech to the employees about how the key to life was that you should never be satisfied. I thought that was the most ridiculous advice I had ever heard. When I was traveling through Burma, I spent a month in a monastery, and my attitude is that you should always be satisfied. I thought to myself, "I'm getting the hell out of here." The next day I walked into Reed's office, gave him back my signup bonus money, and left.

Tell me about your monastery experience in Burma.

I went to Burma to check it out. At that time, it was just opening to foreigners. The monastery sits in the middle of Inle Lake, which is the largest lake in Burma. The only way to get there was by longboat, which the boatman rowed standing up using his leg.

I remember sitting on the floor in the monastery eating from a bowl of peanuts they had there. A monk came over, sat beside me, and spoke to me in perfect English. After talking for a while, he invited me to stay. I ended up staying for a month.

I shaved my head and sat in a room meditating without talking to anyone. But the thing that impacted me most was going out with the monks every morning to receive alms. The monks don't work or cook. They depend on the people to give them food to eat. We had to go out every morning with our alms bowl and walk through these villages, and the people would fill our bowls with rice and fish, and that is what we would eat for the day. That experience had a big effect on me. I was a kid from an upper-middle-class background who was given everything he needed and took advantage of it to the extreme. And here I was walking around in Burma, and these people who didn't have two dollars to their name were giving me food to eat every day. It was a very humbling experience.

Did your experience at the monastery change you? Do you think you were a different person after the monastery experience than before it?

There is no question about it. When you sit in a place for a month with nothing to do but think, and the only things you eat are what's given to you, it changes your attitude as to what is important. At that point in my life, what seemed important was professional success and getting a big house. Afterward, I never cared about any of that. It helped me calm down from the idea that money is everything and is so important—because it's not.

So what is important?

Happiness—spending your day doing what you want to do. If I'm good at what I do, I make money, and that's great, but it's not the driver. The driver is the satisfaction I get from being good at something. People say, "It's easy for you to say that now because you have money." OK, that's true, but there have been quite a few times when I was deadass broke. When I started managing money for Helmut, I had two kids, and we lived in a two-bedroom apartment—and my office was in one of the bedrooms! I couldn't even afford a desk; I used one of those IKEA TV stands. My kids were little then. I still remember going to the store to buy a camcorder. It was $700, and I couldn't afford to buy it.

While there was some pressure in not having money, the truth is that I was as happy then as I am now. I couldn't believe it: Helmut Weymar, who had hired some of the greatest traders who have ever lived, was giving me money, and I was trading for a living. Happiness is believing that the future will be better than the past.

Even now, I just bought this house, and it's great, and I love it, but it is not a mansion on the beach. I drive a 1998 Toyota 4Runner. It doesn't mean anything to me; it's just a piece of transportation. I don't need to be driving around in a Land Rover. I think it all started with my being in that monastery in Burma.

What did you do after you left Cranmore Capital?

I went back to Helmut, and he gave me some money to manage. I also got some other investor money, and I restarted my CTA with about $3 million. I did that for almost two years, making about 10% to 15% a year. With only $3 million under management, it is tough to raise any more money. You need infrastructure, and I couldn't afford infrastructure. It's the whole catch-22 thing. Also, I'm not exactly a marketing guy.

An acquaintance I had became the CIO at Walter Garrison and Associates, a large multistrategy hedge fund. He offered me a job as a trader for the firm with a $250,000 salary, a starting account of $50 million to manage, a full-time quant working for me, and a big office with a window overlooking Park Avenue. So, I closed my CTA again and went to work for Walter Garrison.

Having a full-time quant assigned to me allowed me to quantify a lot of what I was doing. We ran the program mostly systematized, but sometimes I would override a system trade, and sometimes I would take a trade the system wasn't putting on.

Were those non-systematic trades helpful or detrimental?

They made money. My trader would argue with me all the time, saying, "Why are we doing this?" And I would tell him, "Because it makes money." We tracked what happened when I overrode the system. If it didn't make money, I wouldn't have continued to do it.

What types of trades were you putting on that weren't part of the system?

They were mostly stock index trades. I spoke regularly to this guy James Vandell, a former colleague. James was a perennial bear. Whenever James would get super bearish, I would go long, and when he would get bullish, which didn't happen very often, I would go short. It's hard to see what a winner looks like, but it's easy to see what a loser looks like. I thought to myself, "I've been there." The things James was saying and doing were exactly what I was thinking and doing when I blew up in Thailand. I recognized it because I had done the same thing before. I'm not saying that I was smarter than him; I'm saying that he was doing exactly what I did, and I knew how that would end because I went broke. So, this time, I was going to do the opposite of what was essentially a proxy for me back in Thailand and make money off it instead of losing money. When the COT wasn't providing a trade signal, and James had a strong opinion, he was my contrarian indicator.

So, instead of using the COT numbers as the basis for a trade, you were using a human COT.

It's precisely the same thing. People ask me all the time, "What would you do if they stopped publishing the COT numbers?" I tell them that I can trade right off of CNBC. You can watch CNBC or Bloomberg all day, and 10 people will come on and say the exact same thing.

Have you actually done that—place trades based on fading opinions on CNBC?

I do it all the time. Most of the time, the COT will line up with the opinions on TV anyway. If everyone is saying you have to buy gold, it's no coincidence that the COT is showing everyone is long gold.

I don't just make these trades on a whim, though. These guys may all be talking about something, but I still need the market to provide confirmation. If they are all super bearish, and the Dow goes down one thousand points and closes on the low, I'm not going to be a buyer. But if they are all super bearish, and some really negative news came out that day, but the market closes higher, I'm buying. I learned my lesson. You don't fight the tape. Be patient, and the market will tell you when.

The low of the reversal day will be my stop. I'm not going to argue with it. If I go long, and the market goes back to the low of that day, I'm out. I'm so disciplined with this stuff. It's not just that I have a stop on every trade, which I do, but that I have a stop that is based on some meaningful market move. The news came out, the market gapped down, and then it closed up. OK, that low is going to be my stop forever. If that low is hit, I'm out.

So the contrary opinion indicators you use only tell you what direction you should be looking for a trade in a given market, but to actually get a trade, you have to wait for a signal based on the market action. And if that market action subsequently gets contradicted, the premise for your trade is eliminated, and you're out.

Yes, that's 100% correct. You need both the market positioning and the market action. I don't know which is more important, but they are both extremely critical.

That explains how you can be a contrarian in the market without having open-ended risk.

If you pay attention to both the positioning and market action, you won't get run over.

I understand that if the market goes back to the low or high of the day you view as the reversal point, you will stop out of the position, but what gets you out if your stop is not hit?

I will take profits when the market positioning that got me into the trade goes back to neutral.

What constitutes a neutral reading?

I have a sentiment-based oscillator I developed. When it goes to zero, I look to be a buyer, when it goes back to 50, I'm out.

Is your oscillator based just on the COT reports, or does it include other inputs?

I prefer not to put the answer to that question in the book.

Earlier, you mentioned using CNBC as a contrary indicator. Is there any particular program that you pay the most attention to?

I watch *Fast Money* religiously at 5 p.m. EST every day. I can't tell you how much money I've made off of that show. It's the greatest consensus show ever. They have four people on who give their opinions. All I watch is the first five minutes when they come up with their excuses for why they think the market did what it did that day, and the last two minutes in a segment called *Final Trade* when they all come up with their trade idea for the next day. There is one guy on the program named Brian Kelly, who I have now watched for years. He is wrong by such a larger percentage than random that it is hard to believe. I will never have a position on if he is recommending it.

Do you watch CNBC during the trading day?

I have it on in the background all day. If someone comes on talking about something I'm interested in, I'll turn the volume up. I already know what they're going to say because they all say the same thing. If the market has been going down, they will make the bearish argument. Recently, on this rebound off the March low [the March 2020 low, which followed the huge selloff triggered by events related to the COVID-19 pandemic], you kept on hearing lines like: "The market doesn't make any sense right here." "The low is not in." "The market has gone up too far, too fast." In the meantime, the market has continued to rally further. All these people think they are smarter than the market. Again, I've been there. They are not. No one is.

The most powerful word in the markets is "despite." If you hear or see a comment like, "Despite the increase in oil inventories being much higher than expected, oil prices closed higher," that is the tape telling you what is going to happen. Everyone saw inventories were much higher than expected. Why did the market close up? The tape knows more than anyone else.

Were you long on the rebound off the March low?

Yes, at the lows, the COT data was in a bullish zone for the Dow futures, and we had an upside reversal on a day when all the news was negative. Funny enough, that previous evening, I was on a chat group started by a former colleague. One of the guys on the call, Adam Wang, is one of the greatest fades that I know. Adam is one of those Ph.D., smarter-than-everyone-else type of guys who works as a risk manager. He doesn't trade any money because if he did, he would blow out.

It was one of those days when the S&P was down sharply again to a new low for the move. Adam came on the group chat and said, "I haven't seen any panic. This market has a lot further to go. There hasn't been any capitulation yet." It was the same thing everyone on TV was saying that week. This is a guy who hadn't mentioned anything about the market going down before. Now that the market is down 30% in three weeks, he's saying it's not the bottom because there is no capitulation.

As soon as Adam opened his mouth, I knew the market was going to run. The market went limit down to new lows that night. I put on a partial long position that night. I put on the full position the next day as the market rallied sharply off the lows, closing up for the day, despite a preponderance of bearish news.

Was it a coincidence that this chat was on the same day that the market spiked to a major relative low?

It's never a coincidence. That's the point. Adam was a sample of everyone else. The fact that the chat started lighting up was itself a sign that the market was at a capitulation point. If all these guys were talking about how bearish the market was, then everyone was talking about it.

We got off on a tangent in your career story. What happened with your position at Garrison?

I went from $50 million to $600 million under management in two years. I was there five years and did really well, making money every year, including 2008. I thought the 2008 performance was my finest moment since trend following did exceptionally well that year, and I used a countertrend approach. Everything was great. I had a few million in the bank, and I lived in a big house in Westport, Connecticut.

If everything was going so well, why did you leave Garrison?

I left because the political structure in the firm changed in a way I thought would be problematic. At that point, I was working from home. I would go into the office only once a month for a portfolio managers meeting. I didn't want to be a partner or a boss; all I wanted was to be left alone and manage money.

As I was trying to figure out what to do, the former marketing director at Garrison, who had left to join The Henton Group, contacted me. He wanted me to manage money for them. I went to Walter and asked him to start a separate CTA that I would manage. He didn't want to set a precedent because then the other portfolio managers would also want their own fund. I totally understood his point; you can't run a business on exceptions. So I left.

Were you managing close to $600 million when you left Garrison?

No, Garrison lost a lot of assets after 2008. So, when I left, I was managing only about $150 million.

How long were you at Henton after you left Garrison?

I wasn't at Henton; I managed their account through a CTA I set up.

How much money were you managing?

I managed $150 million for Henton, and I raised another $60 million from other investors. I managed those accounts for three years until I shut down my CTA.

Why did you shut down your CTA?

It was a life event. I got divorced—the divorce I never got in Princeton.

I guess the divorce was the catalyst, but were there other reasons why you decided to shut down the CTA?

I was not enjoying what I was doing at all. I like to trade, and I wasn't doing any trading. I was running my trading program totally systematized for marketing purposes. Investors would ask, "Are you 100% systematized?" I could just answer the question, "Yes." Initially, it had seemed like a good idea. It was an easy life. I didn't even have to think. I could hire a trader whose only job was to execute the orders the system generated. Although the returns were still good, they were degrading from what I had done before. And I couldn't go back to doing a discretionary overlay because we had marketed the program as being fully systematic, and investors had put us in their fully systematic fund products.

Also, I was really bothered by the return degradation. My CTA was making money, but it wasn't doing anything special. My annual return to maximum drawdown ratio had always been in the 3 to 4 area, now it was in the 2 area. I had spent so many years trading, blew out so many times, and learned so many lessons that I felt I should be one of the top traders in the world. And, if I wasn't going to be that, then screw it.

I had six people working for me, and I hated it. I didn't like managing people and being responsible for their success. My staff looked to me to go out and help with the marketing, which I didn't like doing.

Why did you have so many people working for you?

Because, when I started the CTA, I was planning to build an institutional asset management firm. I was going to raise a few billion dollars. So, I had to have a trader, a marketing guy, a quant, etc.

What was the name of your CTA?

Perbak.

Perback?

P-E-R-B-A-K.

Did Perbak stand for something?

The night we had to name the CTA, I was reading a book called *How Nature Works* by a famous physicist named Per Bak. I liked the things he had to say about human nature, so I named the firm after him. We would give out his book to people who came to our office.

After you shut down the CTA, did you stop trading altogether—even for your own account?

Yes, I bought a farm in Rhode Island.

What was your plan?

I didn't have one. I just felt I had to reevaluate my life. I figured I would live like Thoreau for a while. It took me six months to throw out my back chopping wood.

Why did you pick Rhode Island?

It was close enough to my kids and far enough from my ex-wife, who lived in Connecticut. I also picked Rhode Island because of a business opportunity. Marijuana had just become legal in Rhode Island, and it looked to me like an incredible opportunity. There was so much money to be made, and there was a significant barrier to entry.

What barrier?

Most people didn't want to have the stigma of being involved in the pot business. I didn't care about any stigma.

What was the opportunity that you saw?

A lot of people wanted to grow pot, but they didn't have any money to start an operation. We're not talking about doctors, lawyers, or hedge fund managers looking to grow pot; these are 24-year-old kids who didn't go to college and are working at some blue-collar job. They didn't have the $150,000–$200,000 startup cost for setting up a growing facility that could generate $400,000 a year in revenue. I started building these facilities and then renting them out at $6,000 a month. I knew what the operators were making and that they could easily afford that rent. It would take me about two years to make back my investment.

I guess the people who were running these operations also did quite well.

They were making $200,000 or more a year, and I did a six-year lease-to-own deal with them, so they owned the business after six years. It was definitely a win-win situation and a good business idea.

How many people did you set up in this business?

About 40.

When did you get back to trading?

About a year and a half after I had shut down my CTA. Even though I was very happily remarried and had all the money I needed, I went through a weird depression. I felt that something was missing in my life. The only thing I could think of was trading. It was what I had done for 25 years of my life, and it was what I was best at. I thought I could be one of the best traders in the world. So why was I not doing it? Through all the ups and downs in my life, I had never gone through any depression.

Didn't you get depressed at all those times you lost all your money?

I may have been sad temporarily, but I was never depressed about it. My reaction always was, "OK, what do I have to do now to make sure this doesn't happen again?"

How did you figure out what was causing your depression?

It was obvious. I loved trading.

Was there a catalyst that got you back into trading?

I visited an old friend and neighbor and talked to him about how I felt. He put me in touch with a contact he had at Bryson Securities, and they gave me an account to trade. Bryson's attitude is, "We don't care what you do; just make money." If you lose money, you're gone; if you make money, they love you. They never questioned my trades or what I did. Not trading for 18 months clears your mind. I used my system and overlaid my discretion and risk management on top of it. I was able to use everything that I knew from my 25 years of experience. It was great.

Besides the times you blew out early in your trading career, are there any trades that stand out as being particularly painful?

No. I don't get stuck in bad trades; I just get stopped out. I may miss trades because I am stubborn. But I will never, ever violate my stop. So, I don't get myself in those situations anymore.

Obviously, a critical component of your risk management is placing a stop on every trade at a point that negates your hypothesis that the market has peaked or bottomed. Are there other elements in your risk management strategy?

When investors talk to me about my risk management, they ask, "Do you use value at risk?" I tell them that I don't because I think it is garbage. Value at risk is based on historical correlations, whether it is 30 days, 60 days, 90 days, or longer. When you get markets like we've seen recently [the interview was conducted April 2020], correlations can break down in 48 hours. The value at risk will have nothing to do with the current risk. By the time value at risk catches up to reflecting an abrupt shift in correlations, it's too late.

I am my own risk management. I look at the market all day. I'm paying attention to the market correlations, especially the correlations of the positions I am in. If I see that I am concentrated in positions that are all moving together, I will either reduce my position or put on a position that will be inversely correlated. That is why my volatility hasn't gone up despite the explosion of market volatility during the past couple of months. I saw what was happening and what my positions were, and I reduced my positions. Did I make money? Yes, but what's even better is that my volatility didn't go up one iota. If you look at my daily returns, you wouldn't have any idea that what had just happened in the markets happened.

Was that because you reduced your positions or because you added uncorrelated positions?

It was mostly due to my reducing positions. However, when correlations suddenly increase, as they did recently, I will be more inclined to add an inversely correlated position without necessarily having an official signal. As an example, after the February 2020 top, I took a short trade in the stock index, even though it wasn't my typical type of signal, because being short the stock index, when I was long other markets, reduced my risk.

The February top in the stock market was unusual. Typically, the market goes up, up, up, and speculators get more and more long. In this case, the speculator position wasn't meaningfully long at the top. But then the market came down 5%, and everyone got long. And I saw the same thing on TV where everyone was saying you have to buy the dip. Then the COT report came out, and it showed everyone had bought the dip. It was the largest long speculator position in years. That was when I realized that the market was a massive short, and whatever the impact of the virus was, it was going to get a lot worse.

I assume that was an atypical trade because even though you had an extreme COT reading, you couldn't have had a reversal day signal here since the market had already declined 5% from the high. What was the trigger that got you short? Was it just the COT reading?

The trigger was that I was long across the board. I have a system for trading stock indexes that I don't use very often, but I will use it as a risk mitigator when needed. The idea is that if NASDAQ, a higher beta index, is lagging the Dow, a lower beta index, when the market is up—which is not the price action you would expect—and I'm long equity-correlated positions, then I will short NASDAQ. After the COT report came out, we had a one- or two-day bounce in which the NASDAQ lagged the Dow. That price action was enough to get me short since I was looking for an offset to my longs anyway.

Do you sometimes put on trades that are not based on the COT numbers?

Sometimes, I will put on a non-COT trade. The COT is not a perfect indicator. There has never been and will never be a perfect indicator. But, because I have lost so much money in the market and made such terrible trades, I physically cannot put on a non-contrarian trade.

There are days when I'm sitting here, and everyone on TV is saying the same thing: "The market is going down." Then I get a call from someone who I know is always wrong, and he's telling me how the market is going down. Then I'll see something on LinkedIn from another guy who is wrong all the time, saying the same thing. This type of day will happen a few times a year. And while everyone is saying the same thing about how bearish the market is, the market is going up, and it doesn't make sense. I'll put that trade on because I have seen it so many times. It's all that I do, so I have developed an instinct for those types of situations. I think intuition is just experience.

Do you think you have been successful because your inner core is contrarian?

Yes, definitely. Being a contrarian is instinctive for me. I've been a contrarian since I was a kid. It's part of my DNA. Fortunately for me, it is a valuable trait to have as a trader. I try to see when everyone is doing the same thing, and I go the opposite way. By definition, everyone can't make outsize returns. So if everyone is doing something, the only way to make outsize returns is by being on the other side. The great thing about the markets is that I can wait until there is a confirmation before taking the opposite position.

Do the lessons you have learned in the markets spill over in the way you live your life?

It spills over in every way I live my life, and that's the problem [he laughs]. Being a contrarian works in the markets, but it doesn't work in social situations. People want to be liked; they want to be part of a group. Being a contrarian doesn't win you any friends. It's a lonely place to be. My wife calls me a pathological contrarian. I'm not saying it's healthy. I'm not saying everyone should live that way.

Give me an example of how you are a contrarian outside of trading.

I get into arguments with my friends who are Democrats, and they all think I am a conservative Republican. I get into arguments with my friends who are Republicans, and they all think I am a bleeding heart liberal. It's automatic for me to take the other side. People get into such one-sided views that their logic disappears. If you ask me on a personal basis whether I think Donald Trump is an asshole, yes, I think he is an asshole. But does that mean every single thing he says has to be lambasted, every single time? That's illogical.

OK, I'll bite. Give me an example of something Trump said that he was lambasted for that actually was right.

He said he would win the election, which everyone thought was ridiculous, and he is the president.

I assume when you argue with someone, whether they are liberal or conservative, it is because you believe in the opposing view on that particular issue, or do you actually argue just for the sake of it?

Sometimes, I will argue just for the sake of it because I think it is important for people to hear the other side.

So, if you are at a party where most of the people are liberals, you will argue the conservative side, and if you are at a party where most of the people are conservatives, you will argue the liberal side.

100%. I have done that so many times, I can't even tell you.

Besides being a contrarian, what else has been critical to your success?

I succeeded because I have failed so many times, and I had an open mind about failure and was able to learn from it. I failed because I sucked, not because the market was wrong or because someone screwed me, or any of the other excuses you hear.

People fail, and they quit; they get scared. For some reason, I have a risk instinct. I hate failing, but I don't mind taking the risk and then failing. I have a good friend who is a wonderful human being. His risk appetite is basically zero. He is a lawyer, making a good living, but he hates what he is doing. He'll call me up complaining and say, "I know this guy is guilty, and he is a racist, and I have to defend him." I tell him, "Why don't you just quit, take your money, and do something else." But he just can't process that. And I can't process not doing that. Why not take the risk? You're going to die one day anyway.

Is your approach as effective now as it was 20 years ago when you first started using it, or has it been affected by all the structural changes in the market since then?

I don't think it's any different now than it ever was in history. Everyone is short; the market doesn't go down on bad news; the market starts to go up. That is what a market bottom is. The market doesn't bottom on good news; it bottoms on bad news. Also, there is a sound underlying reason why the COT has remained and should remain a useful indicator.

My daughter just took a job with one of the physical commodity companies. She doesn't know any of this stuff. She didn't study finance; she majored in international relations. I was talking to her recently.

"Let me ask you something, Dad," she says. "I'm learning about hedging. If they [her company] own mines, then they know what the supply is, right?"

I answer, "Yes."

"And, if they are talking to customers all the time, then they know what demand is, right?"

I answer, "Yes."

"Wouldn't they have inside information on their hedging then?"

I say, "There you go!" [He claps his hands as he says this.] "That's exactly what I do. They are the commercials, and I trade on the same side they do."

"But I thought you did your own thing," she says.

I say, "That *is my own thing*. I'm going with the people who have the most knowledge. That's the whole point."

You were extremely reluctant to do this interview. In fact, you turned me down at least twice. What changed your mind?

My wife is continually telling me that I should write a book with my ideas, so people could learn from it. I know I am never going to write a book. So I think it is a good idea for someone to write down these concepts. It's not my story that is important but rather the idea of how markets really work. I don't want to sound pompous like I'm the only one who understands how the markets work. Some people get it, but not a lot, which I guess is fortunate. If everyone agreed, the game would be over.

If I have any message to the world—and it is the reason I agreed to do this interview—it is to convey the importance of participation. Everyone understands that the market is a discounting mechanism. What they don't realize is that the discounting mechanism is not price; it's participation. It's not that the price has gone from 50 to 100, and therefore the bullish fundamentals are discounted. Instead, it's everyone is long, and consequently, the bullish fundamentals are discounted. Amazon stock provides a great example of this principle. When it reached the $700–$800 level, everyone thought the price was ridiculous. There was lots of talk about Amazon being a bubble. It was clear, though, that the majority of people did not own it, or they wouldn't be calling it a bubble. The stock is now trading above $2,300.

The critical role of participation is a concept that applies well beyond trading. An example I like to use, which is outside the sphere of trading, is football betting. If you have the best team in the NFL playing the worst team in the NFL, everyone knows who is probably going to win. But that is not what you are betting on; you're betting on the point spread. I don't see how any type of analysis you could do could tell you whether the point spread is overvalued or undervalued. To me, the answer lies in participation. If everyone is betting on one side, then the point spread will have to move, and it will probably move too far. In fact, I have a football betting system that looks at 30 guys who make picks versus the spread. When 25 or more of them pick the same team, which happens only about six times a year, the other team will win 80% of the time. Now, is that because I have any ability to pick football spreads [he laughs]? No, it's because if over 80% of the guys in my sample are choosing the same team, then everyone else must be doing the same thing too, and the point spread is probably too wide.

The concept that a market's discounting mechanism is based on speculator participation, not price, is the most important thing that I know.

Given the developments of the past few decades—algorithmic trading, high-frequency trading, artificial intelligence, the proliferation of hedge funds—is it still possible for the individual trader to beat the market? Jason Shapiro provides the perfect illustration of why I believe the answer to this question is "yes."

At its core, Shapiro's trading success is grounded in exploiting the flaw in the emotion-based trading decisions of other market participants. Shapiro seeks to go short at times when bullish euphoria reigns supreme and to go long at times when bearish sentiment has become prevalent. It is noteworthy that the efficacy of Shapiro's approach has not deteriorated one iota in the two decades he has used it, despite all the significant changes that have occurred during that time. While the structure of markets, the nature of the participants, and the available trading tools have all changed dramatically over time, the one thing that has not changed is human emotion. And it is the immutability of human emotions that assures that trading opportunities will continue to prevail, notwithstanding the changes above.

To trade like Shapiro requires going against your inherent human instincts. You need to be able to sell when your natural instincts would be more inclined to fear missing out on a soaring bull market, and to buy when any imminent end to an unrelenting bear market seems unimaginable. Of course, by itself, going short in a roaring bull market or long in an unabated bear market is an invitation to financial ruin. As expressed in the famous adage of uncertain origin (questionably attributed to John Maynard Keynes), "Markets can stay irrational longer than you can stay solvent."

To make a contrarian trading approach work, a method for timing entry into markets is absolutely critical. There are two essential components to Shapiro's approach:

1. Taking positions counter to the extremes of speculator market positioning;

2. Timing the entry into such positions based on market action.

Shapiro relies primarily on the weekly Commitment of Traders (COT) report to determine extremes in market sentiment. He looks to be on the opposite side of extremes in speculator positioning, or equivalently, on the same side as commercial positioning. As a supplemental input, he will also use financial TV shows. So, yes, watching financial TV programs can be useful in your trading—*as a contrarian indicator!*

For timing his contrarian positions, Shapiro will look for market reversals that occur despite a preponderance of news in the opposite direction. Markets bottom on bearish news and top on bullish news. Why? Before interviewing Shapiro, my answer to this question would have been that fundamentals are only bearish or bullish relative to price, and at some price, the news is fully discounted. Although this answer is still valid, Shapiro has a better explanation: participation. Markets bottom because speculators are already fully positioned short—a condition that will naturally occur in an environment of pervasive bearish news. A similar explanation would apply to market tops.

Early in his trading career, Shapiro blew out his account twice: once by assuming a bull market would go on forever and once by fighting a bull market. The common denominator in these opposite circumstances was the absence of risk management to prevent an account-damaging loss on one wrong idea.

If there is one absolute in Shapiro's trading methodology, it is that he will have a stop-loss on every position. This rule will prevent substantial losses when the implications of the COT report are wrong. Shapiro will select a stop point that contradicts his hypothesis that the market has bottomed or topped.

Risk management is not merely essential for individual trades, it needs to be applied at the portfolio level as well. Specifically, traders need to be cognizant of those times when markets become highly correlated. In such situations, the risk for any given portfolio may be much greater than normal because of the higher probability of simultaneous adverse price moves in multiple positions. Shapiro manages the increased risk of higher correlation markets by reducing his overall position size and by seeking inversely correlated trades to add to the portfolio.

One of the most profitable periods in Shapiro's early trading career occurred when he went on a three-week vacation in Africa—a trip that made monitoring his market position impossible. Before leaving, Shapiro provided his broker with instructions for liquidating his position in the event of an adverse price move. When he returned, Shapiro was pleasantly surprised to discover that his position had accumulated a hefty profit while he was gone. By not being able to watch his position, Shapiro avoided the temptation to take profits, which was hugely beneficial. He realized that his "sitting" with the position had turned out to be far more profitable than his daily trading. This lesson proved long lasting and is manifested in the trading methodology Shapiro ultimately developed. If Shapiro is not stopped out of a trade, he will hold it until his COT-based oscillator turns neutral—an approach that will often require holding a position for months and through multiple market gyrations.

I have frequently admonished traders not to listen to other people. As one representative quote: "If you listen to anyone else's opinion, no matter how smart or skillful the trader might be, I guarantee it is going to end badly."* After interviewing Shapiro, I feel that I need to include a qualification in that prior advice. Namely, if you know or can identify traders or commentators who are reliably wrong—a task far easier than finding those who reliably right—then their opinions could well be useful *in a contrarian sense.*

---

* Jack D. Schwager, *The Little Book of Market Wizards* (New Jersey, John Wiley and Sons, Inc., 2014), 72.

RICHARD BARGH

The Importance of Mindset

I T is ironic that although Richard Bargh was consistently profitable from his start as a trader, he still came perilously close to failing several times. The reasons why are detailed in the interview. Bargh began his career trading a proprietary account. Officially, the starting equity in his account was marked at zero. Monthly withdrawals that averaged near £3,000 kept his account equity within £15,000 of zero for the first 14 months, making it impossible to calculate returns for this period. Then, a giant winning trade permanently moved his account equity into meaningful positive territory.

Bargh's annualized return for the six-plus years since that juncture (the last 4½ years trading his own account) is an astounding 280%. Bargh's average return is amplified by the fact he traded his futures account at a high margin-to-equity ratio, keeping a much smaller amount of cash in excess to margin requirements in his account than is typical for most futures traders. However, the extremely high margin-to-equity Bargh employed commensurately amplified all his risk numbers as well. Therefore, it is noteworthy that Bargh achieved a 280% average return with an end-of-month maximum drawdown of only 11% (19% using daily data). As might be inferred from these two statistics, Bargh's return/risk metrics are extraordinary: adjusted Sortino ratio—25.1; daily Gain to Pain ratio—2.3;

and monthly Gain to Pain ratio—18.3.* His adjusted Sortino ratio is more than seven times as high as his Sharpe ratio (for most traders, these two statistics tend to be reasonably close), implying a huge *positive skew* in his return distribution (that is, the largest gains are much greater than the largest losses).

Bargh maintains a spreadsheet with columns for different attributes, which he monitors daily in a self-awareness ritual. These items include focus, energy, risk management, process, counter trading (trading against the price move, which he considers a negative), ego, fear of missing out, and happiness rating (either extreme—depression or euphoria—being adverse for trading). Some entries require further elaboration, such as "sugar trades." *A sugar trade*, Bargh explains, is a trade that you get into, and you don't even know why you are in the trade. When Bargh judges that he has exhibited weakness in any area, he will fill in the appropriate column for that day. At the end of each week, Bargh reviews the spreadsheet looking for columns with any fill-ins as a roadmap to the areas he needs to work on for further self-improvement.

Bargh also does daily journaling to record what he is thinking and feeling—a routine that he considers essential to identifying weaknesses in his mindset, which he then works on in his continuous quest for self-improvement. Commenting on the importance of daily journaling, Bargh says, "You very quickly tend to forget about last month, last week, or even yesterday. By keeping a journal, you can see what was going through your mind at any point in time and track how your mindset changes over time. If I showed you my journal entries from 2015 versus now, you would see they are worlds apart. My 2015 entries were replete with comments like, 'I'm a crap trader. I'm useless.' All I was doing was constantly berating myself. My entries now are entirely different."

Bargh credits the Trading Tribe Process (TTP) created by Ed Seykota, whom I interviewed in *Market Wizards*, as an essential influence in helping him achieve emotional balance in both his trading and life overall. As a massive oversimplification, TTP seeks to create harmony between

---

* See Appendix 2 for an explanation of these performance metrics.

the subconscious and conscious minds. The process focuses on feelings and specifically avoids questions and advice. TTP requires a group, which is called a *tribe*. There are tribes practicing TTP worldwide, and Bargh runs the London group. Readers can find a detailed description of TTP at seykota.com.

Bargh was the first of a week-long set of interviews I conducted in London. I slept only three hours the night before my London flight and then less than two hours the subsequent night in London, as I experienced my worst case of jet lag ever. I was fortunate that Bargh's honesty and forthrightness made this an engaging interview, allowing me to maintain my focus despite the lack of sleep. I interviewed Bargh on a Saturday in a conference room adjacent to the trading floor where he works. The interview lasted the full day. When we finished, I was still more alert than I had any right to be. I accepted Bargh's dinner invitation, and we went to an excellent Peruvian restaurant (Coya), just down the block from his office. The combination of the chef's tasting menu, a few beers, and the informal conversation made for a pleasant evening. I slept soundly that night.

Did you grow up in London?

No, I grew up in Yorkshire on a dairy farm.

At what age did you know you wanted to do something different?

One day, when I was four or five years old, I turned to my dad and said, "You don't have a real job. I want to get a real job." Funny enough, what I'm doing now is not a real job.

So since you were a small child, you knew you wanted to do something different. How did your dad respond?

Oh, he was fine with that. He always said, "Don't be a farmer."

When you were in your teen years, did you have any idea what you eventually wanted to do?

All I knew was that I wanted to be rich. We lived in a village. There was one wealthy family in the village, and one day when I was about six or seven, my mom took me to visit them. We didn't have much money, and when I saw their house, I thought it was incredible. They even had an outdoor swimming pool, which is ridiculous in the north of England because it barely gets above 20° Celsius [68° Fahrenheit] in the summer. I remember walking away with my mom and telling her, "I'm going to buy that house one day." That experience set my ambition. I had no idea how; I just knew that I wanted to be rich.

The other thing that got me interested in trading was the movie about Nick Leeson [*Rogue Trader*], who broke Barings Bank. The part about him being a shady character, of course, is not good. But I remember watching him on the trading floor with all the shouting and screaming, thinking, "That looks so cool."

How old were you then?

I was in my young teens.

I think you are the first trader I ever met who was inspired to become a trader by that movie.

Yeah, I know. It's not good, is it? [He laughs.] I started asking my mom and dad about how you make money in currencies, and they said, "You're too young to understand." I never took it any further than that.

What did you major at in school?

I got a Masters in math from Imperial College in London.

Were you naturally good at math?

Yes, but I was also bad at writing and didn't enjoy it.

Did you have any idea what you wanted to do with a math degree?

No, I didn't.

Did you have any career goal?

I was still interested in trading, and I applied to banks for internships. But I quickly realized that I was way behind the curve. I was competing against people who had been doing internships all through their college years. I got nowhere with my efforts, and, after a while, I gave up. It was the aftermath of the financial crisis, and there were still job cuts going on in the banking sector. The year before I graduated, I took an internship for an actuarial position at a pension company.

I guess that was a natural extension of your being a math major.

I thought it was something I could do, but I didn't enjoy it all. I hated the corporate environment. I couldn't make a joke because everything was so PC. I probably offended some people there, and I didn't come across very well. On top of that, I didn't put much effort into the work they gave me.

Why is that?

I thought the actuarial work was boring. I actually don't like statistics.

So what kind of math did you study or like?

Applied mathematics.

What happened when you finished your internship?

They didn't offer me a job.

Do you remember your reaction?

I took it badly. I was pretty arrogant. I expected the firm to offer me a job at the end of my internship because I went to one of the world's best universities and was smart. I thought, "How could I not be offered a job here?"

Is Imperial College that difficult to get into?

Yes, at the time, it was ranked fourth in the world.

Did they tell you why they weren't offering you a job?

Yes, they said something like, "It didn't seem like you were that interested in the job."

Well, they were right.

Yes, they were quite right. I think they were shocked when I looked upset at not being offered the job. It is just that with my competitive personality, I expected to get the job. I don't take losing or rejection very well.

So what did you do then?

I know this sounds clichéd, but I thought that if I was going to fail, I might as well fail at something I wanted to do. I decided to give trading another shot.

And your goal of becoming a trader was primarily motivated by a desire to get rich quick?

Yes.

That's odd. In previous *Market Wizards* books, I can't recall other traders who indicated their primary motivation to get into trading was the money. Yet, for this book, you are the second trader I have interviewed so far who mentioned that getting rich was the primary motivation.

I raise my eyebrows when someone says that something else was their primary motivation for becoming a trader.

Most commonly, the traders I interviewed in previous books mentioned their love of trading, often viewed as some sort of game, and a desire to beat the game as their driving motivation.

I have never looked at it that way. I never felt there was something to beat. I just saw it as a way to enhance the quality of my life. I don't feel there is a market to beat. The more I trade, the more I realize that the only thing to beat is myself.

How did you get your first trading job?

I worked like crazy in my final year at university. I applied to loads of banks again, and I got rejected by all of them. I had just about given up when I saw this job posting that sounded perfect to me. You got to trade from day one. You were backed by capital and got a split on profits. That sounded great because if I went to a bank, I wouldn't be trading from day one, and presumably not trading the way I wanted to trade. Instead, I would be boxed into what and how I should trade. I applied online and got an interview.

How did the interview go?

I almost screwed that up as well. I was interviewed by one of the three partners in the firm who wanted to gauge my level of interest in the job and how motivated I was. At that point, I was like a starved dog. I was desperate to get the job. I told him I was the type of person who would never quit.

That all sounds fine. Why do you say that you screwed it up?

After the interview, he took me over to the trading desk to meet the other two partners at the firm. I don't remember this, but, apparently, as one of the other partners was speaking to me, I put my tie in my mouth. I think it may have been a leftover habit of mine from when I was in school. When I was very focused on something, I would put my tie in my mouth. After I left, the partner at the desk said, "We can't hire him." The guy who interviewed me convinced his partner to give me another chance. So I got invited back again for another interview, and, luckily, I was able to persuade them that I wasn't a complete idiot.

That tie habit is probably something you do unconsciously.

Yes, entirely unconsciously. I only found out about it years later when one of them made a joke about it.

Did you know anything about trading or the markets when you interviewed for the job?

I knew absolutely nothing. I never traded my own account because I felt I would build bad habits. And I am glad I didn't do it. I thought I needed someone to teach me how to trade.

Didn't the firm care about your complete lack of knowledge and experience?

They were more interested in finding people who were hungry to make money rather than people with experience. Based on my background, they also knew that I was smart enough to grasp anything relevant to markets. I think they believed that personality was more important to being a good trader than what you knew about markets.

Once you started the job, how did you learn to trade?

The standard procedure for the firm was to take on two trading trainees each year. The first two weeks were an intensive training course where you came in at 6 a.m., and the instruction lasted until 4 p.m. They taught us how to use the trading software. They also taught us about fundamentals, such as understanding how critical central banks were to moving the markets. Their business model was trading event risk. They would work out an expectation for each event, such as a Federal Reserve announcement, and then if the Fed did something unexpected, they would trade the event and try to make a profit. By the time I arrived, however, the firm was trying to diversify away from that approach because all the traders were doing mostly the same thing. In the past, they had a few traders who were exceptional at trading intraday technical analysis. In hindsight, I think they were hoping that I would be good at pattern day trading.

Did they teach you anything about how to use technical analysis in trading?

One of the partners used technical analysis. He taught us how to identify support and resistance levels using Fibonacci retracements, trendlines, and other indicators. The basic concept was that you would put in your bid at a technical level of support and place a stop five or six ticks lower, hoping you would get a 20-tick bounce out of it. The firm would tell us, "Focus on the technicals because the fundamentals are easy." Being quite green to it all, I believed it. I thought, "Yeah, I'm going to make money as a technical trader. Screw the fundamentals; they're easy."

Which markets were you trading?

The firm traded futures markets, primarily currencies, bonds, and stock indexes.

When did you start trading?

Typically, trainees spent the first six months on a simulator. The firm monitored your P/L. They wanted to see that you were consistent before they let you trade real money. They made it very competitive between myself and the other trading trainee. They switched the guy who started with me to trading real money after only two months. I was left trading on the simulator for the full six months, and that was hard to take. There were some excellent markets during the time I was trading on the simulator, and the other new hire was trading real money. During that period, the Swiss Bank pegged its currency, which was a huge event, and there were also coordinated central bank rate cuts.

I assume you made money during the simulation period since they eventually gave you money to trade.

I found the first six months very difficult because of extreme paranoia. People used to joke about how I was only a few days away from getting fired. They would try to rile you up, and I took that to heart.

How were you doing on the simulator?

I was making money, but I didn't know if that was good enough for them.

Were you trading on both fundamental events and technicals?

My profits were coming mostly from technicals.

What kind of technical analysis were you using?

We learned about this pattern called the "open drive." The pattern forms when the market gaps and then drives in that direction. The assumption is that the market will continue to drive in the same direction.

Does that pattern still work, or did it just work then?

I think I was just lucky with using that approach at that time, which allowed me to make money on the simulator. As soon as my trading went live, I never made a penny off of intraday technical trading. For about four years, I tried to make it work. It was stupid. I was so stubborn.

But you did make money in those years.

Although my main focus was on technical analysis, I was still making fundamental trades, and those trades accounted for almost all the gains.

Were you more attracted to technical trading than fundamental trading?

Initially, I was.

Why?

I thought the firm wanted us to focus on becoming good technical traders.

Was that because they didn't want people to duplicate the same trades?

Yes, it was because they wanted more diversification among their traders.

So, was your initial focus on technical analysis a matter of trying to please your bosses?

I think so. Also, because I was so naïve, I thought that if my boss could trade this way, so could I. He had a gift for intraday technical trading, which I didn't.

Did the firm give you an amount of money to trade?

They didn't actually give you a line of money to trade. In the employment contract, there was a £10,000 stop-out point. In theory, if you lost £10,000, you were out.

How were you paid?

You would get 50% of trading profits, but you had to pay a desk rent of about £2,500 per month. The desk rent covered stuff like Reuters and trading software. They gave you the first three months for free.

One thing I didn't mention that is important is that I had been dealing with depression since secondary school [ages 12 to 16]. During the simulation period, I realized that I was only going to be good at trading if I became happy. I recognized early on how mentally tough trading could be, and I thought that if I was not mentally right, I had no chance of succeeding in trading. From that point on, I spent a lot of time focusing on trying to be happy.

How do you do that?

I read an excellent book that I recommend to anyone who has a problem with being unhappy: *Depressive Illness: The Curse of the Strong* by Tim Cantopher. Something about that book was very therapeutic and resonated with what I was going through. It allowed me to start a journey towards becoming happier. In the book, the author describes how you can chart getting out of depression. In the chart, time is on the x-axis, and happiness is on the y-axis. You tend to go like this when you're coming out of it. [Bargh draws a string of upward trending scallops with his hand waving through the air.] Essentially, he is trying to tell you that you can't expect to go from zero to happy in a straight line. It takes time. You start out very unhappy; your happiness improves; you drop back down but to a slightly higher level than before. What particularly resonated with me is that the author described how many people who get depressed tend to be quiet, ambitious, and hard-working. That description fits my personality very well.

Can you recall what it was about the book that helped you get out of your unhappy state?

It resonated with me because it made me feel that I was not alone. It helped me understand that the same thing happens to other people, and there is a strategy for getting out of it.

How did you get out of that mental state?

I got out of it by brute force self-talk. I remember sitting on the bus back from work and thinking, "You have got to be happy! You have got to be happy!" I psyched myself up to get out of it. I found that if I didn't do that, I would slide back into a hole, and it is tough to get out of a hole.

In a sense, did trading save you in that you realized you weren't going to be successful unless you were in a proper mental state? Did that give you the motivation that you didn't have before?

It definitely gave me motivation.

Was trading the catalyst for getting that book?

Yes. It took many years to get completely out of feeling unhappy. I haven't had a depressive episode for about three years. It never entirely leaves you, though. You never forget.

What was your mental state at the time you started trading real money?

Mentally, I was all over the place for years, mainly because of the pressure of not getting a salary. Essentially, you have a mindset that you have to make money trading.

What were your trading results in the first year?

I made about £20,000 in 2012, but I was negative on the year when you factor in all the costs.

You made £20,000 with a £10,000 risk line. That's actually pretty good for the first year of trading.

I guess so, but I never really viewed it that way. I saw it as, "I'm not very good at this."

But you were only negative because of the expenses.

That was one of the things that kept me going. I always felt that, since I was making money, all I had to do was beat the expenses. So, I knew there was something there, and that I had some kind of ability.

In 2012, you made money but didn't cover your expenses. What happened in 2013?

At the start of the year, my bosses reset my account to zero, so it would no longer show a negative amount. During the first half of 2013, my trading was profitable but not by enough to fully cover the monthly expenses.

Since you weren't making enough in trading to even cover your monthly office charges, let alone get a profit split, how were you paying your living expenses?

I was living off of savings. I had saved the money that I made from the summer jobs I had been doing for years. Since I lived on a farm, I didn't have a temptation to spend much, and I saved most of the money I made.

What kind of jobs?

When I was 16, I got a job as a waiter, but I was awful at it. I was very clumsy. I would drop dirty knives and forks on people. I got sacked at that job. After that, I had a job of putting up tents at events like weddings. I was very good at that job because I am so tall [Bargh is 6'8"].

Were your savings from summer jobs enough to live on?

I had also saved money from my intern job. Also, my parents helped out by paying my rent, and I paid my other expenses from my savings.

Speaking of that, how did your parents feel about your taking a job that had no income?

They weren't too happy about it.

Did they try to talk you out of it?

Eventually, they did. By mid-2013, I had used up almost all my savings. I told my parents that I had only enough savings left to cover one month of expenses. My parents were genuinely concerned. They didn't want to be financing what they thought was a gambling addiction. They said, "We're not going to continue supporting you. You need to sort it out and get a real job."

What was your performance for the year at that point?

As of the end of July, my gross profits were £26,000.

£26,000 on a £10,000 risk line is pretty good performance.

Maybe, but one thing the return statistics don't show is missed trades. I made my money mostly by trading events, and with the ongoing European debt crisis, there were many opportunities to make money trading events. Monetary policy was changing a lot in those days, forward guidance was introduced, and quantitative easing was restarted. There were so many events to trade, and I kept screwing up. I wasn't well prepared for them. It was a vicious cycle of missing a trade, feeling like crap for missing the trade, and then watching everyone else making loads of money off of it.

Did you feel like a failure at that point?

Massively.

That's ironic because, objectively, you were doing very well in percent return terms, excluding the expenses being charged against your account.

My theory is that for human beings, everything is relative. You are always comparing yourself with everyone else.

If you felt like a failure, did you consider giving up and doing something else?

Even when I felt like a failure and that I was bad at trading, I could never think of anything that I would rather do than being a trader. I still really enjoyed it and wanted to make it work. So it was tough being in a situation where I was almost out of money, and I felt that my parents were giving up on me. I didn't think getting a part-time job was a good idea because I was spending all my energy on trading. I felt that if I got a part-time job, I would get even worse at trading.

What did you do?

I spoke to the bosses and told them straight up what the situation was. I said, "I am out of cash, and I don't know how much longer I can keep doing this. Is there anything you can do to try to help me out?" And they did! It was amazing. They said, "We'll pay you a salary. How much do you need?"

How much did they give you?

They gave me a salary that was enough to cover my monthly office expenses. I later found out that my bosses took Amrit to dinner to get his opinion on me. [Amrit Sall, who is interviewed in Chapter 4, had started at the same firm a few years earlier.] They said, "He looks like he's struggling. We're not really sure about him. What do you think?" And Amrit told them, "I think he's going to make it." It was Amrit's backing that convinced them to give me a salary. Once I got that salary, I thought I had till Christmas to push my trading to more than cover the monthly costs. And, luckily, I did.

[I interviewed Amrit the next day and asked him about this episode and why he believed Richard would succeed. He replied, "Richard is a hard worker. He has an amazing work ethic. If you are that committed to something and keep your focus on that one task, it's only a matter of time before it starts working for you. He is that guy. He plugs away. He is proactive about dealing with anything that is holding him back."]

Why did they ask Amrit?

Amrit was one of their most successful traders, and I think they valued his opinion. I didn't really know Amrit at the time. I sat in another part of the office. I had barely spoken to him.

Several years later, though, Amrit did become a mentor. He helped drive into me the importance of mindset in trading. Amrit helped me realize that I was getting in my own way. I was always a glass-half-empty type of guy, and I would continually beat myself up for making mistakes. Amrit kept saying to me, "Look, you can't think that way. You are only going to trade well if you have a good mindset."

Did your concern about losing your trading position diminish once you started receiving a salary?

Not right away. I thought I had bought myself some time and had till Christmas to push my trading to more than cover my monthly costs. By the end of October, I was up about £40,000 for the year, which may sound OK, but I didn't feel good at all because my account was still negative once you factored in the office costs and my salary draw. I thought that I didn't have much time left.

So, as of the end of October 2013, you still thought that your trading career could end that year.

Yes, barring some miracle.

What happened?

In November 2013, the general market expectations were that Mario Draghi, the president of the European Central Bank (ECB), would cut rates in December, but not as early as November. I was praying he would cut rates in November.

Why, because that would be a surprise?

Yes, because that would be a surprise, and I thought I could make good money on it. I know this sounds like a cliché, but I remember thinking, "If there is a God, please, this could be my last chance." When Draghi announced a rate cut after the ECB's monthly meeting, I immediately bought several hundred European short-term interest rate futures contracts.

How were you able to take such a large position given your modest risk line?

My bosses assigned position limits based on their confidence in the trader and the level they thought the trader could handle. They had seen that I was making money throughout the year and had raised my limit. The trade was simple. I aggressively bought short-term interest rate futures and exited the position when the rate cut was priced in. I made nearly £90,000 on that trade.

It may have been simple, but it was a perfect trade. You had anticipated the possibility of the trade. You were utilizing the methodology you believed in—betting on an event—instead of using technicals. You were ready for the trade, and you put on the maximum position size. You did everything right on that trade. It was your first giant winning trade. How did it feel?

It felt incredible. I remember thinking, "I have saved myself. Now I can turn this into a career." Amazingly—and this is what made it so sweet— my parents were visiting me that same night. I took them out for a meal.

They didn't know anything until the meal?

No, they didn't.

You had been doing better. Did they even know that much?

No, they just knew I was getting backed by some guys at work.

So, they had no idea. Your parents thought you were probably near the end of your trading job.

Yes, they did.

How did you tell them what happened?

I just told them that I made £90,000 that day. They couldn't believe it. It was a great moment.

Did that change their perspective on trading?

I think so, but I don't talk to them about trading anymore because my mom is a big worrier.

After that trade, did you feel you were now set?

Yeah, but every time I feel like I am set in this game, something strikes me back down.

The market will do that. Did that trade get you off of using technicals, or were you still trying to make technicals work?

I was still trying to make technicals work, but, by that point, the majority of my focus was on getting better on the fundamentals. On paper, the method is really simple. You work out what will move the market. You find your trade, and you execute. What stops traders from performing well is themselves. Most of my problem was psychological. I would have a good day, become complacent, and then be unprepared for the next event, which turned out to be an excellent trading opportunity. It was hit and miss.

I am much better now, but there are also far fewer opportunities now than back in 2013 and 2014. Back then, many things were still relatively new, like quantitative easing and forward guidance. There was more uncertainty about what the central banks were going to do and how they were going to do it. Whereas now, the markets have central banks so nailed down that there is not as much opportunity to make money on central bank actions as there once was. The markets now are good at pricing in events before they happen. I make money by pricing in a surprise, and with fewer surprises, there are fewer opportunities. You can still make money on these events, but you have to do it differently. You have to be smarter about how you do it.

Can you give me an example?

I don't want to get into that; that's more proprietary.

Fair enough. You mentioned that, in later years, Amrit acted as a mentor. Did you have any other mentors at the firm?

You are interviewing Daljit, aren't you? [Daljit Dhaliwal, who is interviewed in Chapter 5, started as a trader in the same firm a couple of years before Bargh.]

Yes, I am.

I sat next to Daljit. In those early trading years, he was the only person I spoke to.

Did he help you?

There were both good and bad aspects to it, but, on balance, I would say that it was mostly good.

What was good, and what was bad?

Daljit was incredibly motivated. I don't think I ever met anybody more motivated than Daljit. He was very good at understanding what moved markets. He gave me tips here and there, which helped me out.

Can you give me an example?

Because he did intensive fundamental research, he was very good at anticipating market events. He would say something like, "There's going to be a coordinated rate cut. Be prepared for it." Whereas I, at the time, was more focused on trading technicals because I had been told by the bosses to shy away from fundamentals. However, without making money on fundamental trades here and there, thanks to Daljit's help, I wouldn't have made most of the profits I did make.

That all sounds very positive. What was the bad side of having Daljit as a mentor?

I wouldn't blame Daljit for it, but we were encouraged to be aggressive as a group. To build your account, you have to be aggressive. Daljit was always pushing me to do more size. I would take his advice too literally. I would take a 30-lot position in the Bund and sit there petrified because if I got it wrong, I would be cooked. But what I really should have been doing is trading five-lots and building up confidence over time.

Did you then put on larger position size trades than you otherwise would have because of that influence?

Actually, it worked exactly the opposite way. I ended up not trading a lot because I felt that when I did put on a trade, I had to put it on in large size. Then when the moment came to put on a trade, I wouldn't do anything.

Was that because you saw the choice as being between making a very large trade or doing nothing?

Exactly. I would end up doing nothing because I was too afraid to lose. I am not blaming it on Daljit because he would tell me that I needed to trade more. He was trading a lot and learning a lot. One of my regrets is that I didn't trade more. I was pushing my size to levels that were more than I could comfortably handle, which made me afraid to trade. I wasn't trading, and by not trading, I wasn't getting experience.

Interestingly, you, Amrit, and Daljit all know each other, and I am interviewing all of you for this book. I don't think I have had that circumstance before except for Marcus and Kovner in the first *Market Wizards* book.

And Seykota as well.

Yes, you're quite right. Seykota was a mentor to Marcus, who then later hired Kovner. So that was another instance of three connected traders in one book.

I just recently reread the Marcus interview to get a sense of how you write. It is interesting how new things pop up when you reread one of those interviews years later. It seems like with more experience, you see things in a different light. One of the trades Marcus discussed in that interview was a long soybean position in which he got out early, but Ed Seykota stayed in, and then soybeans proceeded to go limit up day after day after day.

Yes, I recall that well. Interestingly, despite Marcus losing money repeatedly in his early trading years, my impression was that his most painful experience was not any of the losing trades but rather missing that opportunity.

I never appreciated the pain of missing out until I experienced it myself. I've had a 12% down day, and even that was not as bad. It's a different feeling when you miss a great trade opportunity. It's awful. I struggle with it.

Was there one such missed trade that was particularly painful?

I mentioned earlier that I was still on the simulator when the Swiss National Bank pegged its currency to the euro. Well, ironically, I also missed them dropping the peg in January 2015. Up until that point in my career, I had worked from 6:30 to 16:30, like clockwork. I hardly ever left the office during the day. I even brought in food and ate at my desk. That evening I was scheduled to fly to America to attend a trading conference. I left the office when the bank opened to pick up some USD. There was a problem with my card, and I spent about an hour at the bank trying to get the problem sorted out. When I returned to the office, everyone looked completely shell-shocked, and a coworker who sat next to me told me what had happened. That was one of the best risk/reward trade opportunities in my trading career, and I missed it. I was heartbroken.

You mentioned Daljit was an early mentor. Did any of your three bosses give you advice or any other feedback?

They were reasonably hands-off, although they did monthly reviews.

What did they tell you?

They had started on the LIFFE floor before switching to screen trading, and that experience still influenced them. They would say things like, "You need to be more consistent. Try to make £100 a day." I never really thought that is how trading worked. It's more like you make nothing for a while, then you have a spurt.

That is what your record eventually ended up looking like. So you are quite right about that. What was working for you in those early years?

I had a couple of big wins. The first one was a short crude oil trade. At the time, oil prices were very high, and I was on the lookout for a potential release from the US Strategic Petroleum Reserve. I was just waiting for it to happen. I don't remember if they did it, or there was just talk about a release, but the news caused oil prices to move a few dollars lower. I was able to make £7,000 on that trade. I remember coming home and telling my girlfriend (who is now my fiancé), "I just made £7,000 today!" I quickly learned to stop coming home and telling her about my P&L. I didn't want to put my pressures on her. Then I had another big win shortly afterward. Some European economic data came in shockingly bad, so I bought the Bunds and made another £4,000.

Oddly enough, all those trades were fundamental.

I know. I know. I think I am a slow learner. It takes me a long time to get things into my head. But once I do get it, I get really good. I think part of it is that because I am very scientific, I want a lot of evidence. In an ideal situation, I would like to see ten examples of US releases from the Strategic Petroleum Reserve.

That's probably another thing that impeded you from embracing fundamentals: You don't get a statistically significant number of observations.

Exactly. I struggled with that. One thing that hurt me is that I am too arrogant.

You were too arrogant in what way?

I wouldn't listen.

What would people tell you that you weren't listening to?

They would tell me that I needed to pay more attention to the fundamentals.

But I thought your bosses were telling you to pay more attention to technicals.

They were telling me that, but my coworkers were telling me the exact opposite.

You were getting conflicting advice. By definition, you could only listen to one side.

I know, but I didn't think for myself. I should have sat down and thought it through. I never did that. Most of my mental energy was spent on worrying about whether I was good enough, and whether I would get fired. Instead, I should have been focusing on the process. It took me a while, but eventually, I realized that I had to focus more on the fundamentals.

Is all your trading now based solely on fundamentals?

No, ironically, I trade technicals again after all these years, but I trade them on a longer time frame. I don't trade technical analysis alone; I combine it with the knowledge I have about the fundamentals.

What prompted you to go back to using technicals?

One thing about event-driven trading is that if there isn't an event to trade, there is nothing to do, and it is really boring. You can feel like you're wasting your life.

I guess then, simply out of boredom, you could be tempted to make trades you really shouldn't do.

Exactly. I have found that I trade much better when I have a side project. If I have nothing else to do but trade events, and there are no events to trade, my mind runs wild. I need to focus my attention on something; otherwise, I will focus on the wrong things.

A couple of years ago, I started looking into trend-following systems and testing some of them. I wanted to see for myself whether trend following worked. I ran simulations over many different parameters and periods. I played around with varying stop sizes and target levels to see what effect those changes would have.

How did you do that testing?

I wrote programs in Python.

What kind of trend-following systems did you test?

I tested Donchian-type systems and moving average systems. [Richard Donchian was a pioneer in trend-following trading. The basic rule of the system he developed was to buy when a market closed at a new four-week high and to sell when it closed at a new four-week low. This type of system is called a *breakout* system. Basic moving average systems signal a buy when the market price or a short-term moving average rises above a longer-term moving average, and they signal a sell in the reverse case.]

What did you find?

I found that trend following does work, but the problem is that you can incur huge drawdowns.

It worked way better back in the 1970s and 1980s.

I found that out as well. The results were much, much better back then than they are now.

Yes, the trends are still there, but the markets have become much whippier, making the return/risk performance of basic trend-following systems marginal. How did you resolve that inherent limitation in trend-following systems?

I don't use trend following alone. I combine it with my knowledge of events. So far, the results have been satisfactory.

In doing your system testing, you must have found that shorter-term breakout systems, such as Donchian's four-week rule, are subject to whipsaw losses and don't work very well.

Yes, that's true.

I imagine you must have gone with a longer-term trend-following system, or is it a matter of something more complicated?

I don't use a computerized system. One of the principles that I had when I started this research project was that I didn't want something a computer could do. My hunch was that if I could easily duplicate the basic trend-following systems, so could anyone else.

That is precisely the problem with basic trend-following systems—everyone can do it. In the 1970s, or better yet the 1960s, when very few people were using trend-following systems, they did very well. I think of Ed Seykota, who back in the 1960s was running trend-following systems on an IBM 360 mainframe. He didn't have much competition. But once you get to the stage where PCs are commonplace, and anyone can buy trend-following software, the efficacy of the approach starts breaking down. So, how are you using trend following to a positive effect?

Trend following by itself is insufficient. The critical elements are how you manage risk and how you take profits once you are in a trade. Initially, I used to go for the home run when using trend following. I would get in a trend and use a trailing stop to get out. However, I found that when there was a large upmove, and the market then came back down to my trailing stop, I hated giving back so much of my profits. You have to trade your personality. You have to feel at peace with how you're trading. After you get out of a trade, whether it made or lost money, you have to forget about it like that [he snaps his fingers]. If you feel uncomfortable, you have to explore that feeling because there is a reason why you are uncomfortable, and you have to find out why. That feeling of discomfort is what led me to develop my methodology for exiting trend trades.

So, even though you did system testing, I assume you are not using technical analysis as a system but rather as an input.

The only significance of my trend-following testing was that it gave me confidence that it was possible to make money off the charts. But I don't trade any automated signals; all my trading is discretionary. I would describe my trading approach as some combination of event interpretation, insights I have gathered from trend following, and lessons I have learned from the way Peter Brandt manages risk. [Peter Brandt was interviewed in Chapter 1.]

I have interviewed Peter Brandt for this book. What specifically did you learn from Peter?

I learned that keeping losses as small as possible is critical to capital preservation. The most crucial thing in trading is mental capital. You need to be in the right headspace for the next trade. I find that when I go into a deep drawdown, my mindset is not right. I might start forcing trades to try to make money back. I might get gun-shy about taking the next trade.

The way Peter Brandt manages risk is incredible. I am so happy I studied what he does. [Bargh showed me a thick binder he maintains of annotated copies of Peter Brandt's trades.] When Brandt gets into a trade, he expects it to work straightaway if he is right. The best trades just go. If there is any sign that the market isn't doing that, he tightens his stop for getting out. That approach fits the way I trade the fundamentals. When I put a trade on in size, I expect it to work immediately. If it is not working straightaway, I get the hell out of there fast.

If you have a high-conviction trade and put it on in size, how long will you give it to work?

The longer I am losing money in a trade, the more concerned I become, and the more aggressive I become in tightening my stop.

Do you know how much risk you are taking on a trade when you put it on?

I have a rough ballpark estimate. I know how much I will lose every time the market goes ten ticks against me.

Do you have a predetermined number of ticks you will give a trade before you get out?

It depends on the trade. The more confident I am, the more aggressive I will be with the risk I take, but, equally, the more aggressive I will be with my stop. I made 100% in one day on a Brexit trade. You can only make that type of return if you're using substantial leverage on the trade. So I don't want to see any pain in that type of trade. If I see pain, it is a massive red flag.

So when you put on a large trade, you expect to be ahead instantaneously.

I should be. Sometimes, I may be behind for a split second, but most of the time, if I'm behind on those trades, it's not safe to stay.

Do you then get out right away?

I do.

Is it a matter of minutes?

Seconds. Sometimes if it's not that large of a position, I may give it minutes. But if it's a significant position, and it's not working in 20 or 30 seconds, I'm out.

People have difficulty in cutting losses because they are afraid of getting out of the trade and then seeing it go in their direction. It's an ego thing. I was making the same mistake for years. I would get into a trade, put in my stop, and see the position trade at a loss for ages but without hitting my stop. I would wait for my stop to get hit, even though I knew that 90% of the time, the trade was not going to work. But I couldn't bring myself to get out because I couldn't bear to get out and then see the trade work. And, sometimes, when I did get out, the trade would then go to the target. When that happens, it teaches you to do the wrong thing, which is to hold on. The problem is that you only remember the times you got out, and the trade then went to the target; you don't remember all the times when you got out, and it saved you money.

Why do you think that is?

It's human nature to always bias the negative and not the positive. Traders will fail because they will just stick with their stop, even if the trade is not working. The really bad traders won't even have a stop, or they will pull their stop away from the market.

That is what I call a CIC stop order—cancel if close. So you're saying that it's not enough to have a stop on every trade.

That's right. Traders will stick with a losing trade going sideways for five days, and just wait for the market to hit their stop. To me, the longer a trade is not working, the more likely it will lose.

You mentioned you made 100% on a Brexit trade. Tell me the story behind that trade.

All the traders in the office, including me, were expecting that the Brexit vote would not pass, but we all came in around midnight just on the off chance that it would.

I assume that if the Brexit vote had failed, there would not have been any trade.

Exactly. The results were announced region by region. As the night wore on, it became increasingly clear that Brexit was going to win. The market had not priced that in at all. So there was money to be made. The obvious trade was to sell the British pound. The problem, however, was that the pound was incredibly volatile, and I was afraid that if my timing was a bit off, I could wipe out half my account.

That concern is quite understandable. I remember the British pound was flipping around wildly that night. It was not like one of those situations where the news comes out, and then the market moves in a single direction.

That's right. One region could have reported making it look like Brexit was going to happen, and then the next region could have reported and made it look like Brexit was not going to happen. I could have been caught with my pants down and lost a lot of money.

So what did you do instead?

I bought US Treasurys. I figured that the shock of Brexit passing would cause a market shift to risk-off trades, which would trigger a rally in US Treasurys. The difference was that if I were wrong, I would probably lose only a few ticks in a long T-bond position compared with a couple of hundred ticks in a short British pound position—a critical distinction given that I was putting on a highly leveraged position.

How much did T-bonds rally?

I believe it was something in the range of 60–100 ticks.

Given those numbers, the long T-bond position probably offered an even better return/risk profile than the more direct trade of selling the British pound.

The Treasurys looked a lot easier to trade than the pound.

Can you give me an example of a trade where you combined your event trading with technical analysis?

Earlier this year [2019], gold wasn't doing very much. When Trump did something like impose tariffs on China, gold was the least reactive market. Then, one weekend, Trump decided to increase tariffs on China. The following Monday morning, gold had a strong upmove. I thought to myself, "That's different." Also, the price move coincided with the breakout I was looking to trade. So I put on a long position.

Are you still in that position?

No, I got out.

What got you out?

I have predefined rules about where to take profits and how to ride trends.

Are these rules that take profits because the trade reaches a certain level of profitability or because the pattern changes in some way?

It's a bit of both. I'm monitoring the situation day by day. I'm looking to get as much as I can out of the trend. If there is an explosive upmove, I will tend to take profits because any meaningful stop would risk giving back too much of the open profits. If, however, the market has a steady trend, I will move my stop up gradually. Every situation is different.

What did you do in this gold trade?

I took some of the profits during the uptrend and took the rest when it started to pull back. I always want to try to keep a bit of the position when I am getting out in the middle of an ongoing trend.

Earlier, you talked about the importance of having the right mindset when trading. Can you expound on the mental side of trading?

My goal as a trader is to always be in harmony with my process. So, I am using my feelings as an input to trading. I try to spot in real-time when I am trading poorly. In analyzing my past drawdowns, I found that I would start to trade poorly but then keep on trading because I was afraid of missing the next trade. I now have a straightforward method for dealing with this situation. If I feel like something is not right, I just leave work early, or I might take the next morning off. I will do whatever I can to put my mindset back in the right place. I want to be trading from a state of calm and inner peace; I don't want any internal conflict.

So, it's like a circuit breaker for when you feel your trading is out of sync with the market.

Yes, and I couldn't do that before because I was too afraid of missing a trade.

What was your worst trade ever?

My worst trade was not my worst in terms of loss, but it was my worst because of the way I managed the trade. At the time, the eurozone PMI (Purchasing Managers' Index) releases were moving the market a lot. One month, either the German or French—I don't remember which—PMI hugely beat market expectations. I thought that the bond market would break sharply and stocks would rally sharply. I sold 200 Bunds and bought 200 Euro Stoxx. I was immediately offside by about £20,000. I said to myself, "I can't take this loss," and I sat with the trade. Luckily, the market bounced back, and I was able to get out with only a £3,000 or £4,000 loss. Shortly after I got out, the markets moved violently against my original trades. It was terrible.

Actually, the trade didn't work out badly, but if you didn't have that short-lived correction—

I would have been cooked.

It's one of those situations where the outcome wasn't bad—in fact, it worked out much better than if you had immediately taken the loss—but it could have been a disaster if there hadn't been that brief correction. You did the wrong thing, but the mistake worked in your favor. However, since you termed it your "worst trade," you clearly recognize that even though you were lucky, it was the wrong decision.

Yes, that trade shook me up because it made me realize I was capable of doing what I did. It scared me because I thought, "I could do this again."

You drew the right lesson out of that experience. Most people would probably have learned the exact wrong lesson: "Boy, that was smart of me waiting for the correction instead of panicking out." Interestingly, what you label as your worst trade was only a small loss, and, ironically, the very thing that made it a bad trade made it a smaller loss than it would otherwise have been. I think the ability to differentiate between the action and the outcome is one of the reasons you've been successful as a trader.

I'll never, ever forget that trade because I couldn't believe it. I never thought I would act that way. Just the realization that I was capable of having the mentality of, "I can't take this loss," scared the hell out of me. It must have scared me enough because I never made that mistake again.

What you term your "worst trade" actually didn't lose much money. What was your worst loss on a single trade?

In September 2017, I was listening to the ECB press conference, and Mario Draghi made a statement in which he mentioned the strength of the euro in the opening paragraphs. I thought that comment was significant and that he was going to devalue the euro. It was a trade that I had prepared for, and I immediately sold 200 euro contracts. I had a profit very quickly, which is what I look for in these types of trades. Then I got greedy and bought 200 Bunds. It wasn't a trade for the Bund because Draghi's comment was about devaluing the euro, not about easing rates.

So, in effect, you were trying to pyramid the position in a less risky way by adding an indirect trade.

Exactly. As soon as I bought the Bund, the euro started coming back, which was a big warning sign for my original trade. As I was getting ready to bail out of the euro position, the Bund moved sharply against me. I immediately got out with a loss on both positions, with most of the loss coming from the impulsively added Bund position.

So, if you would have just stayed with the originally planned position—

I would have had a small loss. It was just greed. The next day there was an event-trade opportunity when the Bank of England switched to a hiking bias, and I was too gun-shy to pull the trigger because I had just lost 12%

the day before. I hadn't mentally recovered from that loss and couldn't take the chance of another loss. The market had a big move, and the other traders in the office had a great day, while I was sitting there still reeling from the day before. It was a double whammy of pain. Then to make matters even worse, that weekend, the traders in the office went to Spain to celebrate Amrit's bachelor party. I felt like my world had just ended, and I didn't feel much like celebrating.

Your weakest performance seems to have been in January through July 2018 when you were about flat. Nothing horrible about that, but for you, it represented very significant underperformance. Was there anything different about that period?

I had a very good 2017 and came into 2018 with the mindset that I could push it. I was taking too much risk. I came back after a trading break and decided to put my size back to where it was. My mindset went from, "I need to push it," to "I need to just focus on keeping my capital together and not incur any more significant losses."

Did working with Steve Goldstein help you? [Goldstein is a London-based trading coach who worked with several of the traders in this book and was my source in finding some of these traders.]

Steve helped me see a part of my personality that I hadn't noticed.

Which was?

I tended to compare myself with others a lot and judge my performance against them. If I missed a big trade, but no one else in the office traded it, I didn't care. But if one person traded it, I hated it because I felt he beat me in some way. That feeling is what kept tripping me up. I felt like I was behind, and I kept trying to make up for it by taking too much size on the next trades. That flaw was a big part of the explanation of why I did poorly during the first half of 2018. Steve helped me become aware of what I was doing.

Weren't you cognizant of that before?

I kind of knew it but wasn't fully conscious of it.

What advice did Steve give you?

The strange thing is he didn't give me any solutions. He pointed out what I was doing, though, which was the valuable part. He shone a light on the situation and helped me see how what I was doing was a problem.

Did the awareness of how you responded to missing a trade that someone else caught help you change how you reacted?

It did. My ingrained response to missing a trade and seeing someone else do better than me was just a bad habit, and bad habits can be changed. Once I was aware of the problem, I was able to change. For example, on the day I missed the Swiss Bank peg trade we talked about earlier, other traders in the office had a great day because of that same trade. In the past, my response would have been, "I hate them. They are so lucky." My attitude now is entirely different: "Shit for me, but good for them." I'll process it and move on.

Has your trading methodology changed over the years?

Yes, I am better at running my profits now. One of the things I did was take a picture of every trade I did in size. I then went back and analyzed different ways of exiting those trades.

What did you find?

For a long time, I didn't have rules for getting out. It was more like, "Oh, I'm up by this amount; I should take profits." I found that I could do better if I held on to a portion of the position.

How long might you hold that extra position?

It depends on how strong the trend is, but it could be as long as a month.

How much of the position do you hold on to?

I will keep about 5%–10% of the position. I still take a large majority of the risk off because I don't want to deal with the volatility implicit in holding large positions overnight, let alone for longer periods.

I guess even that small percentage makes a difference.

It's a nice feeling to add a few extra percent on a trade without adding any significant risk.

What are the lessons you learned as a trader?

⚡ To be a good trader, you have to have a high degree of self-awareness. You have to be able to see your flaws and strengths and deal effectively with both—leveraging your strengths and guarding against your weaknesses.

⚡ It doesn't matter if I miss a trade because there will always be another opportunity.

⚡ Mental capital is the most critical aspect of trading. What matters most is how you respond when you make a mistake, miss a trade, or take a significant loss. If you respond poorly, you will just make more mistakes.

⚡ If you take a trade that results in a loss, but you didn't make a mistake, you have to be able to say, "I would take that trade again."

⚡ Opportunities are dispersed. You might have an opportunity today and then have to wait three months for the next opportunity. That reality is hard to accept because you want to make a steady income from trading, but it doesn't work that way. In 2017, nearly all my profits came from two weeks in June and one day in December. That's it. The rest of the year amounted to nothing.

⚡ Have a long-term focus and try to increase your capital gradually rather than all at once.

⚡ You have to forgive yourself for making a mistake. For a long time, I would beat myself up anytime I made a mistake, which only made things worse. You have to accept that you're human and will make mistakes. It took me four or five years to understand that. I don't know why it took me so long.

⚡ Staring at these screens all day long is like a casino inviting you to click. You have to guard against the temptation of taking impulsive trades.

⚡ If a bad or missed trade destabilizes me, I have rules for bouncing back: Take some time off, exercise, go out in nature, have fun. I used to have a habit that whenever I lost money in the markets, I would spend less money. I would tell my girlfriend, "I don't want to go out tonight because I lost money today." That type of attitude only causes your mindset and body to get tight, which stops you from trading well because you don't want to take any risk. A counterintuitive concept Amrit taught me is that I should spend more when I'm losing money. After I had a losing day, he would say, "Go out and treat yourself." The idea is that you empower yourself by still going out and spending money. I found that advice very hard to accept and ignored it for a long time.

Do you do that now?

Now, I am at a stage where trading doesn't affect anything else.

Any last words?

One thing that being depressed made me conscious of is the importance of being happy. I want a happy life. Before, my goal was to make a lot of money. Now my focus is on having a happy life. Funny enough, I'm still making money. I'm a big believer in focusing on your happiness first; nothing else matters.

———

A lesson that comes up repeatedly in interviewing great traders is that you have to find a methodology that fits your personality. In his early trading years, Bargh tried to make technicals work, even though he gravitated more naturally to fundamentals. Although Bargh was spending most of his time on technical analysis, he found that virtually all of his profits were coming from his fundamental trades. Ultimately, Bargh switched his focus to his preferred methodology—fundamental analysis—and his trading improved dramatically. He later even found a way to incorporate technical analysis effectively by using it as an adjunct to fundamental analysis.

Bargh believes that mindset is critical to successful trading. He says, "I want to be trading from a state of calm and inner peace." When Bargh finds that he is trading poorly and doesn't have the right mindset, he will stop trading and take a break. Losses will beget more losses if you continue to trade when you are off balance because of recent losing trades. When you are out of sync with the market, the best advice may simply be to take a temporary break from trading and resume trading only when you feel ready to do so.

In his earlier years, by trading a standard position size that was larger than what he was comfortable with, fear of taking trades caused Bargh to miss many excellent trading opportunities. If he were trading a position size more in line with his comfort zone, he would have made and profited from many of these trades. The lesson is don't trade so large that fear dominates your trading.

If you feel uncomfortable about your trading, you should seek to identify that source of discomfort and then modify your methodology to eliminate it. Bargh's discomfort in giving back large open profits on trend trades when the market moved dramatically in his favor spurred him to change his exit methodology on such trades. Instead of using trailing stops to exit trades, he adopted a more price-sensitive approach—a modification that improved his overall performance.

Bargh advises guarding against the temptation of taking impulsive trades. Impulsive trades are often triggered by impatience—an urge to do something while you are waiting for a trade that legitimately meets your criteria. The market rewards patience and trades borne of impatience are usually detrimental.

Trading to earn a consistent amount steadily may be an admirable goal, but it is not a realistic one. Market opportunities are sporadic. Sometimes, the market will provide great opportunities; other times, months will pass without a good trading opportunity. Bargh mentioned that in one very successful year, virtually all of his profits came from a two-week period and one other day. If you try to force consistent profitability, you will be prone to take suboptimal trades, which will often end up reducing your overall profitability.

If a trade is not acting as expected, cut losses immediately. Bargh will get out in seconds if a big trade is not working as anticipated. Such instantaneous risk cutting will not apply to most traders, but the idea of cutting risk quickly relative to the methodology used is still critical advice.

Using stops on every trade is one way to control losses. But if a trade isn't showing a profit in a reasonable period (the definition of "reasonable" will be dependent on the specific methodology), Bargh insists there is no reason to wait for the stop to be hit. He believes that the reduced losses that can be achieved by not waiting for a stop to be hit will outweigh the gains from trades that are negative for the initial period and then recover without the stop being hit.

You don't have to exit a profitable trade all at once. Even if a trade reaches your target, it may make sense to keep a small portion of the position, so you get some additional profit if the market keeps moving in the direction of the original trade. Bargh will routinely maintain 5%–10% of a position that he liquidates because it has met his target. He finds that maintaining such small partial positions increases his overall profits without meaningfully increasing his risk.

Missed trades can be more painful—and more expensive—than trading losses. Bargh missed a major trade opportunity by, atypically, leaving the office to take care of a bank errand. Over the long-term, trading success depends not only on trades made but also on minimizing missed trade opportunities.

The obvious way to execute a trade idea may not always be the best approach. Sometimes, a related market can provide a better return/risk trade. For example, when the evolving voting returns increasingly pointed to a surprise win for the Brexit referendum, the straightforward trade would have been to sell the British pound. However, the problem was that the British pound was swinging wildly as the voting returns were coming in, meaning that a short British pound trade could easily get stopped out, even if the trade ultimately proved correct. Bargh surmised that another consequence of a surprise win for the Brexit referendum would be a market shift favoring risk-off positions. So, instead of selling the British pound, Bargh bought US Treasurys, which were far less volatile and could be traded with meaningful stops that required much less risk. In effect, long T-bonds (the indirect trade) provided much better return/risk than the direct and obvious trade of selling the British pound. The lesson is that the way a trade idea is implemented can be more important than the trade idea itself.

Bargh's worst loss occurred when he tried to double his market exposure by adding a large position in a related market—a position that didn't share a justification for the trade, as did the original position. It was an action that Bargh readily admits was motivated by greed. The unplanned position resulted in turning what would have been an acceptable small loss into a large loss, with most of the loss coming from the added trade that lacked the criteria for being implemented in the first place. Trades motivated by greed usually end badly.

The day after this worst loss, which was a direct consequence of a trading mistake, a change in Bank of England monetary policy provided the exact type of event-trading opportunity Bargh seeks out. The trade worked spectacularly well, except that Bargh didn't take it. He was still destabilized from the previous day's costly trade error and couldn't bring himself to take on any new risk. This experience illustrates an important trading lesson: The damage from a bad trade often extends well beyond the loss on the trade itself. By shaking up a trader's confidence, such trades can lead to missing winning trades the trader would otherwise have taken. The resulting missed profits can often even exceed the loss on the original trade.

Traders need to distinguish between trade outcomes and trade decisions. Sometimes, a good decision may have a poor outcome, and a poor decision may have a beneficial outcome. The trade Bargh labels as his "worst trade" was one in which he couldn't bring himself to take a large loss and just held on to the position. The trade temporarily recovered, and Bargh liquidated it. Soon after, the market moved violently against his original position. By hesitating instead of acting to cut his loss quickly, Bargh turned a large loss into a smaller loss. Although the outcome of this decision was favorable, Bargh recognized that he was just lucky and that if a short-lived recovery hadn't occurred, his original large loss could have turned into a disastrous one. Bargh realized he had made an immense trading mistake, even though that mistake turned out to be beneficial.

Many traders erroneously evaluate their trading based solely on outcomes, whereas meaningful evaluation should be based on whether trading decisions were consistent with their methodology and risk control rules. Winning trades (or smaller losing trades, as was the case in this example) can be bad trades if they violate trading and risk control rules that have been responsible for a trader's longer-term success. Similarly, losing trades can be good trades if the trader followed a process that has demonstrated efficacy in generating profits with acceptable risk.

AMRIT SALL

The Unicorn Sniper

A MRIT Sall has one of the best track records I have ever encountered. Over a 13-year career, Sall has achieved an average annual compounded return of 337% (yes, that's annual, not cumulative). And return is not even the most impressive aspect of his performance. His return/risk numbers are nothing short of astounding: an adjusted Sortino ratio of 17.6, monthly Gain to Pain ratio of 21.1, and a daily Gain to Pain ratio of 3.6. These numbers are 10 times the levels of what could be considered excellent performance (see Appendix 2 for the definitions and context of these statistics).

Sall also provides a perfect example of the deficiency of the Sharpe ratio. His Sharpe ratio is 1.43, an excellent level, but not a particularly exceptional one. The Sharpe ratio's primary pitfall is that its risk component (the standard deviation) penalizes large gains equivalently to large losses. For a trader like Sall, who has many spectacularly large gains, this penalty is severe. Sall's *adjusted** Sortino ratio, a statistic that only penalizes downside volatility, is 12 times as large as his Sharpe ratio. This extreme imbalance between the two ratios is extraordinary. Most traders have

---

* The adjustment allows for comparing the Sortino ratio with the Sharpe ratio (see Appendix 2 for an explanation).

an adjusted Sortino ratio to Sharpe ratio closer to 1:1. Even traders with excellent return to risk have adjusted Sortino to Sharpe ratios closer to 2:1 or 3:1. A ratio of 12:1 indicates that Sall's large gains are tremendously greater and far more prevalent than his large losses. You can see the stark asymmetry between gains and losses in Sall's daily returns: He had 34 days with returns greater than 15% (three of them with returns greater than 100%—yes, that is not a typo) and only one day with a double-digit loss. And even that one double-digit loss (discussed in the interview) was primarily due to circumstances beyond his control.

Sall is a senior member of a group of traders who trade independently but share information and opinions. His colleagues hold Sall in high esteem. Richard Bargh (see Chapter 3) says, "Amrit has an amazing mindset. He is very mentally strong and always has an optimistic outlook. He really knows where his edge is and knows when to push it and when not to. So he keeps his losses very small. He has no apparent weaknesses as a trader." Another colleague describes Sall's trade execution as "a thing of beauty."

Sall has a unique trading style—one that I have not come across among any of the traders I interviewed in previous *Market Wizards* books. Although in this book there is another trader with a similar trading style (Richard Bargh), a resemblance that is related to Sall being a mentor to Bargh in his early trading career. Sall focuses on trading market-moving events, seeking to capture large gains over short time intervals—typically only minutes— by identifying events that signal a high probability of accelerated price swings in the anticipated direction. He implements this core strategy in large-sized positions because his preparation for these trades gives him high confidence about the short-term market direction implied by different event scenarios.

Sall is meticulous in keeping comprehensive write-ups on every trade he has ever taken and the significant trades he has missed. He groups these trade logs by category, filling multiple binders with trade descriptions. These write-ups provide analogue models that aid Sall in determining whether a prospective trade is more likely to be a major opportunity or subpar. The knowledge base provided by his compilation of past trade summaries also allows Sall to create a trading plan for both the execution and management of an anticipated trade. After a trade is made, Sall will summarize what he did and what he got wrong and right. At the end of each month, Sall reviews the trade summaries for the prior month. Before any significant expected trade, he will review similar past trade write-ups as analogues for how the market might be expected to react.

Once he has done all his research, Sall will do mental rehearsal in preparation for a trade, so that he can respond unhesitatingly whatever the details of an anticipated event prove to be. As he describes it, "I will spend some time visualizing and internalizing how the trade might play out. This mental rehearsal allows me to act instantaneously. It includes not only triggers for getting into the trade but also a plan for managing the trade. I will also envision different scenarios where the trade goes horribly wrong or where it goes very well and know how I will react in each case."

I interviewed Sall on a Sunday, the day after my interview with Richard Bargh, in the same conference room adjacent to their trading floor. Apparently, Bargh must have warned Sall that I guzzled sparkling water, as he had several large bottles on hand. The interview lasted the full day. After we finished, Sall took me to dinner at what could best be described as an Indian fusion restaurant. Since I eat virtually everything, I let Sall, who is Indian, do the ordering. I hesitated about one of his choices—barbecued chicken wings—because I hate sweet foods. I needn't have worried; apparently, Indian barbecue has nothing to do with American barbecue. Although we had spent the entire day talking, it was relaxing to have a conversation that had nothing to do with trading, while enjoying a delicious meal.

———

Did you have any career aspirations in your childhood or teen years?

Not at all. I was all over the place. I didn't even have any idea what I wanted to study at the university level. I stumbled into economics. My grades weren't exactly great in college, which is hardly surprising since I never even looked at a textbook. At that point, I wasn't motivated by academia. I was more interested in playing soccer with my friends. My first choice was to pursue a degree in business information systems because it was what my friends were doing, but that is a popular course, and my grades weren't good enough to be accepted into the program. However, I was able to get into the economics program. Ironically, looking back at it now, what I thought was a failure in my life at that time—not getting better grades in school—was exactly what needed to happen to facilitate my becoming a trader.

That's one thing about life: You never know what is good and what is bad. Sometimes things that seem bad end up being fortunate and vice versa. How did you go from earning an economics degree to becoming a trader?

I enrolled in a master's program in investment banking and international securities at the University of Reading, and I put my all into it. They had a simulated trading room, which was my first exposure to markets and trading, and I fell in love with it. While I was at Reading, there was a presentation by a couple of guys who were ex-LIFFE floor traders from Refco. After the presentation, I shoved a pen and pad at them and said, "Tell me everything I need to know. What books and articles should I read? What blogs should I follow? I'm interested in everything and anything about the practical side of trading." One of them gave me his card and said, "Call me on Monday." I was accepted into a trader training program before I graduated.

Tell me about the training program.

Initially, it was full-time classroom instruction. The firm taught us about technical analysis, fundamental analysis, and the psychology of trading. After about two months of instruction, they transitioned us to trading on a simulator.

How many people were in your training program?

About 20.

How many ultimately survived?

Two.

That's about what I would have guessed. Initially, did you feel more comfortable trading on technical analysis or fundamentals?

Neither. For the first year, I didn't feel comfortable with anything. I was trying everything, and that is what you should do.

What methodology did you use when you first started trading?

I tried trading breakouts from trendlines and intraday consolidations, looking for a quick buck.

How did that work out?

I made money initially, but over the longer term, it was a net negative strategy. It is an approach that feeds into your impulsive nature. You're trying to make easy money. Eventually, you realize that is not how it's going to work.

I actually find trendline breakouts to be one of the most unreliable signals. What trips people up is that when you look at a chart, it seems like trendline breakouts work. But that perception is a consequence of knowing where to draw the trendline with the benefit of hindsight. What most people don't realize is that, in real-time, there were often multiple other trendlines that experienced what proved to be false breakouts, which, effectively, redefined the trendline. What did you gravitate to after you gave up on trading trendline breakouts?

I tried several other technical approaches, none of which appealed to me. I don't like putting on a trade where as soon as I put it on, I feel that I have to be lucky for it to work, and technical-based trades made me feel like that.

Since you really didn't have any methodology at the time, what was your experience when you first started trading real money?

I was profitable straight off the bat.

Since your forays into using various technical signals didn't pan out, how were you making money?

I was trading fundamental events a lot. I saw the potential in the volatility around these events, and I wasn't shy. I would jump in headfirst when I thought something was a trade, whereas I think most junior traders tend to hesitate when they see a lot of volatility. They will prefer less volatile trades like buying or selling on breakouts.

So you were attracted to the volatility.

I was attracted to the volatility, and I was aggressive with it.

Back then, when there was a significant headline, how did you trade it?

If it was a surprise that the market wasn't pricing in, I would get in as quickly as I could and with as much size as I could, anticipating that the market would have to adjust to the new information. Over time, the opportunities to do these types of trades diminished, and it became necessary to rely more on trades where the expected outcome in response to the news flow was not black and white.

Were these expected headlines, such as scheduled economic reports or announcements, or unexpected headlines?

Both.

For the latter, I assume you had to be watching the newsfeed continuously throughout the trading day. Moreover, I assume you had to be so informed on the fundamentals driving a given market that you could instantaneously assess the price implications of any news item.

Yes. There are only a handful of factors driving any particular market at any given time. It is a matter of being aware of what is relevant to a market and what is priced in. If a key central banker came out and said something contrary to what was priced in, that would be a big trigger. I would react without hesitation and place an aggressive trade.

How long would you hold the trade?

I would hold it anywhere from minutes to hours.

How large was the account they gave you to trade?

There wasn't actually a specific amount of money you were given to trade. Instead, you were given a risk line of £30,000.

So, if you lost that amount, you would be shown the door.

That was what we were told.

You said that you were immediately profitable. How much did you make that first year?

By midyear, I had made about £150,000. At that point, I took out £50,000, and the company took out the same amount. We had a 50/50 split arrangement, and whenever you withdrew profits, the company withdrew an equal amount.

So, after the withdrawal, your trading account was back to £50,000. What happened during the second half of your first year of trading?

I managed to blow the entire £50,000 and went into a negative balance.

Did something change that explains the drastic reversal in your performance during the second six months of your trading versus the first six months?

I think in the first six months, I hadn't been challenged by tough markets.

In the first six months of trading when you are doing so well, did you get cocky?

Oh yeah. I was straight out of school, and I thought, "This is great. This is so easy." That's why when I was served humble pie by the market, it was a real wake-up call.

Since your account had gone negative and there was a cutoff point at £30,000, were you concerned that you might be knocked out of the game?

That was always a fear in my mind. Even though I didn't want to exit, I knew I could still be pushed out. I remember feeling quite miserable at the time. Trading was all I really wanted to do. I had no backup plan. It's like the old saying, "If you want to take the island, burn the boats." I was all in. I had no plan B. I had no aspirations to do anything else other than trade. There was no way I was going to fail.

Did being so close to a knockout point make you more cautious in your trading?

You have to become cautious in some sense. When your drawdown reaches a certain level, you have to cut your size. That said, I'm in the game of catching unicorns. They're not on every corner. When a unicorn turns up—a trade where everything lines up exactly the way I want it—I have to go for it aggressively, even when I am in a drawdown. I am only going to get about 10 of those trades a year, and I can't afford to pass up one of those opportunities. That perspective puts me in a position where I am never more than one or two trades away from getting out of a drawdown.

Were you doing anything wrong during the second half of the year? Were you losing money because you were making trading mistakes or because the market was just unfavorable for your strategy, even though you were still following your methodology?

I got cocky and relaxed with my discipline. I loosened my entry criteria by not sticking to my type of trades. It was the classic mistake of doing well and then loosening up. Back then, I was vulnerable to experiencing drawdowns after periods when I had done particularly well. Fortunately, I have transcended that pattern.

Did the losses come primarily from taking trades that were deer instead of unicorns, or did they come from unicorn trades that didn't work?

It was definitely the former. It was a matter of being impatient and trying to force trades. I was trying to make money out of nothing. I remember one time during that drawdown period, in response to an ECB [European Central Bank] announcement, I put on my risk-limit positions in the Bund, Bobl, and Schatz [10-year, five-year, and two-year German interest rate contracts]. The risk manager came over, crouched down at the side of my desk, and said, "Amrit, what are you doing? What are you going to do with these positions?" I froze momentarily, and then I snapped out of it. That was the first time I realized how dangerous it could be to become lax in my trading.

You had your maximum allowable position in three extremely correlated contracts. Effectively, you had a triple position. What was the catalyst for taking such an aggressive approach?

It was a comment that I can't even remember now, but I know that it was a marginal comment. I was in a significant drawdown, and I was hoping I could come back.

So, you not only put on a marginal trade that was questionable, but you did it in triple size. What did you do after the risk manager came over to your desk and made that comment?

I realized that I was in a position, *hoping* for it to work. The second I realized that I was hoping and not trading anymore, I immediately liquidated everything. That lesson has stuck with me to this day. I never want a position where I am hoping that it will work. I had to go through that experience to know the difference between a trade where I have full conviction and a trade where I am hoping.

The obvious lesson from that experience was beware of trades borne of hope rather than conviction. Were there any other lessons?

I learned the importance of being patient. Market opportunities are always going to be there. With the benefit of hindsight and experience, I can now say that the big trades are pretty simple. You don't have to go looking for them, but you do have to wait for them. Trading opportunities in the market ebb and flow. There will be periods in the markets where opportunities dry up, and there will be nothing to do. In those nothing periods, if you are looking for something to do, that is when you can create real damage to your account. That is what I was doing; I was still trying to do something when nothing was happening. Instead, I should have been waiting for opportunities. It's the same idea expressed by Jim Rogers in one of your books when he said, "I just wait until there is money lying in the corner, and all I have to do is go over there and pick it up. I do nothing in the meantime."

I like to cite Debussy's quote that "Music is the space between the notes," because an analogous statement about trading—Trading is the space between trades—is so strikingly apropos.

I firmly believe that is true. To facilitate the outstanding trades, you need to be doing nothing in between. I always ask myself: Am I in a state of readiness? Am I fully prepared? Am I wasting my financial capital and mental capital on subpar trades instead of waiting patiently for the real trade opportunities?

Ironically, implicit in your statement that the big trades are simple is the idea that it's the *not* trading that's difficult, whereas making good trades is easy.

I completely agree. Any idiot can make something complicated. When I look back at the trades responsible for my best return months, they just scream out to me, *This is a big trade opportunity.* Had I taken only those trades and none of the others, my returns would probably have been double what they were. But trading doesn't work that way. You have to learn to not be impulsive and to not do silly things in the interim periods—"the space between the notes," as you term it. One of the mistakes I made in those early years was that when nothing was going on, I forced marginal trades, wasting mental and financial capital, instead of waiting for the unicorn that would eventually show up. Learning from that mistake was one of the pivotal lessons in my trading career. I now know that 90% of the time, the market is not going to provide any opportunities, and 10% of the time, I will make 90% of my profits.

Now we are sitting here with the comfort of knowing your subsequent history. But, back in your first trading year, when your account went negative, you wouldn't have known that you would eventually succeed. You had some early success followed by failure, and you were in danger of getting knocked out of the game. Where was your mental state at that point?

It's an odd thing to say, but I knew I would succeed. I knew it was going to work out. I just had to stay in the game.

So, even back then, with your account underwater, you were still confident.

Yes, because I had a taste of what it was like to have good trades on, and I knew there were going to be more of them. I just had to stay in the game long enough for my stars to be aligned again.

We are talking about the lessons you learned during the second half of your first year of trading. Did those lessons register then, or are they insights you realized later and are referencing now in retrospect?

I realized even then that I couldn't carry on doing what I was doing. I knew I was close to the exit door, and I couldn't afford to take any marginal trades. I stopped trading technicals. I didn't make any trades unless I had a lot of conviction.

To follow the ensuing dialogue, readers need to understand the term "quantitative easing." The following is a short primer intended for readers who may not fully comprehend this term.

Typically, the Fed seeks to adjust interest rates by targeting the Fed funds rate, which is the overnight rate at which banks lend money to each other. The Fed's primary tool for targeting the Fed funds rate is termed *open market operations*—the buying and selling of short-term Treasurys to increase or decrease the quantity of money and, in turn, reduce or raise interest rates. For example, if the Fed wanted to reduce the Fed funds rate, it would "print" (electronically create) money to buy short-term Treasurys, increasing the price of Treasurys, which is equivalent to reducing interest rates.

In a sense, quantitative easing is an extension of normal open market operations. When short-term interest rates fall to near zero, the standard tool of buying short-term Treasurys to provide economic stimulus no longer works because short-term interest rates are already near zero. This situation was the dilemma the Fed faced during the financial crisis in 2008 and its aftermath. The Fed responded with quantitative easing, which meant increasing the supply of money, as in normal open market operations, but without the objective of decreasing short-term interest rates, which were already near zero. In practical terms, quantitative easing meant the Fed created money to purchase non-traditional assets (i.e., assets other than short-term Treasurys). Specifically, the Fed bought longer-term Treasurys and non-government assets, such as mortgage-backed securities. By purchasing longer-term Treasurys, the Fed reduced longer-term interest rates—an action that could still provide economic stimulus. The Fed's motivation for buying other types of assets, such as mortgage-backed securities, was to mitigate the meltdown in these other sectors during the financial panic.

The Fed's first quantitative easing move occurred in November 2008 when, to support the mortgage and housing market, it purchased mortgage-related government agency assets and private mortgage-backed securities, a financial asset class for which buyer demand had virtually disappeared. At that point, the Fed had still not applied quantitative easing to the purchase of longer-term Treasurys, although there was speculation that it would at some point.

———————

Your trading history contains many days with exceptional gains. I counted 34 days in which you made a return above 15%, 15 days with returns above 25%, and five days with returns above 50%. But even with this history of days with huge gains, one day stands out: March 18, 2009, when your return exceeded an unbelievable 800%! How was that even possible? What is the story behind that trade?

In November 2008, when the Fed first announced quantitative easing, it purchased mortgage-backed securities to stabilize the markets during the financial meltdown. I expected the Fed to eventually expand quantitative easing to include the purchase of longer-term US Treasurys. I thought that if and when such an announcement occurred, it would trigger an instantaneous, massive rally in T-bonds. March 18, 2009 was the day when the Fed announced an expansion in quantitative easing, which, for the first time, included the purchase of longer-term Treasurys.

Did you take a large position immediately after the announcement was made?

Not as large as I would have liked. At the time, my permissible limit in T-note futures was 300 contracts. In anticipation of the event, I explained to the risk manager why I wanted an increase in my position limit in T-notes to 600 contracts. I was only requesting the increase in my risk limit for T-notes for this one anticipated trade, and I even offered to reduce or give up my position limits in other markets as an offset to this higher requested risk level. The risk manager, however, refused to increase my risk limit because I was still a relatively new trader and in a drawdown at the time. Because of this limitation, I also took a limit position in the

Bund as a proxy for what I really wanted to do: double the T-note position. While not as profitable as the T-note trade, the Bund trade contributed significantly to my outlier return that day.

How big was the move in T-notes after the announcement?

[Amrit pulls out the relevant chart and shows me the day of the announcement. The price bar for that day is four full points wide. I am struck by two observations: First, the rally occurred within an ongoing downtrend in the T-note market. Second, the high of the announcement day was within a few ticks of the rebound high and was followed by a large continued price slide.]

Ironically, going long was a great trade for the day, but it would have been buying near the high for any longer-term trade. How long did you hold the trade?

Minutes. I was very quick to get in because I was poised for that one trade. The order was prepared, and my finger was ready to click. My mind was totally focused. There was no obstruction between the newsfeed and me. There was no self-doubt or excitement to compromise my acting on the trade. I was in a state of flow. I was looking for one trade, and I didn't care about anything else. When the market surged after the news, I intuitively knew that the price move was so quick and so big that I should immediately take profits. I ended up selling the position near the high.

So, the high of the move was made only a few minutes after the announcement.

Yes.

How much did you make on that trade?

I made over $1 million in two or three minutes of trading! This was the moment that opened my eyes to the opportunity trading offered to a young, hungry, and disciplined risk-taker.

Do you remember your emotional state after the trade was completed?

It's embarrassing thinking back on it now, but I had a very ungrateful reaction. It was a mixed bag. Of course, it was nice having such a great day. However, almost instantly, I fell back into a negative mindset.

Why?

I didn't feel like I made $1 million; I felt like I lost out on making $1 million. It was such an easy trade that I wish I had more, and I did try to get more.

So, you were actually upset because you didn't have double the position you wanted?

Looking back at it now, I am filled with gratitude, but that was not how I felt then. That was another part of the journey.

When you put on a huge position like the quantitative easing trade, do you use a stop?

Back then, I didn't necessarily, but I do now. Getting a stop in place is a hard-and-fast rule for me now.

Do you enter the stop at the same time you place the order?

No, because I don't want the market whipping back and immediately taking out my stop. Once there has been enough price movement to avoid getting stopped out artificially, I will put my stop in. It is essential to have that protection on because once you have a position, there is always the possibility of news coming out adverse to your position, and you may not be able to get out quickly enough. Having a stop in eliminates that tail risk.

When did you start using stops religiously?

After I had my worst daily loss, a 24% hit.

When was that, and what happened?

The trade occurred in June 2013, and it was a comedy of errors. The ECB had been touting the possibility of negative interest rates for some time. It was my belief that if and when they went to negative interest rates, it would be very bearish for the euro.

You felt that way even though the prospect for negative interest rates had been widely discussed and people were sort of expecting it?

Yes, because it would still have been a market shock in my time frame. It would confirm the action, and once the ECB went to negative interest rate territory by any amount, it would raise the question of whether even more negative interest rates might be in the offing. It would open up Pandora's box. I am always looking for a trigger. I am looking for a moment in time that allows me to place a leveraged position for what I consider to be a potential big intraday move. If the trigger looks like the start of a longer-term price move, I will try to hold part of the position. My approach doesn't stop me from putting on a position on an event that may be somewhat priced in because it can still trigger a big move on the day of the event, which is all I need to place the trade.

So what went wrong in this particular situation?

Mario Draghi, the president of the ECB, was giving a press conference, and I was expecting him to announce a move to negative interest rates. When he was asked whether the ECB was ready to move to negative interest rates, he began his answer by saying, "I told you we are technically ready…" At that point, I went short without waiting for him to finish his reply. It was not necessarily a mistake to go short in anticipation of his answer because I knew I could get right out if I was wrong on the trade. However, the moment after I entered my sell order, my computer suddenly powered down. At the same time, I am still hearing Draghi on the TV as he continues and says the magic words, "but we won't pre-commit." I knew the euro was going to soar and rip my face off.

What did you do?

I panicked. I said out loud, "My computer has gone off! My computer has gone off!" The risk manager walked over to my desk and calmly said, "I can see what your position is. Come over to my desk, and you can trade out of it." I am used to getting in and out of trades quickly, and I would've been out of that trade instantaneously because as soon as I heard Draghi finish his sentence, I knew it was a bad trade. Even worse, I knew there was a lot of speculative money caught on the wrong side of the trade, and I would normally have gone long after I heard Draghi say, "but we won't pre-commit." My best trades come from being on the other side of the type of trade I was in—namely, trades in which short-term speculators have it wrong, and I can go against them.

Are you implying that if your computer hadn't gone down, you would have reversed your position?

I would definitely have attempted to reverse my position very quickly.

What happened after you went over to the risk manager's desk to trade out of your position?

I saw that the euro was being bought quite aggressively, and I had no stop in. That moment ingrained into me the rule that I have to get my stop in as soon as possible. [Sall hits the desk with each word when he says, "I have to get my stop in."] If I had a stop on that trade, my loss would have been minimal. Also, now that my trading size is much larger, I will no longer take anticipatory trades.

Did you get out right after you went to the risk manager's desk, or did you wait and watch the position?

I got out right away, but the market was moving so quickly that I had already taken an enormous hit.

What caused your computer to power down?

I believe it was some Windows issue.

That has got to be the worst bad luck trading story I have ever heard. How did you feel after that loss?

What could I do? I realized that I could either accept it and move on or let it affect me emotionally in ways that were not going to serve me well. I put it behind me as quickly as I could. I left the office, and later that day, I got together with some of my friends at the local bar. We had what I called a "celebration" because I wanted to shift my focus to the positive aspects of my situation rather than sulk over my loss. I was grateful to be in a position that offered so much potential for earnings. The fact that I could lose so much money, so quickly, only reinforced the opportunity I had. I felt I was in the right job, but that I just had an unlucky moment.

Your choice of the word "celebration" strikes a chord with the conversation I had with Richard yesterday [Richard Bargh, who was interviewed in Chapter 3]. He said that his natural tendency after a bad day was to stop spending money and that one of the things he learned from you was that he should instead go out and treat himself.

Richard and I had those conversations. After a bad trading day, I have two options: I can sit there, dwell on it, and let it hold me back, or I can flip it on its head and take control of it. After a big hit, I try to minimize the impact on my emotional capital by returning to a calm and centered state as soon as I can. I do a postmortem on the trade, learn the lessons, and move on to the next opportunity. After processing a big loss or drawdown, I have often treated myself from a place of gratitude for all that I have achieved to date. Through this process, I avoid the trap of repeatedly replaying the same negative story, reliving the pain multiple times, and taxing my mental capital.

Is the thought of rewarding yourself or celebrating after you have experienced trading losses a concept you instinctively realized was a good idea from the beginning?

I think I realized it after doing it a couple of times. There was a guy in the office who used to say, "Whenever you have a good period trading, make sure you treat yourself, so you know why you are doing it."

But you were treating yourself after you had a bad period. That's precisely the opposite.

That's true. For me, it's all about shifting your mindset. You want to get your mind back to a calm, rational place rather than being in a negative and stressed state. You want your decisions being driven by your prefrontal cortex rather than your amygdala. If I realize I am having a tough time, I will ground myself and be grateful for the journey. Then I can go out and treat myself.

The ocean provides a good analogy. The ocean surface is covered with waves and turbulence, but if you dive down, it is calm. We all have the ability in us to dive down into that calm region. If you are worried about missing out on a trade, you will be prone to take trades you shouldn't be taking. If you are emotionally agitated, you may snatch your profits instead of letting them run, or you may hold onto your losers. You need to pull away from all those primitive reactions to a higher self—a calm and centered person.

Your response to negative trading periods is 180 degrees opposite to what the natural reaction of most traders would be. Most traders would sulk and feel horrible if they had a terrible trading day, like your huge loss because your computer went down at a critical moment.

That's what trading is; it's going against standard human emotions. As a trader, you are continually going up against your own emotional limitations. That is why so few people succeed in trading.

How long did it take you to get centered again after you took that 24% hit because of the computer glitch?

Instantly. I made all the money back within seven days.

Was there a big trade that helped you recover the loss?

No, it was more the cumulative effect of taking multiple trades that fit my criteria.

You mentioned the importance of shifting your mindset to a calm state. When did you come to this realization?

I noticed that, periodically, I would go through losing periods for no discernible reason. So, I started to keep an error log of marginal trades that were resulting in losses.

Underlying subconscious thoughts, emotions, and behaviors can drive our actions and adversely impact trading. I came from a working-class family where money wasn't abundant the way it is for me now. In the early days, I felt I often self-sabotaged and took subpar trades following record winning periods as a way to self regulate and "come back down to earth." Keeping a log of these subpar trades allowed me to become aware of these automatic response patterns.

[Sall pulls out a chart to illustrate the connection between emotions and losses. The emotional state is on the x-axis, with descriptions ranging from "calm" on the left end to "fear of missing out" on the right end. The magnitude of the loss on marginal trades, which Sall labels as "leakage" to indicate the losses were avoidable, is on the y-axis. The graph shows a clear pattern of the magnitude of losses moving from near flat in the calm region to increasingly larger levels as the emotional state becomes more excited.]

This chart helped me realize the underlying cause of these losing periods. To make the most of your trading opportunities and to minimize making bad trades, it all comes down to your state of mind, which is probably the most critical factor to trading success once you have your methodology down. I want to stay in the calm region—that zone where things flow through you. The only way I could be successful in making millisecond decisions for large amounts of money is by accessing that calm state.

I once read that the US Navy Seals use neurofeedback and biofeedback to help them access flow states on demand when in combat. I also read that the hardest part of a Seal's job was knowing when not to shoot. These observations resonated with me. I thought that if I could learn to access a similar state of mind on demand, it might allow me to process a lot more information and get better at knowing when "not to shoot." This goal led me on a journey of understanding the interconnection between the mind and body, and exploring meditation and flow states.

Expound on how you get into a flow state and how it impacts your trading.

Before a significant trade event, I go through breath work and meditation to center in on the present moment and transcend the chatter in my mind. Over time, I have learned how to access flow states within a few minutes. The ability to access flow is fundamental for success in trading and many other endeavors, such as professional sports. When I am deeply present, everything feels easy. In this "deep now" state, I'm reacting from a subconscious level that represents 95% of the mind's potential versus 5% for the conscious mind. In this state, I'm creative, and I can process large amounts of information and react without hesitation. I'm open to new information and evolve my positions accordingly. Trading feels easy, and I'm not trying to force anything, I have no attachment to my position or the outcome. I cut losses without hesitation, and I run my winners without any impulse to snatch profits.

In contrast, when I have difficulty transcending my mind before an event, everything I do will feel like a struggle. I will miss out on valuable bits of information. I will hesitate to put on correct positions because of self-doubt, and I will get out of winning trades way too soon.

Through experience, I have learned that when my gut tells me that something is off, regardless of what my research indicates, my gut is usually right. Learning to trust my gut has been pivotal to my success; it tells me when a trade is a unicorn, and I should go all in, and when there may be unseen danger, and I should hold my fire.

Before, you said the opposite side of your worst losing trade, which was caused by your computer going down, was an example of your best type of trade. Can you give me an example of this type of trade that was a big win?

I always look for situations where the market initially moves in the wrong direction in response to an event, and then I can go the other way. This is the same type of trade I was on the wrong side of when my computer went down. A perfect example occurred recently [September 2019] when the ECB announced a package of quantitative easing measures.

The speculative money was fixated on the amount of monthly purchases with expectations in the €30–€40 billion area. But, I had an appreciation that the total purchase amount was more important than the monthly flow. My gut told me that the fast money was looking for any excuse to sell disappointment. When the newswires reported that purchases would equal €20 billion per month, the fast money reacted in disappointment, with the Bund selling off, and the euro rallying. I had decided that, in this instance, it was best to wait to review all the information before making a trade, and I maintained a calm, flow state, digesting the full statement. When I saw that the monthly purchase commitment was open-ended, I knew that all the weak shorts would have to quickly unwind their speculative positions. At that moment, and just at that moment, the market was mispriced, so boom, I took the killer shot and went against the herd. The trade worked for a couple of hours before disappointment set in once more, and the market again reversed. But, by that time, I had made my money and was out of the trade. You could argue I was ultimately on the wrong side of the trade, but I was trading against a mispricing of speculative positions, and in my time frame, I was right.

The thing with short-term trading is that you can be "right" and lose money. The traders who went short in response to the initial announcement were ultimately right, but unless they were able to hold onto their positions through a sharp pullback, they would have lost money. Looking at the trade from a longer-term perspective, I was technically on the "wrong" side of the trade. Nevertheless, because I had an appreciation of how the positioning of short-term traders might impact prices, I was able to place a very profitable short-term trade.

What percent of your profits come from one-day trades?

Probably around 75%.

What is the characteristic of the minority of trades you hold for a longer period?

The longer-term trades are still triggered by the same type of events as my short-term trades, but a small percentage of those trades have long-term potential.

Yes, but what is the characteristic of those trades that suggest they have long-term potential?

Entirely unexpected events that have significant long-term implications for the economy can fuel long-term price moves. The unanticipated outcome of the Brexit vote and its aftermath provide a perfect example of a trade that had legs.

How do you decide when to get out of a trade?

I have an uncanny knack for picking half-decent places to liquidate. I'm working on translating my discretionary liquidation decisions into systematic rules, but I am not there yet. Also, if there is a parabolic price move on an intraday time frame on a position I hold, I will lock in the profit. I learned this rule the hard way when I have held onto such positions, thinking they would go much further, only to give back a chunk of the profits.

Except for that one trade when your computer went down, you have been very effective in managing risk, especially considering the magnitude of your returns. I know an essential element of your risk management is getting out immediately if a trade doesn't act as you expected. What are the other ingredients in your risk management?

In terms of individual trades, I vary my risk between 1% and 5%, depending on my conviction level. As I mentioned earlier, I get stops in on my positions as soon as possible. I will also take partial profits on trades rather than holding the full position until exit. Taking partial profits allows me to lock in "free trades" that offer unlimited upside but zero downside after I've taken profit on part of the position. It's like owning a free call option in a market I think should rally hard.

At the portfolio level, when I hit a 6% drawdown, I *may* start scaling back my size and become much more selective on new trades I put on. It depends on the circumstances. At times I have lost 5% in one trade and felt OK about it and kept my trading size unchanged. At other times, I have been on a slow bleed losing money over a long period, which usually means the market is in a lull period, or I'm out of sync with the market. In such instances, I will begin cutting size back and tighten up my criteria to take only dead certain trades.

Have you made any significant changes to your trading approach in recent years, and if so, why?

In the past, I have tended to implement trading ideas in a single market. I now try to execute trade ideas in multiple correlated markets. For example, I will place simultaneous positions in the Bund, Euro Stoxx index, and the euro, or at least two out of three, rather than just one of these markets. The reason for this change is that, sometimes, if the trade is not working in one of these markets, it doesn't mean there is something wrong with the trade hypothesis; it may just be that something is going on in that market that is keeping the trade from working. A good example occurred after an FOMC meeting that suggested the potential for lower rates. I bought T-notes and the S&P. The T-note position didn't do anything initially; it was even down a bit. That didn't mean the trade was not valid. If I was only in the T-note position and wasn't also in the S&P, which rallied, I would have been more inclined to conclude that my trade hypothesis was wrong, which turned out not to be the case. What had happened was that there was an impending auction weighing down the interest rate markets, and once the auction was out of the way, T-notes never looked back. So I have learned not to concentrate my trade ideas in a single market.

Over time, increased market automation and high-frequency-trading algorithms have made execution harder and eroded my edge on some very short time frame strategies. As a result, I focus primarily on higher conviction trades and trade less frequently during the month, but take on more risk per trade to reflect the conviction level.

What are some trading misconceptions you have seen that cause people to fail?

A lot of losing traders I have known thought they had to make money consistently. They had a paycheck mentality; they felt they had to make a certain amount every month. The reality is that you may go through long periods when you don't make anything, or even have a drawdown, and then have a substantial gain. Entrepreneurs understand that. They will invest in a company for a long time, and the payoff comes in one hit after many years of hard work. If you are looking for outsize profits, you can't approach that goal with a mindset of consistency. At best, I am right only 50% of the time, and sometimes I am right only 30% of the time. However, when I'm right only 30% of the time, I am earning eight times as much on my winners as I am losing on my losers. Traders have to ask themselves whether they can handle being right only 30% of the time, or do they feel they have to be right day after day? It is that latter perspective that holds a lot of people back.

What else causes traders to fail?

Losing traders will get locked into a state of negativity. They will let their losses affect them. It is a snowball effect. They will have a loss, and another loss, and another loss, and then, all of a sudden, they are in this really dark place in their heads where it is too late to escape because they have compounded all those negative thoughts. If they had killed the negative reinforcement process at the root by controlling their emotions after the first loss, they would've been in a much better position.

Also, working in a trading office for 13 years, I've seen a lot of people just trade and hope; they don't last long. You need to manage risk.

How about successful traders—do they share any common traits?

⚡ Successful traders take care of the downside and know that the upside will take care of itself.

⚡ They never give up. Even when things go badly, they will find a way to push through and know everything will be fine.

⚡ They are competitive within themselves and are always looking for ways to improve performance month after month.

⚡ They believe in their edge and realize that each trade is mutually exclusive—a perspective that allows them to pull the trigger every single time, regardless of the outcome of the preceding trades.

⚡ They embrace failure as feedback. They understand that failure is a necessity on the path to success in any endeavor. They realize that something is a failure only if they miss the opportunity to learn from it.

Your return/risk performance represents one of the best track records I have ever encountered. What skills or personal qualities do you believe have enabled you to achieve these results?

⚡ I am very aware of the characteristics of a good trade, and I don't hesitate when such a trade presents itself.

⚡ I am always looking for asymmetric return/risk trade profiles. I want to cap my risk every time, and when I capture a unicorn, I want to ride it until it throws me off.

⚡ I'm not looking for instant gratification; I put in the work and then wait patiently for the right trade. I can stay in a state of readiness, so when the big trade comes, I don't hesitate. I can go from zero to a hundred instantaneously. That approach works for me. Other people may feel they have to be doing something every day; I don't.

⚡ I am rigorous about managing my downside and preserving my mental capital in between big winning trades.

⚡ I don't attach myself to the outcome of a trade. I keep my focus on following a process.

⚡ I am good at discerning between high conviction and low conviction trades, and I vary my position size accordingly.

⚡ I am aggressive when there is a trading opportunity, and I back away from the market just as quickly when the opportunity passes.

⚡ I am disciplined, which allows me to leverage aggressively when there is a major trade opportunity.

⚡ I am always trying to learn from my mistakes, and I have a process to avoid making the same mistakes again.

⚡ I never give up. In the first seven months of this year [2019], I was in a drawdown. That hasn't happened to me since my early years of trading. You need to have the resilience to last through the difficult periods.

⚡ I am willing to outwork everyone else. In my early years, I used to get up at 4 a.m. or 5 a.m. to get fully updated on any overnight news. I used to sometimes put in 15- to 18-hour days.

⚡ To succeed as a trader, you need to have a fire in your belly; it's the only way you'll keep coming back after being kicked down repeatedly. I have that determination.

⚡ I think the most significant single factor to any success I have had as a trader is my inner focus: self-reflection, self-awareness, journaling, meditation, and breathwork. In particular, my ability to get into a flow state is the essence of who I am and, when combined with in-depth research, is my edge.

What do you know now that you wish you knew when you started?

It's what you don't do that counts. Patience is the key word. Successful trading is the art of doing nothing. It's what you don't do between the real trade opportunities that will determine your success over the long run. You can do so much damage to your mental capital between trades that when the big trade turns up, you are not ready for it.

So, it's not so much the losses you might take on suboptimal trades that is the problem, but rather the major trade opportunities you will be prone to miss because of the adverse impact of such marginal trades on your focus and mindset.

That is exactly right.

Do you have any last words?

Trading has been a wonderful journey of self-discovery and growth for me, and I am happy to share the story of my ups and downs and what I believe it takes to succeed over the long run. The last decade of trading feels like a warm-up, and I'm excited to see my growth in the coming years ahead.

———

Sall's incredible success as a trader is due to a trading process that combines three essential components:

1. **Trade Research and Planning**—Successful trading is not a shoot-from-the-hip approach; instead, it is a matter of hard work. Sall prepares assiduously for every trade. He has compiled thousands of pages of notes, chronicling all his past trades. For each of these trades, he documented his trading plan, the details of the relevant event and market response, and what he got right and wrong. These trade notes, which are categorized, allow Sall to identify and study historical analogues to prospective trades. Using this personally compiled research library, Sall prepares a highly detailed write-up for each contemplated trade—a plan that encompasses a wide range of scenarios as to how the trade might evolve in real time. Sall also vigilantly watches the newswire all day for any unexpected events that might offer trade opportunities.

2. **Trade Execution**—The types of trades that Sall terms "unicorns," which account for the vast majority of his profits, require instantaneous discretionary decisions. There is no time for contemplation and analysis. Sall has to know what he will do for each possible circumstance as an event, such as a central bank statement, unfolds. Even taking a

minute or two to think the trade over would typically result in missing the trade opportunity. To make sound trading decisions virtually reflexively when an event happens, Sall prepares by conducting in-depth research and planning, described in item 1. In addition, Sall engages in visualization and mental rehearsal as to how he will respond in a variety of circumstances, much as some professional athletes do before a big game or major competition. He also gets into a "deep now" state through meditation and breathwork.

3. **Emotional Calm**—Sall considers maintaining the appropriate emotional state—calm, centered, focused—as absolutely essential to being a successful trader. He is scrupulous in avoiding a negative mindset or allowing a trade loss or trading mistake to impact, let alone derail, a subsequent trade opportunity. Sall will short-circuit any potential negative mental spiral before it gets going. When he is in a drawdown or has experienced a particularly bad trading day, Sall will break any burgeoning negative mindset by focusing instead on all the things he is grateful for. In Sall's words, "It's all about shifting your mindset. You want to get your mind back to a calm, rational place." Maintaining a positive mindset and a calm emotional state is not an auxiliary component of Sall's trading process; it is an absolute core part of it.

The idea of treating yourself when trading is going poorly is a unique piece of advice. It is a concept that was never mentioned by any of the traders I interviewed in previous *Market Wizards* books. It has worked well for Sall, but is it good advice for traders in general? I don't know, but individual traders can experiment with the idea. However, what is certainly good advice for all traders is Sall's more general point that successful trading requires a positive mindset and a calm, focused emotional state.

Patience is an inherent trait shared by many of the great traders I have interviewed. For Sall, patience lies at the very essence of his trading success. This assessment is best illustrated in Sall's own words describing his trading style in our email correspondence before the interview: "My style has often been referred to that of a sniper. I am in a constant state of readiness waiting for that perfect shot. I don't want to waste my bullets doing anything else because it will jeopardize my ability to take that perfect shot. I wait for a trade that I intuitively know is right, and then I will take the shot. The rest of the time, I sit still and patiently wait."

Sall believes that doing nothing between the genuine trade opportunities is far more challenging than executing the trades responsible for the bulk of his profits. Having the patience to avoid the temptation of taking suboptimal trades is essential for two reasons. First, these trades will tend to be net losers. Second, and even more importantly, the negative impact of these trades on a trader's mental state and focus may result in missing the really big trade opportunities. The lesson is: Only take trades that fit your rules and avoid the marginal trades.

Ironically, striving for performance consistency, which sounds like a worthwhile goal, can be a flaw rather than a virtue. Sall says that a common trait he observed among traders who failed is that they had a goal of making money every month. Why is this an undesirable objective? The explanation lies in the fact that the markets don't provide opportunities on a regular schedule. Consequently, a goal of making profits every month will entice traders to take trades that are based more on hope than methodology when genuine trade opportunities are lacking. In effect, the quest for consistency will lead traders to act in diametric opposition to the sound principle of patience.

The trades that Sall has the patience to wait for have two essential characteristics:

1. They are trades he perceives have a high probability of moving in the anticipated direction.

2. They are asymmetric trades: the potential gain far exceeds the risk taken.

Sall will take large positions on these high-conviction trades. The wide variation in his position sizing—specifically, taking much larger positions on high-conviction trades—is an essential factor in Sall's ability to generate outsized gains.

To limit the loss on any single trade, Sall will always place a protective stop order as soon as practical. Because Sall trades large positions based on events—times when markets are particularly volatile—placing stops at the time of order entry would run too high a risk of a position getting stopped out on a meaningless, momentary price gyration. Instead, Sall will wait for the market to move enough in his direction so that his stop will only be triggered if the trade idea fails. What if the market moves against him before he can place a stop? Since Sall is very quick to liquidate his position if the market fails to immediately react as anticipated, a straight market order will serve to contain his loss in these instances.

Winning breeds complacency. When trading is going particularly well, many traders will tend to get lax in both their trade entry and money management. They will be more prone to take trades they normally wouldn't and to be less rigorous in their risk control. After one strong winning period, Sall found himself falling into this trap when he placed limit positions in three highly correlated markets on a marginal trade. A query as to what he was doing by the company's risk manager brought Sall back to his senses, and he liquidated all his trades. The risk manager's intervention helped avert a possible significant loss. Still, the experience helped Sall learn the lesson to caution against getting cocky and loosening trade discipline after extensive winning periods—a valuable lesson for virtually all traders.

If you ever find yourself in a trade based on hope, get out. You need conviction, not hope, to stay in a trade. Sall's use of technical-based trade triggers early in his career resulted in trades with little conviction that he hoped would work. His unease with hoping trades would work convinced him that technical trading was the wrong path for him.

Sall provides an excellent example of a trader whose exceptional success was greatly abetted by an extreme work ethic. I am often asked whether hard work alone is enough to become a successful trader or whether great traders succeed because they have some innate skill. Although hard work and risk management are critical to trading success, they are not sufficient to explain the magnitude of performance achieved by exceptional traders. These traders also possess innate skill. Sall's comment about how he decides where to get out of trades is telling: "I have an uncanny knack for picking half-decent places to liquidate." The words "uncanny knack" reflect an intuitive skill that cannot be taught or learned.

Running a marathon provides a good analogy. Most people, if they are sufficiently committed and work hard enough, can run a marathon, which is an impossible task without lots of preparation and training. However, regardless of the degree of dedication or amount of hard work, only a small fraction of people have the body type that would permit running a marathon at a world-class pace. Similarly, with enough work and dedication, combined with effective risk management, a significant percentage of people could become at least marginally profitable traders, but only a small percentage possess the intrinsic skill to become Market Wizards.

Sall creates detailed write-ups of all his trades and periodically reviews these trade logs. One reason he performs this exercise is to compile a historical record of market behavior in specific situations to serve as guidelines for what to expect in future similar circumstances. However, another critical reason he creates and reviews this trade documentation is to learn from his past mistakes so he can avoid repeating them. Maintaining and periodically reviewing a written analysis of your trades that includes reasons for entry and exit, as well as what you did right and wrong, is a valuable exercise for all traders. It provides a useful tool for recognizing trading mistakes, which is the first step to avoid repeating the same mistakes in the future. Learning from mistakes is how you become a better trader.

Great traders tend to be very confident in their abilities. Yes, I know they may be confident simply because they are successful. However, I think for these traders, confidence is an inherent trait that may precede and be independent of success. Sall provides a good example supporting this premise. Even after his account balance went negative in his first trading year and his trading career was in peril, he was still confident he would succeed. An honest assessment of your degree of confidence in your trading ability is one way to gauge whether or not you are likely to succeed as a trader. If you are ambiguous or doubtful about whether your trading methodology provides an edge, you should be particularly cautious regarding the amount of money you are willing to risk.

If you have the skill and genuine confidence that you can be a profitable trader, then one other trait is necessary to succeed: resilience. Never give up.

DALJIT DHALIWAL

Know Your Edge

DALJIT Dhaliwal's track record is extraordinary. In his nine-plus years of trading, he has achieved a remarkable average annual compounded return of 298%. He trades aggressively, taking large positions when he has a high degree of confidence in a trade. His average annualized volatility is extremely high at 84%.

So, you might think, "Sure, his returns are amazing, but his risk must be off the charts as well." And, this presumption would seem to be supported by his stratospheric volatility. But, here's the thing: His volatility is super high because of his many huge gains; his downside has actually been remarkably controlled. Given his return and volatility levels, it would be reasonable to expect to see multiple drawdowns of 50% or more. But Dhaliwal's maximum drawdown, based on monthly ending equity levels, is under 20%. He has been profitable in all years, 95% of quarters, and 70% of months. As implied by his combination of mammoth returns and controlled downside, Dhaliwal's return/risk statistics are exemplary: an adjusted Sortino ratio of 10.3 and a monthly Gain to Pain ratio of 8.5—numbers that are five times the levels of what could be considered excellent performance. (See Appendix 2 for the definitions and context of these statistics.)

Dhaliwal's initial passion was tennis, not trading. As a teen, he was a promising junior player in the UK, and he had hopes of becoming a professional. When Dhaliwal is committed to a goal, he goes all out in achieving it. He started playing tennis at the relatively late age of ten (late for an aspiring professional). Dhaliwal practiced relentlessly, receiving instruction from professional coaches five days a week. The reasons why he abandoned his quest to become a tennis professional are discussed in the interview.

While Dhaliwal was in university, the 2008 financial meltdown and its aftermath sparked his interest in markets. By the time he was in his final year of studies, Dhaliwal knew he wanted to be a trader. The problem was that he attended a mid-ranked university, and trading jobs went almost exclusively to graduates of top universities. This obstacle was especially acute when he graduated in the post-financial-crisis period when trading jobs were particularly scarce and competition for these positions fierce. By all logic, it should have been impossible for Dhaliwal to land a trading job—but through sheer determination, he did.

Dhaliwal attacked trading with the same passion and commitment he had for tennis as a teen. He devoted himself to learning everything he could about markets and trading. Dhaliwal had the sound sense to realize that he didn't know anything when he started, and therefore, he did not harbor any preconceived notions. Instead, he studied market price moves and their causes, to learn from the markets how to interpret different events.

Dhaliwal's methodology went through many changes as he evolved as a trader. Initially, he primarily used technical analysis, but he quickly shifted to a fundamental focus when he realized that the smaller number of fundamentally based trades were the source of nearly all his trading profits. For most of his career, Dhaliwal placed day trades based on his interpretation of fundamental events, such as central bank announcements. In recent years, he has shifted increasingly to longer-term trades based on macroeconomic models he and his research assistant have developed.

Dhaliwal spent most of his trading career as part of the same group as Richard Bargh (Chapter 3) and Amrit Sall (Chapter 4). A desire to operate more independently without being influenced by other traders prompted

Dhaliwal to move to his own London office, which is where I interviewed him. I mentioned to Dhaliwal that I was interviewing Michael Kean (see Chapter 10) the following day. By coincidence, Dhaliwal invests with Kean. The next day Dhaliwal invited both of us to a terrific dinner at Goodman, a steakhouse in the City of London.

How would you define your trading strategy?

I would say that I am a macro, event-driven trader. On the quantitative side, I am using leading economic indicators and historical analogue models we have developed. On the qualitative side, I use a short-term strategy of trading headlines as a tactical tool for getting positioned in the market. Also, on the qualitative side, I use my understanding of narratives that may be driving the market, which, at times, could overwhelm the fundamentals.

Did you have any career aspirations as a teen?

Probably more than anything else, I had hopes of becoming a professional tennis player. Tennis was a big part of my life in high school.

Did you compete professionally?

I never made it to the international level. My top ranking was about 80 in the UK.

What happened to that career pathway?

When I was about 16 years old, I had a pivotal conversation with one of the coaches, who had been a world-ranked player. He said he loved the experience of competing at the international level and the opportunity it gave him to travel the world, but that there was no money in it. At that point, he was in his 30s and studying for a degree to start a new career.

Was it his comment about the limited earning potential that dampened your enthusiasm to pursue a career as a professional tennis player?

More than that, it was the idea of having to start a whole new career at that stage of your life. I didn't have a love for tennis the way some of my peers did. My interest in tennis didn't extend beyond the possibility of becoming a pro. I knew I didn't want to become a tennis coach. There was also another formative moment about a year later. One day, my coach brought in someone for me to play against. We played a set, and I beat him 6-4. Afterward, my coach told me the player I had just beat was world-ranked the previous year. He hadn't told me beforehand because he didn't want me to be intimidated. At that moment, I should have felt the spark and thought, "Hey, maybe I can do this." But I didn't. I still didn't see myself having a career as a tennis pro.

When did you give up on tennis?

In university, I injured my ankle playing football [soccer]. My tennis coach told me to take the winter off and come back, but I never did.

Is there anything about your experience playing tennis at a serious level that relates to your trading career?

In tennis, you must take every shot, whereas, in trading, you don't have to take every potential trade. You can wait for a trade where everything lines up in your favor. It would be like playing tennis and only having to take the shot when you were set up for a perfect smash. One thing I realized about trading is that I don't have to trade if I am not in the right frame of mind or the opportunity cycle is not in line with the way I trade, and I quite like that.

That is more an observation about the contrast between playing tennis and trading. Is there any connection between reaching a high level of proficiency in a sport like tennis and being a skilled trader?

It comes down to the psychological similarities between excelling in a sport and trading. You need to have discipline in both. You need to manage your rest and nutrition. As a trader, you need to make optimal decisions, and it's difficult to make the right decision if you're stressed or tired.

What sparked your interest in the markets?

When I was in university, the markets were a big part of what was going on in the news.

What years are we talking about?

2008 to 2010.

Oh, the financial meltdown and its aftermath. What did you major in?

Economics and finance. I felt that finance was an exciting field. I liked not knowing what would happen the next day. I didn't want to be in a mundane job.

When did you start trading?

While I was in university, I started spread betting on currencies. I think it is illegal in the US, but it is legal in the UK and also tax-free.

How much were you betting?

Tiny amounts—only a few pounds. I didn't have much money.

On what basis were you placing bets?

I was just using basic technical analysis, such as chart breakouts and moving averages.

What did you learn during that phase?

I made 5k and then lost 2k very quickly. I realized I didn't know what I was doing. I decided to bank my remaining gains and focus on my studies. Going into my last year, my grades weren't that great. I wanted to get a job as a trader when I graduated, and I realized that I needed to improve my grades if I was going to get into the field. I studied hard in my final year and managed to get a good grade overall.

One day, someone from one of the banks came down to our university to give a talk. His topic was primarily about the operations department. After the talk, I went up to him and said, "I really would like to get a job trading. How can I do it?" He replied, "To be honest, there are probably 200 jobs in the operations department and less than half a dozen in the trading department, and the trading jobs are only going to go to candidates from top-tier universities."

I take it that you were not at a top university.

No, it was a mid-level university.

What did you do then?

At that point, I thought I might as well try to apply for as many trading positions as I could anyway. I felt if I could just get an interview, then maybe I could sell myself. I applied to about 30 different places, mostly banks, but also proprietary trading firms. I was rejected by all of them except for one proprietary trading firm that gave me an interview.

Tell me about that interview.

I was interviewed by the risk manager who had been a floor trader before he decided to switch from trading to management. I had just finished my final exams, and it was the only interview I had. I was determined to do well.

Were there any pivotal questions or answers in the interview?

We just had a long conversation about what was going on in the markets at the time. I think he was impressed with my genuine interest in the markets and desire to learn. At the end, he asked me if there was anything else I wanted to ask for or say. I told him, "I have applied to 30 different places, and I *really* want to be in this field. If you just give me this job, I will be the hardest worker you will ever see." I think it was my enthusiasm more than anything else that got me the job.

Tell me about your experience when you joined the trading firm.

The first three months were a big learning curve. They taught us about both fundamental analysis and technical analysis in classroom sessions.

Did you have a methodology when you started trading?

In the beginning, I was just testing things out. I didn't have much of a process. Initially, I gravitated more toward technical analysis. I used Market Profile [a type of price analysis that attaches particular significance to the price areas that witnessed large trading volumes] and combined it with chart analysis. I didn't like indicators; I thought they were backward-looking. Whereas, I quite liked chart patterns because they would tell you where you were and give you some context for what to expect. For example, if the market was in a trading range, you knew that eventually there had to be a breakout in one direction, even if that breakout proved to be a false breakout.

I agree. After all, indicators are derivatives of price and, therefore, can't give you more information than already exists in the price chart itself.

Looking at your track record, I noted that you were profitable pretty much straight off the bat. Apparently, you were doing quite well with technical analysis, since that is the approach you started with. I wonder what motivated you to switch from technical analysis to fundamental analysis, given that you were trading profitably using technical analysis?

I felt uncomfortable with technical analysis because I didn't understand why it should work, and, consequently, I didn't have the confidence that it would continue to work in the future. Whereas with fundamentals, I had a much clearer understanding of why prices moved from one level to another. I also found fundamental analysis way more interesting. Actually, reading your first *Market Wizards* book was a formative influence in my early career. I don't remember who said it, but the advice to trade a method in line with your personality had a significant impact on me.

I don't remember who said it either because that same message came up either explicitly or implicitly in multiple interviews. When I give talks about the lessons of the *Market Wizards*, the importance of trading an approach compatible with your personality is one of the first points I tend to stress. How did you start using fundamental analysis as a trading tool?

It was mainly headline trading—typically, trading on the comments of central bankers or other officials.

How did you trade those headlines?

I had a view of what the market was expecting for any event based on reading various comments and news stories. Back then, I would trade headlines based on whether they were bullish or bearish relative to market expectations, even trades in which it didn't seem to make any sense to expect a market response because the information was already out there.

Can you give me an example?

The point at which I really started building my account was during the eurozone debt crisis in 2011. That was the time when Greece began blowing up. Every day, you would see a headline referencing a comment by European officials that was either hawkish or dovish towards Greece. I would trade these comments for short-term moves in the euro. At one point, I noticed that an official could say something like, "We're not going to help Greece," and the euro would move 20 ticks. Then later in the day, Chancellor Merkel would come out and say the same thing, and the euro would move another 40 ticks. You would think that the information was already in the market, so there shouldn't be any price reaction. But I would trade it because the market suggested that information was now more significant since Merkel said it. I didn't care whether I fully understood the reasons behind it; all I cared about was the immediate market impact. I try to align myself more with making money than being intellectually correct. In practice, that means letting the market reaction to news guide me as to what is important.

Before, you used the phrase, "back then," implying that you no longer trade the fundamentals the same way. How has your approach changed?

Actually, what I do now is quite the opposite. I will fade the initial reactions to headlines. It is no longer possible to trade for the initial move off the headline because the algos will make the trade before I can. [Dhaliwal is referring to algorithmic programs that are designed to instantaneously take trades based on the words and phrases in news headlines.]

It sounds like these headline-based trades, whether trading in the direction of the headlines, as you did in your earlier years, or fading them as you did subsequently, were all very short-term trades. When did you start taking longer-term trades?

Around 2016, I began to realize that when there was a significant fundamental shift, the short-term moves continued into longer-term moves. Then I thought, "Why am I spending all my time trying to catch the short-term moves when I can just nail one of these big moves and make a significant portion of my annual profits in just one trade?" That's when my trading mentality shifted. I thought, "I don't have to be right all the time; I just need to be right in a big way a few times a year." It's not an easy game trying to trade headlines. Mentally, it's quite tiring. Then, when I analyzed my trading results, I noted that almost all my profits were coming from very few trades, which meant that all the other trades were netting out to close to zero. So why was I bothering to take all those trades?

What was the essential distinction between the trades contributing to your P&L and those that weren't?

The most profitable trades were the ones that were based on entirely unexpected events.

So was the change in your approach basically a matter of being more restrictive in the trades you took and having a willingness to hold those trades longer?

Not entirely. The major shift was a transition to trades that were based on a broader macroeconomic analysis.

Can you give me an example?

This past July [2019], I went short the S&P in what was probably my largest trade ever. I felt the policymakers weren't doing enough to alleviate the downside risks in the economy. Payroll growth and manufacturing were slowing. At the same time, EU economic data was terrible. Based on my historical analogue models, I felt that given the economic regime we were in, the equity market was susceptible to a drawdown.

Where exactly did you go short?

[Dhaliwal shows me the chart pointing to a narrow consolidation forming near the top of a broader range near all-time highs.]

Of course, with the benefit of hindsight, the market subsequently broke back down towards the lower end of the range, but, at the time, a consolidation near all-time highs is a type of pattern that could easily have led to another upswing. What would have happened if the market started rallying into new highs? How much room would you have given the market?

Not a lot because I was timing the market based on some of my short-term fundamental indicators. Also, I split the trade between outright shorts in the S&P and long S&P puts. I gave the puts more breathing room.

When a market trades in a wide range on the same fundamentals, as the S&P did, how do you decide when to initiate the trade? I assume that your stop would have been considerably narrower than the market range.

I wouldn't sell the S&P in no man's land. The entry would be more towards the top of the range.

That is what I was grappling with. So, if you have a bearish view and the market is in a wide range, then when the market gets to the top of the range, where it is unclear whether it will fail or break out to new highs, you would be inclined to trade from the short side because your fundamental models suggest that a failure is more likely. Is that a fair description of how you might determine the timing of a trade based on fundamentals?

Yes, with the proviso that if there is a significant development, it doesn't matter where the market is within the range.

I assume by "significant development," you are referring to a headline event whose impact is likely to be long-lasting. But that raises the question: What if such an event's implications are contrary to your fundamental expectations?

I would go with the event if it were big enough. I want to make money more than I want to be right. Also, I am not looking for confirming signals; I am looking for disconfirming signals. All I care about is how I might be wrong. If there is a meaningful adverse event, it might mean my models are wrong.

———————

Several weeks after our interview, the S&P 500 broke out to new highs and staged a large advance in the ensuing months. This price action prompted a follow-up Q&A via email.

All the economic reasons you mentioned for being short the S&P during our interview would seemingly also have applied in Q4 when the market went straight up. I don't understand why the same fundamentals wouldn't have dictated a bearish stance in Q4 when such a trading position would have been dead wrong. What were the differences between when you put on the trade [late July 2019] and Q4 that would have kept you off the short side in Q4?

My outlook for some key economic indicators for Q4 was indeed bearish. However, in that quarter, the Fed changed its policy stance and switched on the liquidity taps. My research suggested their actions would outweigh my reasons for being bearish at the time (deteriorating economic data). So, I stayed on the sidelines for most of that period.

What was your most painful trade?

In December 2015, there was a big ECB [European Central Bank] meeting. The expectation going into this meeting was that the ECB would cut rates and do quantitative easing. I did my fundamental analysis beforehand and was fully prepared. I knew what the market expected and what would and would not be a trade. We were all sitting in the office waiting for the news. About five or ten minutes before the official announcement was expected, a headline came over the Bloomberg from the *FT* [*Financial Times*] saying, "ECB leaves rates unchanged in shock decision." I saw the attribution to the *FT*, and I thought it had to be correct. The story was such a complete surprise that I thought I could have my best day ever if it was correct. I decided to take a punt and instantly started buying the euro and selling the Euro Stoxx 50. The story was wrong. The ECB cut rates. The markets reversed so quickly that even though I liquidated immediately, I ended up getting out at the extreme of those moves. I went from being up six figures to down six figures in a matter of seconds.

So, initially, the market did move in your direction.

Yes, because the markets started moving on the *FT* headline, but when the actual announcement came out, they instantly reversed.

How large was the percentage loss in your account due to that trade?

About 20%.

Was there any lesson in that trade?

Yes, once it was over, I said, "I'm never going to let that happen again."

What exactly do you mean by "that"?

To have a large position on and not have a stop in.

Why didn't you have a stop?

Because I was so far ahead, I didn't think it would come all the way back.

Was that trade the point of demarcation after which you always had a stop in?

Not only that but after that trade, I also made sure that I took some money off the table when I had a quick, large gain. The euro had already moved a full percent before the ECB announcement came out, and I still had my entire position on.

So is it fair to say that two things changed in your trading after that trade: You always have a stop in, and you take partial profits when possible?

Exactly. Trading is so much about keeping the downside small. The psychological impact of large drawdowns is not worth the upside. You are much better off keeping an even keel.

So what was the story with that *Financial Times* article?

To this day, I don't know. The thing is that I would never have traded on something like that if it wasn't the *FT*. In hindsight, the story should have been implausible because the press is in a lockup room and cannot release any article until the precise time of the actual announcement.

I later found the explanation of what happened in a retraction issued by the *Financial Times*.

> On Thursday, we published an incorrect story on FT.com that stated the European Central Bank had confounded expectations by deciding to hold interest rates rather than cut them. The story was published a few minutes before the decision to cut rates was announced. The story was wrong and should not have been published. The article was one of two

pre-written stories—covering different possible decisions—which had been prepared in advance of the announcement. Due to an editing error it was published when it should not have been. Automated feeds meant that the initial error was compounded by being simultaneously published on Twitter. The *FT* deeply regrets this serious mistake and will immediately be reviewing its publication and workflow processes to ensure such an error cannot happen again. We apologise to all our readers.

I found you through Steve Goldstein [the founder of Alpha R Cubed, a London-based executive coaching firm, who has worked with many excellent traders]. You have done so extraordinarily well. What was your motivation in seeking a trading coach?

Peter Brandt says, "Successful market speculation is an upstream swim against human nature," and I liken coaching to a speedboat that helps me do that. I felt I needed an external check on my own trading, particularly when I was not trading my best or the opportunity set was not in line with my trading style, and Steve plays that role. At those times, I find it helpful to talk to Steve to prevent myself from going into a deeper drawdown. Additionally, working with Steve helped me clarify and solidify my trading rules. He also helped me realize that I was too focused on my weaknesses and that I needed to focus more on my strengths. If you focus on your strengths, you don't leave any time for your weaknesses.

I know from Steve that you bid in a charity auction to have lunch with Ray Dalio. Tell me about that experience.

I read a *Business Insider* article that mentioned that Ray Dalio was offering a lunch meeting for a charity auction. I thought, "That sounds really cool, but I bet that the winning bid is going to be something like $1 million." I checked the website and discovered that the bidding was only in the low-digit thousands. I thought, "I would love to meet him. I'm going to go for it!" I started bidding, and to my surprise, I was actually the leading bidder for quite a while—in fact, I still had the leading bid on the final day of the auction. I left work that day and took the train home, hoping I could get back quickly. The timing was running very tight with the close of the auction, and as soon as I got out of the train station, I checked the website to see if I was still winning. I saw that I had lost the bid. I was devastated. I castigated myself thinking, "Why did I get on the train? I should have waited a bit longer." The next day I received an email from Charitybuzz, the website that had run the auction, saying that Dalio was offering a second lunch and that I could have it if I matched the winning bid, which I happily did.

What was the winning bid?

The winning bid was only $40,000.

Where did you have lunch?

It was an Italian restaurant in the West Village [Manhattan]. I don't remember the name.

How was the lunch?

Amazing. Ray Dalio's book, *Principles*, had a significant impact on me and not only changed the way I thought about trading but also about life.

In what way?

After reading *Principles*, I started questioning everything. I think what Dalio was saying in that book is that your perception of reality is not necessarily the way things are. To reach your goals, you need a strong understanding of the links between the actions you take and the outcomes they produce over time. You can then adjust your actions where needed to reach the desired outcomes. That message prompted me to start doing data analysis on my trades.

What did you learn from that exercise?

I reviewed the trading notes I kept, which represented my perceptions, and then I looked at the data of the outcomes for those trades, which represented the reality. One realization that came out of that review was that although I thought I was good at technical analysis, I discovered that I really wasn't.

Did that insight change your trading?

It did. I started ditching technical analysis.

How did the conversation proceed at lunch?

Dalio said, "This is your time. Ask anything you want."

So what was the first thing you asked?

I was quite nervous. It's a bit of a blur looking back at it now. I told Dalio that I wanted to talk about my trading, markets, and his views on life.

Did he give you any specific advice?

He told me it was essential to go as far back as I could to test my views. Dalio is a master of history. He said that people get blindsided by something that has happened before because they overweight recent history and their own experience and don't go back far enough to backtest their views. He helped me understand that to get conviction, you have to look at history well beyond your own experience.

So now, when you analyze markets, how far back do you go?

As far as I can.

Which means what?

At the moment, about 100 years—but, ideally, I would like to go back well beyond that. Reading is part of my research. One book that I read recently is *Devil Take the Hindmost: A History of Financial Speculation* by Edward Chancellor. That book talks about market bubbles going all the way back to tulipmania.

Is that a good book?

It's fantastic. It's a book that can help you develop the kind of broader historical perspective of markets and speculation that Dalio talks about.

Were there any other insights that you got from your lunch with Dalio?

It was valuable to understand how Dalio thought about expected value. I don't want to misquote him here, but as a rough paraphrase, he talked about all the focus and expenditures on space exploration as the big frontier.

Dalio thought about it the opposite way—namely that we should go down into the ocean, given the ocean depths are still largely unexplored. He framed the argument in terms of expected value. He said we could learn much more from ocean exploration than we could by spending the same amount on space exploration. In other words, the expected value from ocean exploration was much greater than the expected value from space exploration. I found Dalio's perspective fascinating. I started thinking about how I could identify expected value in markets.

How would you define expected value?

For me, it's having a contrarian view on a market that is very out-of-favor. For example, earlier this year [2019], corn was extremely out-of-favor. Prices were at their lowest levels in decades, and the speculative short position was larger than it had been for a very long time. That type of situation suggests there is a high expected value in being on the other side of the market, provided there is a sufficient fundamental shift to support that stance.

Were you able to eat anything at this lunch?

[He laughs.] Dalio was saying, "Hey, you should taste this; it is really very good." I realized that, at that point, I hadn't eaten anything yet.

Were there any other people that were influential in developing your trading methodology?

Yes, Peter Brandt. [Brandt was interviewed in Chapter 1.] I have been a subscriber to Brandt's *Factor* trading service for a long time. I heard he was coming to Poland, and I really wanted to meet him. I emailed his assistant and arranged to meet Peter there. I ended up having dinner and breakfast with him. Peter is so humble about his trading. He is one of those people who understands what he knows and sticks to his edge. Peter told me that it took him 8 to 10 years before he knew he had a definable edge. The fact that it took him that long really struck me. I realized I had a lot more work to do before I understood what my edge really was. After our meeting, I decided I needed to examine the characteristics of my big wins because I have a large skew in my trades. I looked at everything related to those trades: my feelings at the time, the prevailing market characteristics, and my market analysis. I was looking for common denominators in those trades in which I did very well.

You had all that information on all your trades?

I have been maintaining a daily trading journal since 2011.

And Peter was the inspiration for going through your notes to examine the characteristics of your big winners?

Yes, definitely. Peter writes an annual review of what he calls his "best-dressed trades," which are the trades that provided the clearest examples of the classic chart patterns he looks for and subsequently led to the price moves implied by those patterns.

So, you wanted to find out what your "best-dressed trades" looked like.

Yes, exactly.

What did you find?

I realized an unexpected event that ran counter to the news flow was present in every one of my big winning trades. Another characteristic of these trades was that my reason for entering was very clear; I didn't confuse my short-term and long-term views. I also noticed that these trades were never down by much and usually tended to be profitable almost immediately, whereas the trades that didn't work tended to go offside quickly and stay offside.

You mentioned that you record your feelings in your daily trading journal. Can you give me a specific example of how having that type of information helped you improve as a trader?

I think the behavioral side of trading is an underexplored area for improving performance. Certain feelings are symptomatic of trading-related issues. For example, there was a short period when I was consistently recording feelings of frustration and FOMO [fear of missing out] in my journal. When I delved into it, I discovered that the underlying cause of this emotional disharmony was a conflict between my short-term and long-term views. What was happening was that I would have a longer-term trade on, but then I would see a chance to make money on an opposite, shorter-term bet in the same market. I would then end up trading neither view effectively. Even worse, I was leaving significant profits on the table, which was the source of my frustration. I realized this conflict was happening because, at the time, I was transitioning my approach to taking more longer-term trades. Once I objectively understood the issue, I could then develop the right solution.

What was the solution?

I would anticipate possible short-term trades that would run counter to my long-term view in a particular market, and if they developed as expected, I would trade them for what they were, but I would leave my long-term trade on.

Is there anything else that you learned from Brandt?

Yes, he talks about "leakage," which is money that you lose on trades that are not fully aligned with your process. I started tracking those types of trades in my account and saw that they were holding me back from reaching even higher levels of profits. In 2017, all my profits came from 10% of my trading days. It's so critical to avoid marginal trades because they waste monetary and psychological capital.

Peter's trading approach is 100% chart-based, whereas your trading is driven by fundamentals. Is his influence entirely a matter of broad trading principles independent of methodology, such as knowing your edge, avoiding suboptimal trades, and risk management, or is any part of his approach applicable to your trading?

I do use Peter's charting principles because I think the way he looks at markets is timeless. He doesn't use indicators and only looks at charts, a perspective that resonates with the way I look at markets as well.

I take it then that the broad price picture can influence your trading.

It can. I believe that long-term chart patterns are important, especially prolonged consolidations. You can't tell when they will break, but when they do, it can often lead to major price moves.

Can you give me an example of a trade where the chart price action was a significant element?

One trade immediately comes to mind because it is such a classic example. It goes back quite a while, though.

That doesn't make any difference; it's the example that counts.

In early May 2013, the Australian dollar had been in a trading consolidation for a long time. On this day [he points to May 9, 2013 on the price chart], you had one of those disconfirming days where the economic data, an employment report, was very strong, but the market broke out on the downside of its long-term range. The employment report was not just bullish, but *really* bullish. The market had expected an 11,000 figure, and the number came in at 50,000. Also, the unemployment rate went down, while the participation rate went up. The report was bullish in every possible way. The data came out 2:30 in the morning European time. There was an initial rally on the report, but by the time I got into the office at 7 a.m., the market had already sold off, with prices trading below the long-running consolidation pattern that I had been watching. I saw the data that had come out and the subsequent price action, and, straightaway, I just started selling. I didn't think; I just went short immediately.

Do you do anything differently when you are in a losing period?

I have a systematic process for cutting my size down when I am in a drawdown. I consider any loss less than 5% to be just the natural fluctuation required to generate my returns. But once a drawdown exceeds 5%, I cut my size in half.

Is there a point at which you cut it even further?

If the drawdown exceeds 8%, I cut my size by half again, and if it reaches 15%, I would stop trading and take a break.

Has that ever happened?

Aside from that one day with the erroneous *Financial Times* story, there was one other instance. I basically came to work, did research, and didn't trade.

How long did that last?

Not that long—about a week or two.

We talked about the lessons you learned from Ray Dalio and Peter Brandt. Were there any lessons you learned from other traders?

From my former bosses, I learned that trading is not about being right; it's about making money. People are often preoccupied with being intellectually correct, which can be a hindrance to making money. When I started, my attitude was that I didn't know anything. So, I always worked backward from the market moves rather than forward from personal opinions. I wouldn't think, "I have a view on how Greece is going to negotiate with Europe, and, therefore, the market will move in this way." Instead, I would look at market moves and then backtrack to why they moved the way they did. For example, if EU officials made a statement and the market reacted, I would interpret it as, "Oh, they said that, and that's why the market had that move."

What advice would you give other traders about how they can improve?

Compile your trading statistics and maintain a trading journal. Armed with this information, you should be able to define your positive and negative edge characteristics and adjust your trading accordingly. Stay in the sphere of your edge by playing your game and not someone else's. Then, visualize yourself trading at your best. What does that look like? What things aren't you doing that you should be? What actions do you need to guard against? Through this process, you can enhance your positive edge and limit your negative tendencies.

What are the trading rules you live by?

It's interesting, in the beginning, a lot of my rules and principles came from what the traders in your *Market Wizards* book said. Over time, these rules changed to fit my personality and what worked for me. These are the rules I have now:

- ⚡ To paraphrase Adam Robinson, genius is knowing that you have a hammer and only looking for nails. The point is that I need to stick with what I do well.

⚡ The risk/reward on a trade is quite dynamic and can change dramatically as you hold it. Therefore, I need to be flexible in covering part of my position as a trade moves in my favor. Otherwise, I am implicitly assuming that I'm going to be 100% right. I learned this rule through multiple experiences of having a big profit on a trade and then seeing the market reverse quickly while I was still holding the full position.

⚡ I have a drawdown alert, which is a personalized rule. I have noticed that three things seem to be present at the beginning of every drawdown I have experienced:

⚡ a 2% or greater loss in a single day;

⚡ a loss of significant open profits in a trade;

⚡ a big size trade doesn't pay off—a trade that I think is a major opportunity and put on in size and that then ends up being a wash.

⚡ Another personalized rule is to be cognizant of certain feelings that are a warning sign that I may be getting out of sync with the markets. The keywords I watch out for in my daily trading review notes are FOMO and frustration.

⚡ Seek clarity over certainty. Trying to reach for certainty will keep you from acting.

⚡ Always be prepared for what could go wrong. Know what you will do if the opposite of what you think will occur happens.

⚡ Always trade an opportunity for what it is, not what you want it to be. For example, if I receive only a partial fill on a trade, I might be tempted to run the trade further than usual to compensate for the smaller size. Doing so would violate my process and generally lead to worse outcomes.

⚡ Always make sure your stops are set at a point that disproves your market hypothesis; never use a monetary stop—a stop point selected because it is the amount of money you're willing to risk. If you are tempted to use a monetary stop, it is a sure sign that your position size is too large.

⚡ Don't sweat the trades you missed that you weren't prepared to take in the first place. The markets provide a constant stream of opportunities. As long as the sun rises tomorrow, there will be another day I can make money. It is not something I have to worry about.

What advice would you give to a starting trader?

I get asked this question quite a lot, and I find it difficult to answer. I generally advise against seeking a trading career because most people are not willing to put in the amount of effort that is needed to succeed. One problem with markets and speculation is that luck plays such a significant role in the short term, which can fool people into thinking their profits are due to skill, even when they aren't. It takes a medical student six-plus years to qualify as a doctor. Why would you expect reaching a high level of proficiency in trading to be any different? Trading is like any other profession; it requires a long-term effort to succeed. If you are not prepared for that type of commitment, then my advice is don't do it at all.

What do you tell someone who still wants to be a trader after you advise them against it?

Don't be eager to start trading. Do the research, find your approach, and then you can begin trading. This is the piece of advice people listen to the least.

Any final words?

To succeed as a trader, you really need to love trading. To me, playing the markets is like a never-ending chess game. It's the most exciting game you can play. If trading doesn't excite you, I don't know whether the good times will be good enough to offset the bad times.

––––––––––

The one question every trader needs to be able to answer is: What is your edge? If you don't have a clear answer, you won't know which trades to focus on or which trades merit a larger position size. One of the pivotal improvements Dhaliwal made to his trading was identifying the types of trades that were responsible for nearly all his gains. By doing so, he was able to focus his attention on identifying, executing, and managing those trades that really mattered. As an additional benefit, he was able to greatly reduce taking marginal trades, which, on balance, had a net negative impact on his portfolio and were a drag on his focus and energy. Once you identify your edge, you need to stick to those trades that fall in your sphere. It is amazing how many traders are highly proficient in applying a specific methodology, yet fall prey to taking other types of trades, which usually end up with net losses and interfere with the efficient execution of the trades they are skilled at.

Dhaliwal was able to identify the trades that provided his true edge because he kept a detailed daily journal of all his trading, recording not only his market analysis and reasons for each trade, but also his feelings. This detailed journal made it possible for Dhaliwal to categorize trades and define the common denominators in the trades that provided his big wins. Besides providing an invaluable tool for identifying where a trader is making money, a trading journal can also be used to record lessons: correct decisions and actions, and, even more importantly, the mistakes that were made. Periodically reviewing such a journal to reinforce these lessons is one of the most effective ways traders can improve.

To be successful as a trader, you need to be adaptable. Think about Dhaliwal's trading career. He started out using technical analysis primarily but abandoned it as all but an auxiliary tool once he realized virtually all the profits were coming from fundamentally based trades. His original methodology sought to capture the initial price move on significant headline events. However, once algorithmic traders started sparking the anticipated price moves more quickly than he could enter the orders, he shifted to a strategy of fading these price moves—that is, trading from the exact opposite direction after the initial price move. As Dhaliwal developed as a trader and conducted a great deal of research with the aid of a full-time assistant, macroeconomic analysis became the primary driver of his trades. Change has been the only constant in Dhaliwal's trading methodology.

Although Dhaliwal's largest loss was primarily due to a fluke event—a rare, erroneous *Financial Times* news release—an inadequacy in his risk management was also responsible for the loss. Specifically, Dhaliwal didn't have any stop protection on a large position. If he had such a protective order, he would have been stopped out instantaneously when the actual news release contradicted the *Financial Times* story, thereby significantly curtailing his loss on the trade. After this trade, Dhaliwal made sure to always have stop protection on large positions.

Another critical element of Dhaliwal's risk management is a specific process for cutting his trading size if a drawdown exceeds certain thresholds. He will cut size in half if a drawdown exceeds 5%, and cut it by half again if it exceeds 8%. If his drawdown reaches 15%, Dhaliwal will stop trading altogether until he feels ready to resume.

Dhaliwal makes the critical point—one that is often overlooked—that the reward/risk ratio of a trade is dynamic and can change dramatically as the trade is held. As an example, consider that you implement a trade, looking for a 300-point gain and risking a 100-point loss. If the market then moves 200 points in favor of the trade, the reward/risk is now drastically different than when the position was implemented. Dhaliwal manages the dynamic nature of reward/risk in a trade by taking partial profits. He argues that holding the entire position until it is exited is an attempt to be 100% right, at the risk of being 100% wrong. Taking partial profits as a trade moves in your favor not only responds to the fact that the reward/risk of the trade is changing, but it is also another risk management tool. If the market abruptly reverses against your position, the action of having taken partial profits will mitigate the profit surrender or reduce the loss. Although Dhaliwal didn't discuss it, another way of adjusting to the changing reward/risk of a trade that moves in the anticipated direction is to tighten the protective stop commensurately.

Protective stops should be placed at a point that disproves your trade hypothesis. Using a closer stop because it represents the maximum amount of money you are willing to risk is an indication that your position is too large. The implication is that you should reduce your position size so that you can choose a meaningful stop that is also consistent with the amount of money you're willing to risk on the trade.

Know what you will do if you are wrong. Dhaliwal plans out his trades, knowing how he will respond in each possible scenario. Defining your trade management plan before you get into a trade is far preferable to doing so after you have placed the position. Why? Because before you are in the trade, you have the advantage of making decisions with full objectivity. Once you are in the position, you lose this advantage.

Typically, traders will formulate their own opinions about how markets should respond to given events and circumstances and then trade accordingly. Dhaliwal used the opposite approach of having no predetermined opinions but instead looking at market price moves and then identifying the causes of those price moves. In this way, Dhaliwal let the markets teach him what caused specific price moves rather than trading on his own unproven theories and assumptions. Dhaliwal's track record is a testament to the wisdom of this approach.

Market price action that deviates sharply from the expected impact of a fundamental development can be a significant price signal. The Australian dollar trade Dhaliwal discussed provides a perfect example of this principle. An unemployment report came out that was surprisingly bullish. The market initially rallied as expected but then collapsed, with prices falling to new recent lows. The stark contradiction between the fundamental news and the resulting price action provided an excellent signal of the beginning of an extended bear market.

Although Dhaliwal trades primarily based on his fundamental analysis and the study of how markets react to fundamental developments, he does use technical analysis as a supplemental tool. One technical event that he believes has important price implications is a breakout from a long-term trading range. If sustained, such breakouts can lead to extended price moves in the same direction. The Australian dollar trade not only exhibited a counter-to-expected response to fundamental news, but it also provided the technical signal of a breakout from a long-term trading range.

Dhaliwal says, "It's not about being right; it's about making money." The point is that the desire to be intellectually correct leads many traders astray. The only thing that matters is whether you are profitable, not whether your market theories are correct.

One of Dhaliwal's rules is: Seek clarity over certainty. The markets are not about certainty; they are about probabilities. Waiting for trades that approach the ideal of certainty, or near certainty, will lead to inaction and missing many trades that offer good probabilistic bets.

One common trait among many traders who achieve spectacular success is a love of the endeavor. Often they will use gamelike analogies to describe trading, as Dhaliwal does in this interview when he refers to trading as a "never-ending chess game." If you are a trader, it is worthwhile questioning your own motivation. Do you trade because you love the game of trading or because it is a possible means to make a lot of money? Your odds are much better in the former case.

JOHN NETTO

Monday Is My Favorite Day

No one would have pegged John Netto as a likely candidate for career success when he graduated high school. He had poor grades and had failed at every venture he tried. College was not even a consideration. Netto, however, was sufficiently self-aware to realize that he needed structure and discipline. In an inspirational moment, not having given it any prior thought, he decided to join the Marines. Netto waxes effusive about the virtues of the Marines and credits his experience as a Marine as being life-transformational.

After basic and infantry training, Netto requested an assignment in aviation, hoping to be trained as an air traffic controller. The Marines assigned him to be trained as a weather observer, which presumably they deemed to be close enough. After training, he was stationed in Japan. Netto loved the Japanese language and bought language instruction tapes, which he used to achieve fluency in Japanese. He got a particular kick out of seeing the surprised looks he got when speaking Japanese to locals because they always assumed foreigners couldn't speak their language. Netto's fluency in Japanese eventually led to an assignment to the prestigious Marine Security Guard detail at the US embassy in Tokyo.

While still enlisted, Netto attended the University of Washington and was assigned by the Marine Corps to lead Naval Midshipmen as part of the Marine ROTC program. Following up on his discovered love of Asian languages, Netto majored in Japanese and Chinese. Netto planned on a career as a Marine officer with an expectation of an Asian assignment that would take advantage of his language skills. This plan was derailed when chronic knee injuries made the pursuit of a military career impossible. Netto accepted a disability discharge from the Marines before he completed the requirements for an officer commission. His disability discharge check and a small stipend provided Netto with a starting stake for trading.

Netto approached trading the same way he had approached learning Japanese: self-education. Through reading books and accessing information on the web, Netto developed his initial trading methodology, which was entirely based on technical analysis. As his experience grew, Netto realized the importance of also incorporating fundamentals into his analysis and trading. Eventually, he developed a methodology that combined an understanding of the dominant fundamental drivers of market prices with technical analysis as a tool for pinpointing the entry levels for trades consistent with his fundamental view. Netto also developed strategies for trading market events and proprietary software that allowed these trades to be automatically executed in a fraction of a second.

In his office, Netto has an array of 10 large screens. Six screens are linked to one computer and provide price quote pages, market charts in multiple time frames, return/risk monitoring of individual positions, option quotes, trading windows, and general computer applications. An additional four screens are linked to a second computer, which is devoted to Netto's event-trading software.

In the 10-plus years since starting his official track record, Netto has achieved an average annual compounded return of 42% based on his notional account levels. (Using notional account levels instead of the actual account levels dampens both return and risk levels and provides a performance picture that is more representative of the intended risk exposure.) The maximum drawdown during this period was 15%. Netto's return/risk measures have been excellent, with an adjusted Sortino ratio of 4.7 and a monthly GPR of 4.8 (see Appendix 2 for the definitions and explanations of these metrics).

Netto's trading methodology is sufficiently complicated and time-consuming that you would think it would be enough to keep him busy—and you would be wrong. He is currently attending law school as a full-time night student. It is not that Netto seeks to give up trading for a law career. He readily admits that he will probably never use his law degree for monetary compensation. Netto muses that he would like to use it to do pro bono work for veteran advocacy. But his primary motivation is simply a desire to learn the law, just as he had a desire to learn Japanese. Now, I admit that, to me, it seems crazy to take on the workload of law school solely for the sake of knowledge, when you are already devoting full time to the strenuous endeavor of market analysis and trading. But then, I am a linear thinker, and I suspect Netto is not.

Some interviews are more difficult to turn into text than others. Netto's interview was a bear. For starters, Netto talked at a pace reminiscent of a New Yorker trying to wrap up a conversation before rushing off to catch a train. Then, he became so excited when talking about trading that each answer seemed to go off in eight tangents—often, none of which addressed the question. When I asked for a specific example to illustrate a point he had made, the reply often mixed together multiple examples, and not sequentially! In editing this interview, I often found myself pulling together material hours apart in the recordings to construct a coherent answer.

To be fair, during the interview, Netto was repeatedly aware that the answers he had just provided might have lacked lucidity, as evident by his own self-assessment comments during our meeting. "I guess that answer was a bit of a firehose." "This is really esoteric." "That's probably a backstory you don't need." "That's a spaghetti bowl of information." "This may not read well when you play it back." All true.

———

How did you develop your interest in trading?

Speculating on the outcome of events has always been something very intuitive to me. When I was in high school, I was a bookie for students who wanted to bet on sports events. I would post the point spread on all the football games, and I would take either side. I would charge a vig, though, just like Las Vegas does, which is how I made money. I would charge $1.10 for every $1.00 I had to pay out.

So, you were the casino.

Exactly, I was the casino.

How much money did you make doing this?

I was up about $7,000 by my senior year. I was going to turn 18 on December 17, and I had decided to stop acting as a bookie before my birthday because I didn't want to be doing something illegal when I was an adult. That Thanksgiving, which was one of the last weekends I was still going to be doing this, 24 out of 28 favorites won. Most people like to bet on the favorite. On that one day, I lost all the money I had made through high school plus an additional $1,500 that I didn't have.

How did you feel when you realized that you had lost everything you had made over several years, and then some, in a single day?

It was devastating. But the biggest thing I learned from that experience was that no matter how bad things are, the sun always rises the next day.

Did the experience of that weekend when you were a teen have any influence on you when you became a trader years later?

Absolutely. Going through that loss, which I didn't think was possible, made me aware of the potential for outlier events when I began trading, I appreciated that Lehman Brothers could happen. I understood that these seemingly inconceivable macro events could take place in the market because, at some primal level in my formative years of risk-taking, I was hit by an outlier event. Before I ever began trading, I knew it was imperative to manage risk.

Was that knowledge entirely due to the large loss day you experienced when you were in high school?

I knew it from that event and from my experience as a Marine.

Why did you join the Marines?

I was not an academic achiever when I was in high school. I think my GPA was something like 1.8. My only interest was in running my betting operation and an economics class, which I did well on. Although I realized college was important, I didn't feel I was ready for it. About a month before my high school graduation, a Navy recruiter, who had come to our school, asked me whether I had thought of joining the Navy. I immediately told him, "No, I'm going to join the Marines."

At what point before then did you know that you wanted to join the Marines?

I didn't know. It popped into my head when I was asked to join the Navy. I had poor grades and lacked self-esteem. I had some intrinsic sense that I had intellectual potential, but I knew I needed a lot of discipline. And the idea of joining the toughest, most badass service just made sense.

So you preferred to join the Marines because it was the most challenging service.

I chose the Marines both because it was the most challenging and most structured. I was self-aware enough to know that I had slacked off in high school and that I wasn't focused. I knew I needed the structure.

How long were you in the Marines?

Almost nine years.

Tell me about your experience.

It was life-changing. I had never been part of a culture that held me accountable for my actions and pushed me outside my comfort zone.

Was it a difficult experience?

Incredibly difficult.

What was the hardest part about it?

Believing that I could actually finish.

So you had some self-doubt.

Tremendous self-doubt. I had a bad GPA. I lost all the money in my gambling operation. Except for doing well in a state economics test, I had never done anything that worked out. When I was growing up, my brother had a phrase, "AFNS," which stood for "another failed Netto scheme." I was always trying to think of business ideas, and everything I tried didn't work. I had to overcome my toxic thoughts about whether I could do it or not.

Did your experience in the Marines have an impact on you as a trader?

Absolutely. The Marines teach you discipline and the ability to function under tremendous pressure. A lot of the training you do as a Marine is to create such a stressful environment that when the real thing happens, you can function. The first night you are in boot camp, after three hours of sleep, they are banging the garbage can lid screaming, "Get out of the rack! Get out of the rack!" You have 90 days left, and the first day felt like it was three weeks. I've had trading days that didn't go well and felt like three weeks. I go long, and the market goes down; I go short, and the market goes up. Trading is a hard way to make an easy living. The Marines taught me to deal with adversity, and that ability has been essential to my success as a trader. You need to be able to deal with getting stopped out five times in a row and still stick with your process. The Marines train you to deal with setbacks. The Marines teach you the importance of having a game plan and being accountable. Trading is a lot about accountability. You have to be responsible for your losses and not blame them on something else.

Why did you leave the Marines?

I didn't intend to leave. I attended the University of Washington, majoring in Japanese and Chinese, as part of the Marine ROTC program. My plan was to become a commissioned officer and hopefully get the assignment that took advantage of my language skills. Before I graduated, I blew out my knee playing basketball, an injury that required reconstructive surgery. To compound the problem, I had chronic tendonitis in my other knee. It was clear to both the Marines and me that my physical injuries would make a career in the Marines impossible. I accepted a disability discharge.

How did you go from being in the Marines and majoring in Eastern languages to being a trader?

I had invested passively in mutual funds while I was in the Marines, which provided my first exposure to markets. The first pivotal step in my journey to becoming a trader was taking a position as the business editor of the student paper at the University of Washington. I read many books on trading and technical analysis, including Joe DiNapoli's book on Fibonacci analysis, which was very influential.* In 1999, I opened a stock account with $75,000 I had saved from my Marine checks. I ran the account up to $190,000 and then saw the account go all the way back down to $40,000 on the tech stock crash in 2000. I got past the first bear wave in April 2000; it was the second bear wave at the end of that year that got me.

So, you went from more than doubling your money to losing all your gains plus half your starting stake. It sounds a lot like…

[Netto interrupts, finishing my sentence] the high school bookie operation. I'm seeing a trend here [he laughs].

How were you deciding what to buy and sell?

That was part of the problem. I followed the recommendations of a newsletter service that provided specific entry and stop levels on stocks. I will say this: In my entire trading career, adhering to stops has never been a problem. Thanks to my high school experience, I always understood that I could blow up.

So how did you go from $190,000 to $40,000?

I lost the money in successive stop-outs. The sizing was a different issue. I would always get out on the stop, but my position sizing was way too large. I would naïvely think, "I can risk $25,000 on this trade," not appreciating what could happen if I lost six trades in a row.

---

* Joe DiNapoli, *DiNapoli Levels: The Practical Application of Fibonacci Analysis to Investment Markets* (Coast Investment Software, Incorporated, 3rd edition, 1998).

Were you basing all your trades on the newsletter recommendations?

I also made some trades based on my market feel, whatever that means.

So, you had no methodology.

I had no methodology at all. I was still learning. At the time, I didn't think I was still learning. I thought I knew what I was doing because I had taken my account from $75,000 to $190,000.

When did you resume trading?

Not long afterward, I developed a methodology based on trading Fibonacci retracements. [A Fibonacci series is a sequence of numbers in which each number is the sum of the preceding two numbers (0, 1, 1, 2, 3, 5, 8, 13, 21, 34, 55, 89...). The ratio of one number in the series to the following number approaches 61.8% as numbers get larger, and the ratio of one number to the second following number in the series approaches 38.2%. The Fibonacci sequence occurs commonly in nature, such as in the spirals formed by some shells and flower petals. Fibonacci traders will look for potential market reversals to occur near the aforementioned key ratios: 61.8% and 38.2%.]

Were you just placing trades at Fibonacci retracement levels?

I was looking for a concentration of points in the same price area. A basic example of a trade setup would be a 61.8% retracement of a shorter price swing, which coincided with a 38.2% retracement of a longer price swing, both of which coincided with other technical support or resistance levels. I would take positions at these points where multiple support or resistance indicators were concentrated in the same area.

Was this approach successful?

I was profitable in both 2001 and 2002, trading mainly from the short side. But then I had a disastrous day on March 17, 2003, which was the day when President Bush issued an ultimatum to Saddam Hussein to step down under the threat of a US invasion.

That morning, the market opens lower, and I start selling. The market quickly reverses to the upside, and I get stopped out. At that point, I'm down about $14,000 for the day, which is bad, but manageable. Then I go short a second time and get stopped out. Now, I'm down $28,000. I step away and come back. I go short a third time and get stopped out. Now, I'm down $39,000. I step away, come back, and go short again. This time, the market starts falling. When I recover half my loss. I start thinking, "I'm going to pull this out!" I get the account back as far as down only $13,000, and then the loss starts widening again. I get stopped out a fourth time, and now I'm down $40,000. I take one last shot, and by the end of the day, I'm down $63,000.

In that single day, I lost all the money I had made in the prior year or so. It was such bad trading, but that's what happened. I was what we call in Vegas "on tilt."

On tilt?

"On tilt" is a poker term for a player who loses emotional control in trying to recover a loss, making aggressive, bad bets, which end up amplifying the total loss.

Was your trading that day part of your methodology?

The first trade was entirely consistent with my methodology. The market had rallied in the previous few days, reached a resistance point, and then gapped lower on the next opening, confirming a reversal. But after I took that first loss, I should have been done. All the other trades were just tilt.

That day is a classic example of a market going counter to the expected response to a news item.

Completely.

I still kick myself for not going long on election night 2016 when the market initially sold off sharply, as it became apparent that Trump would pull out a surprise victory, but then reversed abruptly, moving steadily higher. I fully recognized then that the market's counter-to-expected price action represented a classic buy signal, but I was so disheartened by the Trump win that I couldn't bring myself to go long.

In our email correspondence before the interview, Netto attached a copy of a letter he had sent to the NFA (National Futures Association, the futures industry's self-regulatory organization) on January 4, 2010. The letter affirmed that he would be trading his account at a notional level of $1 million. He also sent me the NFA's confirmation letter response and an audited track record beginning in January 2010. In futures, the notional account level indicates the account size assumed to be traded and is used when the amount of money in an account is not representative of the risk level being traded. Futures margin requirements represent only a small percentage of contract values. If a futures account is not funded with a substantial amount of excess capital, the amount of money in the account may considerably understate the assumed account size being traded, resulting in exaggerated profits and losses. Using notional account levels, instead of actual account levels, in such circumstances, will reduce both returns and risk metrics (e.g., volatility, drawdowns), and is intended to generate more realistic performance numbers.

———————

The NFA letter and the performance audit you sent me indicates that you started to keep an official track record in January 2010. I have two questions. First, how did you do in your trading between the large loss in March 2003 and the start of your official track record in January 2010? Second, since you had been trading for many years before, why did you decide to start your official record in January 2010?

I was moderately profitable during that interim, but nothing spectacular. I chose January 2010, partially because it was the beginning of the decade, and also because I wanted to take my trading to another level. Although I was trading all along, I made a living primarily from the commissions I was earning as an introducing broker. My goal was to be able to focus totally on trading. I gave up the brokerage accounts in 2011.

Did your methodology change over those years from the Fibonacci-based technical approach you described before?

Yes, the critical change was realizing the importance of the prevailing market narrative and incorporating an understanding of the market narrative in my trading.

Can you give me an example of what you mean by market narrative?

The narrative is another term for the market regime. For example, five-year Treasury notes are paying 1.5% right now. The dividend yield on the S&P is 2.8%. [This interview was conducted in August 2019.] The dominant market narrative is that, given the significant yield advantage in the S&P, money will flow into equities. In this type of environment, it's challenging to be short the S&P. Instead, you want to be buying the S&P near key technical points because real investment flows will be there, providing fundamental support.

As another example, we are currently in a regime where there is a massive chase for yield. There is $17 trillion of negative yield instruments out there. This regime largely explains what is fueling the ongoing bull market in gold. Why? Because, in a sense, gold is a zero yielding currency. The fact that gold yields zero makes it a better asset to hold that $17 trillion of assets you have to pay to own. That factor is the big driver of gold right now.

So, if you have this type of favorable regime for gold, does that imply that you only trade gold from the long side, as long as conditions remain conducive for the market chasing yield?

That's predominantly true, but not always.

What would prompt you to go short in the face of this long-term bullish factor that you have argued is, currently, the driving force behind gold's price movement?

You could get an event that will cause a sharp countermovement in the price of gold. For example, if, unexpectedly, there is talk that Europe will implement fiscal stimulus, European bonds will go through a headline-scare correction. That event would cause gold to sell off because it has been benefiting from a negative yield environment. Also, if a narrative is widely followed, eventually, the trade can get crowded, making the market vulnerable to a sharp countermove, especially if there is a surprise event adverse to the prevailing narrative.

So then you might play a short-term correction in gold, even if you are long-term bullish.

Absolutely, because when you get these sustained, long-term trends, and there is a surprise event, the corrections can be violent.

Can you give me an example of a specific trade that was driven by your interpretation of the market narrative?

In May 2013, then Chairman Bernanke indicated that the Fed was going to move from calendar-based to data-driven decisions in determining interest rate adjustments. What does that mean? It means that any economic data—job numbers, retail sales, etc.—was going to be more impactful than before. Bernanke's comments changed the market narrative. On July 5, 2013, the Employment Report showed a large number of jobs being added. Although I was already positioned short Treasurys before the report, I shorted a lot more because I thought the figure would have a larger-than-expected impact, given the Fed's recent switch from calendar-based to data-based guidance. That was my most profitable day ever. I specialize in identifying shifts in the market narrative that are likely to result in market repricings. I also try to determine what the narrative is, going into any significant event.

Although you weren't incorporating this approach in your trading in 2003, retrospectively, what was the narrative on your big losing day in March 2003?

The narrative was that we were still in a two-year bear market, and with the US about to go to war, the stock market would go back to new lows. The narrative was compelling, and it is what I believed at the time. However, when a convincing narrative is contradicted by the market price action, the reversal from the narrative-driven trading can be violent.

When did you start incorporating the market narrative in your trading?

Probably the first market in which my market narrative played an essential role in my trading was gold in 2008. I will tell you what I did right and what I did wrong. My narrative was: The world is crashing, the Fed will have to ease; therefore, gold is going higher. That was the correct narrative for the first three quarters, and I did quite well trading gold primarily from the long side. But what I missed was that when the world became concerned about deflation, gold would sell off with the rest of the market, which is what happened in the fourth quarter of 2008. I also missed the fact that because they were being hit by large withdrawals, many hedge funds had to raise money, and hedge funds were primarily long gold. So they had to sell gold along with everything else.

So far, we have talked about how technical analysis and the market narrative play a role in your trading methodology. What else is important?

Event trading has probably been the most important contributor to my trading profits during the past 10 years. There are both unplanned events and planned events.

Can you give me an example of each?

Last Friday, while he is flying to a G-7 meeting, Trump tweets some crazy shit about how, when he lands, he will implement retaliatory measures against China. In his tweets, Trump was visibly irate. That is an example of an unplanned event. You cannot afford to be long risk knowing that later that day, Trump is presumably going to announce additional tariffs against China.

How do you respond to that?

You sell risk, and you sell it with abandon.

What was your trade?

I sold the S&P.

But doesn't the market sell off immediately on that tweet?

Not just immediately, but for the next hour.

When did you get short?

Right away. I listen to an audio squawk called Trade the News, which is a website that does nothing but track, filter, and read market-moving news items all day long. I cannot watch a news screen while I'm trading—it would be too distracting—so I have the audio streaming in. As soon as I heard them read that Trump tweet, I went short.

How much was the market down by the time you got your order filled?

The market was down eight full points, which was not a problem; it went down another 50 points.

What is the broader lesson that comes out of that trade?

The lesson is that you have to understand the market narrative, so you know what is and isn't a surprise and act accordingly. But you have to know it is a surprise. If you trade without knowing, you are just a sucker giving your money away, and you will likely be near the high tick on the buy and the low tick on the sell.

So, your event trading is intricately tied to your market narrative.

Absolutely! The narrative will determine how you interpret market events. You can have the same event have very different price impacts depending on the market narrative. For example, if no one expects OPEC to cut production, and they cut production, the energy markets will be caught offside, and you can have a significant price response. On the other hand, if the same size cut occurs, but it is widely anticipated, there may be no price reaction at all, or the market might even reverse once the news is out. So knowing the market narrative is critical to my event trading. It also makes my technical analysis more effective by giving me insight as to when a particular chart formation would be more likely to result in a large price move.

What is an example of a planned event trade?

The USDA's Crop Production report released earlier this month [August 2019] provides a perfect example. As a backdrop, in the June report, the USDA had reported corn plantings at 91.7 million acres. This figure was generally viewed with considerable skepticism because it was widely expected that acreage would be significantly lower, given the severe flooding in the Midwest, which had delayed plantings. The USDA agreed to re-survey plantings in 14 states and update the acreage estimate in the August report. Going into the August report, the market was expecting a *significant* reduction in the acreage estimate. The USDA, however, only reduced the corn plantings estimate by 1.7 million acres to 90 million acres, which was much less of a reduction than expected and a very bearish number. And the kicker was that they also increased the yield estimate. The market was expecting an acreage number closer to 87 million. There wasn't an analyst with an estimate anywhere near 90 million. When you get that type of an outlier, it is almost like the market is giving you the money. The repricing has to happen. There is just not enough liquidity for everyone who wants to get out to be able to get out.

But if the number was that bearish, wouldn't the market go limit down instantaneously? [Limit down is the maximum permitted daily price decline.]

You are assuming markets are efficient, but they are not efficient. The market went limit down, but it didn't go there immediately. I was able to get short almost instantaneously because of MPACT.

What is MPACT?

MPACT, an acronym for market price action, is the software program that I showed you earlier this morning, which reads and evaluates the news in milliseconds and then enters the appropriate order.

So, in your software, you have predefined what trade action to take for each possible estimate value the USDA might release.

Correct. Execution is critical. I invested a substantial portion of my trading profits and net worth in building MPACT, which is an event interpretation application. The software trades the market price action consistent with predetermined scenarios for an event. A big part of what I do is defining 20, 30, 40 potential scenarios before the event, as well as the trade action associated with each scenario.

I can spend a week preparing for a Fed event dissecting multiple qualitative aspects. When I build a score for a Fed event, I'll have a framework to interpret what the Fed says in regards to four things: (1) the economy; (2) inflation; (3) future rate paths; and (4) any idiosyncratic factors. These four factors are dynamically weighted. Accordingly, MPACT will read the Fed release and evaluate it for each of these four areas and generate a score.

Then MPACT will select the prepared scenario based on the score from the statement. Each scenario will also specify the trades to be taken, if any.

Is this software that you created?

I designed it and hired a development team to do the programming. The project took six years to build and refine.

Can you give me an example of how MPACT traded a Fed announcement?

In December 2018, I thought that the Fed would not hike rates—despite the market pricing in nearly a 100% chance of a hike—and that if they did raise rates, the announcement would include some indication that they were done hiking. Instead, Fed Chairman Powell's comments included the line, "It is more likely that the economy will grow in a way that will call for two interest rate increases over the course of next year." That one line was enough to send the markets crashing.

Although it was in total contradiction to your expectations, did your prepared scenarios include the Fed indicating there would be a couple more hikes?

They sure did. I was long the S&P and gold going into the announcement because I was expecting the Fed wouldn't hike. MPACT automatically sold me out of my positions and reversed to the short side.

Okay, that's a clear-cut example. However, what about the case where there are statements with contradictory implications within the same announcement?

Yes, that happened in March 2017, it was my worst trading day ever. I thought that if the Fed left the door open for another hike in June, it would be very bearish for the interest rate markets. The Fed did that, and I went heavily short the five-year T-notes. I lost $210,000 that day, giving back all my profits year to date.

What exactly was the mistake?

Although the Fed indicated the likelihood of a June hike, the overall statement contained a score of other dovish elements, some that I had failed to anticipate in my scenario creation process. At that point, I didn't have the level of detail in my score generation process that I do now. There is a learning curve involved in this process. So, although mistakes cost money, they can also lead to opportunity.

Let's discuss emotions and trading. I know you have a contrarian view on the subject. Can you elaborate on how you see the influence of emotions in trading?

Emotions are your friend, not your enemy. The human emotions that we feel can be used as a signal source. Let me give you a specific trade as an example. In September 2015, the S&P rolled over and broke down sharply to the area of the August relative low. I was overwhelmed by this animalistic sense that the S&P was going to crash. I went short 200 E-mini S&P contracts, which was way too large a position for me.

Part of my trading process is to ask myself where I am on the emotional scale. Am I highly afraid? Am I highly greedy? Or, am I emotionally balanced somewhere between the two? That was an instance where I was at one end of the emotional spectrum—highly greedy. When I asked myself, "What is your respect for the risk level right now?" I realized the answer was, "None." I felt that shorting right there without any process behind me was free money. As soon as I realized that, I covered my entire position immediately.

The best positions for me are when I still have some element of unease. I assess the tension in my body when I am in a trade. I want to be focused and still feel some anxiety. In contrast, if I exhale in relief after a position has gone my way and feel too relaxed, that is a warning sign of a possible impending market reversal. If I buy gold at $1,500, and it then goes to $1,530, and I feel, "I nailed this trade; I better buy more before it runs away," I can assure you, it will be back to $1,518 in no time.

So, ironically, you would be more inclined to add to a position when you still feel nervous about it, not when you feel really confident.

Yes! Correct!

You are saying that people like me who advise traders to get the emotionality out of trading are wrong.

Oh, my God! Why would you want to do that? You would be throwing away a useful signal source. If you have to choose one, would you rather replicate the trades of the three most successful traders you knew, or would you rather do the opposite of the three worst traders you knew? I would always choose to do the opposite of the worst traders. It's hard for good traders to consistently make money, but it's not hard at all for bad traders to consistently lose money. What are the characteristics of bad traders? They have no process. They make their decisions emotionally and are incredibly impulsive, which is why they are swayed by panic and end up buying near highs and selling near lows.

When I tell people to get emotions out of trading, it is because emotional trades are usually wrong. But what you are saying is that your proxy for the worst traders—a valuable indicator—is being aware of your own emotional extremes.

Exactly! You need to understand your own emotionality, journal it, and potentially develop it as another signal source for what you do.

Contrast the characteristics that differentiate winning traders from losing traders.

Winning traders *get the joke*. They realize that they can lose even when they do everything right. Winning traders have a process, the discipline to follow the process, and a commitment to strive for continuous improvement. They understand that even incremental improvements can have a profound effect on their P&L. Losing traders are looking for a silver bullet, and if it doesn't work immediately, they are onto the next thing.

What advice do you have for other traders?

You don't have to make money right away. Sometimes not losing is every bit as important as winning. Risk-taking with a process leads to success, while risk-taking on impulse leads to regret.

Why do you think you've been successful?

I am successful because Monday is my favorite day of the week. When you love what you do, you're going to be successful.

———

I, as well as a number of the Market Wizards I have interviewed, have long advised eliminating emotions from trading. John Netto, on the other hand, takes the provocative view that emotions are one of a trader's most useful tools. Although it appears that we are offering contradictory advice, there is actually no disagreement. Netto also believes that emotions will usually have a detrimental impact on trading decisions. In fact, the tendency of emotions to lead to bad trading decisions is precisely what Netto seeks to tap into as a signal source. Netto strives to be mindful of his own emotional extremes, which will be as deleterious to trading outcomes as anyone else's, as warning signals calling for immediate corrective action. For example, if Netto is in a trade that moves strongly in his favor, and he then catches himself thinking, "This trade can't lose, I better load up on this position before it runs away," he will, instead, liquidate immediately.

Although most traders tend to gravitate to either fundamental analysis or technical analysis, some of the best traders combine the two. Netto provides a good illustration of how fundamental analysis and technical analysis can be used synergistically. Netto will apply his understanding of the dominant market narrative or regime to determine whether he will trade a given market from the long side or short side. Once this fundamental bias is established, he will then overlay his technical analysis to select trade entry points. Typically, these will be reactions to support or resistance levels within what he perceives to be the market's prevailing directional bias.

Event trading is another essential component of Netto's methodology. He trades both scheduled events, such as Fed statements and government reports, as well as unanticipated events. Netto stresses that to successfully trade events, you need to have a good sense of whether any given outcome is a surprise. He will only trade event outcomes that he considers to be surprises relative to market expectations. Execution speed is obviously critical in such trades, since the market will typically respond quickly and dynamically to surprises. Netto has solved this problem by developing his own proprietary software that can read the text related to an event, determine the trade implications, if any, and place the appropriate trade, all in a split second. For this program to work, Netto needs to define the trade implications of scores of possible scenarios before each scheduled event, a work-intensive task. The rapid execution that results from this process means that if his analysis is correct, Netto will capture a substantial portion of the market move, even when the event triggers a near-immediate market response.

After taking a loss—particularly a substantial loss—it is common for traders to experience a compulsion to try to quickly make money back in the same market. Resist this temptation! Early in his trading career, Netto took a large loss in a short S&P position. This initial trade, however, was not a mistake. The trade was consistent with his methodology, but Netto was simply wrong on his directional market call. Had the story ended there, it would have been a bad day, but not a catastrophic one. The problem was that Netto became fixated on trying to make his money back *in the same market*. He then proceeded to go short and get stopped out four more times that day. None of these additional four trades had anything to do with his methodology. Instead, he was caught up in an emotional spiral that blinded him to reasonable trading decisions. To use Netto's poker terminology, he was *on tilt*. By the time it was all over, he had quadrupled his large initial loss and surrendered nearly a year's worth of profits. When you lose money in a market, let it go. Be on guard against the urge to make money back by taking previously unplanned trades.

One theme that has cropped up in several of the interviews in this book, including this one, is the concept that a counter-to-expected market response to a news development can provide a valuable timing signal. President Bush's ultimatum to Saddam Hussein, which signaled the imminent start of the Second Gulf War, was viewed as a bearish development, especially with equities still near the lows of a two-year-long bear market. The market opened lower on the news, as expected, but then reversed, closing sharply higher. This unexpected price action signaled the beginning of a long-term bull market.

Another example of the same principle was provided by the stock market price action on election night 2016. It was widely assumed that Trump would lose the election and that in the unlikely event he won, the market would sell off sharply. When the returns started to make it clear that Trump would win an upset victory, equities began to tank precisely as anticipated. But then prices reversed their initial losses and moved sharply higher throughout the night. This unexpected market response to the news marked the start of a near uninterrupted 14-month run-up in stock prices.

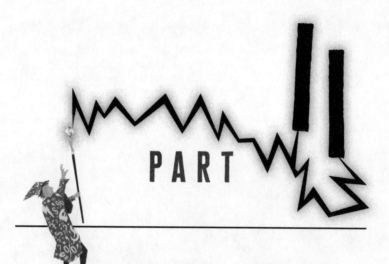

PART II

STOCK
TRADERS

JEFFREY NEUMANN

Penny Wise, Dollar Wise

One day I received the following intriguing email:

Hello Mr. Schwager,

I'm reaching out to you on a whim because I've got what I consider a quite fantastic stock market success story. After years of basic silence, I'm looking for an outlet for my story to be told, and you are what I consider the current best at telling these tales. I've previously kept myself in the shadows of the stock trading community, mainly due to my low-key personality, a little bit due to security (hackers et al.), but more than anything because it keeps life simple for me. Even my best friends have no clue about my success in this industry. Now that I've got two young kids, I think they would one day enjoy my story to have been put down in pen and paper somewhere, somehow, for them to see and appreciate (beyond the material things that they will be the recipients of one day).

I'll spare you the details in this initial correspondence, but I started trading in 2002 with $2,500 and have parlayed it into $50 million in profits (pre-tax). I've traveled the world to many dozens of countries (guessing 60+), culminating with visiting all seven continents the year of my 30th birthday. I'm currently in my mid-30s, and my style has progressed over the years from pattern day trader to swing trader. I'm extremely thematic in my stock selection style and pyramid into positions very similarly to Jesse Livermore. I've never taken a dime of outside invested capital and have only been a one-man operation.

If you have any interest or any recommendation on someone that could help me tell this tale, I would appreciate it greatly!

Thank you for your time.

Jeff Neumann

I replied that I was tentatively planning to do another *Market Wizards* book, but not for a while. As events transpired, six months later, I decided to begin working on a new book and asked Neumann to send me copies of his monthly account statements as evidence. He was able to send me ten years' worth of statements (as far back as available from his broker). To fill in the earlier years, he provided me with the relevant pages of his tax returns. Altogether, his record spanned 17 years. His starting equity was actually $7,700 instead of $2,500, the difference being a stock position his father had left him, which he didn't use to trade. Using the higher starting equity level of $7,700, Neumann compounded his account at an average rate of 80% per annum. This figure is actually understated because it doesn't account for his large net withdrawals during 2002–2008, a period for which the monthly statements that would allow adjusting the return calculations for these withdrawals were unavailable. The percentage returns during his earlier years when his account equity was lower were particularly high and amplified his average return for the entire track record. For the past ten years for which monthly brokerage statements were available and his starting account equity level was $2.3 million in January 2009, his average annual compounded return was 53%.

Turning a few thousand dollars into $50 million is only part of the story. Perhaps the real kicker is that Neumann made a large portion of his fortune trading penny stocks. Now you can fit most of what I know about penny stocks onto—well, a penny. My impression was that penny stocks represented a financial backwater replete with worthless companies and pump-and-dump schemes designed to fleece suckers—a perception that is probably still generally valid for the vast majority of participants. So how does a trader who is not on the inside win so big in a game where the odds are stacked against an outsider? That is Neumann's story.

Neumann picked me up at the airport, spotting me almost immediately after I exited the terminal door (recognizing me from an old book cover photo I assume). We conducted the interview in a sheltered, open-walled seating area in his large backyard, which provided protection from the intermittent afternoon rains. We stopped to take a break for dinner at a local sushi place. Neumann gave me a choice between an Uber and walking via a network of neighborhood trails. I eagerly chose the latter, happy to get in a small exercise fix after a full day of sitting. I am always prepared to record dinner conversation when I am interviewing someone for a book. By experience, I know that sometimes the best stories come up in the relaxed setting of a meal. Although the food was excellent—so good that my request for soy sauce and wasabi proved unnecessary, as it would have interfered with the subtle flavorings of each sushi plate—the decibel level of the restaurant was competitive with the New York subway system. I immediately abandoned any thoughts of recording our conversation and was careful to make sure that our discussions steered well clear of anything to do with trading.

We completed the interview in the guesthouse I was staying at, which also houses Neumann's office. After a couple of hours, I could see Neumann was flagging—he is obviously a morning person, whereas I am a night owl—and I could tell I was not capturing any additional usable material. I ended the interview, much to Neumann's relief, I suspect. We walked over to Neumann's office, where he checked some stock charts on a large monitor. While I stood at his side, he brought up charts of the stock trades we had discussed that day, showing me where he had gotten in and out. As will become evident in the interview, sector themes are an essential component of Neumann's methodology. Neumann defines his own niche sectors. As I stood there, he read an eclectic mix of names off of the tabs for these mostly self-defined sectors: Lithium, pot, cobalt, graphite, alt energy, robotics, homeland security, homebuilders, genetic testing, wearables, agriculture, shipping.

Did you have any inkling at all what you wanted to do when you were a kid?

From the youngest age I can remember, I was going to be a doctor. My dad was a doctor. To me, it seemed that the successful people in town were doctors, and I had the compassion side as well. So it seemed like a good fit.

Were you premed in college?

Yes. I majored in chemistry and minored in biology. I finished my required coursework in three years. The summer after my junior year, I went backpacking in Europe. It was the first time I had traveled in my life. That trip opened my eyes. I had so much fun, and I decided I didn't want to go to school anymore.

Did you go back to college, or did you get your degree after three years?

I could have graduated after three years, but I left myself shy a few credits because I knew I wasn't ready to go on. I didn't know what I wanted to do. I finished my senior year, but the only course I took was scuba diving.

When did you first become interested or even aware of markets?

I had an economics course in high school, and as part of the course, we had a $100,000 virtual stock portfolio. This course was right when the internet was becoming available in school, and I found a way to check the pre-opening market prices, so I could identify which stocks to buy from the day before. I discovered this glitch in the game early on. I turned the $100,000 into something like $1 million.

So, essentially, you gamed the system.

Completely.

When did you first start trading?

I started trading stocks in my college senior year at the computer lab because I didn't own a computer.

What was the motivation to start trading?

To escape med school. To escape more education.

After your summer backpacking trip in Europe, were you drawn to trading because you thought it was an easy way to make a lot of money?

Basically, yes.

Did you know anything? Had you done any reading on trading or markets?

Nothing. I didn't read anything about business, speculating, or statistics until after I started trading stocks.

Then how did you decide what stock to buy and when to buy it?

I started randomly looking at charts, and I found a stock that was trading between seven and eight cents and hadn't moved for a year.

Were you drawn to penny stocks because they were cheap?

Because they were cheap, and when they moved, they moved by a large percentage. When I looked at the biggest gainers on any day, they were always penny stocks.

How much money did you have in your trading account?

Early in the fall, I was caught in a hailstorm while driving, and I received a $2,500 check from the insurance company. I used that money to open my trading account. One of the best things I did was to set a profit goal. I saw that if I could make 3% a day, I could run up my account to $1 million in under a year.

That sounds so incredibly naïve.

Yes, so naïve. I totally agree. I don't know if I just got lucky in choosing a broker that went out beyond the penny decimal in the orders they accepted. I started trading not too long after the change from eighths and sixteenths to penny decimals. My broker went out two decimals beyond the penny decimal. However, most brokers at the time only went out to a penny, which is why my first stock never moved; it was stuck between seven and eight cents.

You mean it was seven cents bid and eight cents asked.

Yes, it was something like 1 million shares bid at seven cents and 1.5 million shares offered at eight cents.

So they didn't take any orders in between?

My broker did. They let me put in an order at 7.01 cents. So I would get filled anytime anybody sold. I was able to cut in line. When I got filled, I would put up my stock for sale at 7.99, and anytime anybody bought, I would get filled. I was almost a market maker. So even though my stock never moved—it was stuck between seven and eight cents—I was making about 13% after commission on every trade.

Did you set any stop on the trade?

I never set stops, but if there ever was large volume hitting below my entry, say at seven cents, in this case, I was able to get out. So my loss would only be .01 cents.

So using this trade as an example, would you always get out at seven cents?

Yes, if it traded at substantial volume at that price.

So even though you were a beginner who didn't know much about trading, you were doing something smart: You were putting on highly asymmetric trades.

From my first trade, I thought, "I could make a living at this." I started out making hundreds of dollars a day, and before I knew it, I was making thousands of dollars a day doing the same thing. I wrote down the account equity levels I needed to reach each successive trading day to get to $1 million. Some days when I did really well, I could cross off five days at a time. At one point, I remember thinking, "I'm only a hundred days away from getting to $1 million." Granted, I still had to make over $900,000 to get there, but the goal seemed attainable.

How long did it take you to get to $1 million?

I don't remember exactly, but not much longer than a year. I made over $1 million before I understood trading at all. I just had this one system down. I was 23, and I had made $1 million. I thought I was going to retire. I was cheap, and I had virtually no expenses. I was eating Ramen noodles. My entire trip to Europe the summer before had cost me only $1,500—and that was including the flight. Interest rates at the time were around 6%, which meant I could make $60,000 a year interest on a million dollars. That was more than enough for me to live on after paying taxes.

So you planned to retire when you got to $1 million?

Basically, at that point, I thought I would travel forever.

During this time, when you were making your first million, did you look at charts at all, or were charts irrelevant to what you were doing?

I just used charts to find stocks that didn't move—stocks that stayed in the same bid-ask range for a long time. That way, I could keep on putting on the same trade over and over.

Was this market-making type of trade the only trade you were doing?

Yeah, except one time, I didn't. I bought a stock that went from 20 cents to $2.00 in a matter of weeks. I started to believe that I was a stock trader. The stock had a really cool story. It was an animal tracking company, and I think this was the time when there was a swine flu breakout. It was the first time I fell for a story. After I bought it, the stock started to break sharply.

How long after you bought it did the stock start tanking?

Almost instantly. The stock went from $2.00 to $1.00 in, literally, a matter of minutes. I remember breaking out into a cold sweat and thinking, "I had such a good strategy going, and I veered from it one time, and I get blown up." I waited and got out on a bounce, but I still lost about 30% of my account on that one trade.

How long did you hold it before you got out?

I got out the same day.

Did you go back to your market-making type trades?

Yes, that was all I did.

Did you always place your buy order .01 cents above the rounded cent bid?

It started that way, but then other people began to catch on and do the same thing, and I had to raise my buy and lower my sell points to levels where I would get filled.

When did that game end?

It ended about a year after it started. The bid-asked spread got so compressed that by the end, I was selling a stock only a few hundredths of a penny above where I bought it.

Where did you go from there?

I was able to use my software program to build in a ticker tape at the bottom of the screen that only showed the stocks that I was interested in following. I watched for stocks that had large block size orders, so I could follow what big money was doing. I only wanted to be in stocks where I saw accumulation by larger entities.

How did you decide when to buy a stock?

I started using technical analysis.

Where did you learn technical analysis?

I just spent a lot of time looking at charts. At that point, I hadn't read any books on it. I looked at charts that had made big moves. Why did a stock launch off a particular point? Was there a volume spike beforehand? I came up with the most simple trendline analysis ever—I still use it.

Which is what?

I look for a steady downtrend, and I draw a line connecting the spikes.

How is that different from a conventional trendline?

A lot of the advice I have seen about trendline breakouts talks about breakouts above a flat line. I felt using my trendline got me in early and gave me a head start.

[Neumann is actually describing a breakout above the horizontal line of a sideways consolidation, not a breakout from a downtrend line. Neumann is not using a different type of trendline, as might be inferred from his comments. Instead, Neumann is making the distinction that he is buying a breakout from a downtrend line rather than an upside breakout from a sideways consolidation formed near lows. By definition, the latter price signal would occur at a higher price.]

I wanted to be the guy who was buying a stock right when it's breaking out above that downtrend line. Often when prices would compress at the downtrend line, there would be large amounts offered. Let's say there were 100,000 shares for sale at 31 cents; I would try to be the guy who was buying the last 10,000 shares.

What if there was no follow-through?

That would be a negative. The stock should be moving like that [he snaps his fingers]. You usually know right away if the trade is right.

So if the trade isn't right immediately, you get out.

Yes, and I get out really quickly. If I bought the stock at 30.1 cents, and it went down to 30.0 cents, I would hit the bid and be out.

Where would you get out if the stock followed through on the upside?

Back then, I sold half right away at the first blip up, which now is where I start buying more, and then if it consolidated and moved up, I would sell the second half.

What time frame were you using for a trendline?

At that time, I liked one-month trendlines because I wanted to be in and out on the same day. For me, a one-month trendline breakout means that the potential move is maybe six to eight hours long. I didn't learn until later to look for breakouts from longer-term trendlines because they led to much bigger moves.

What do you look for now?

I look for breakouts from one- to five-year trendlines so that I can accumulate more significant positions and trade for bigger price moves.

When did you shift from trading to capture the next short-term price swing to trading from a longer-term perspective?

The first time I got into trading the way I am doing it now was when I followed a recommendation posted in a chat room by this great researcher named songw. He posted a news article that there was going to be a bill to increase the amount of ethanol in gasoline blend from 1% to 5%. I remember the immediate response in the chat room was people saying it was no big deal that the gasoline percentage was going from 99% to 95%. Songw immediately reframed the story by emphasizing that for ethanol, it was a 400% increase. It clicked for me. I realized that it was a big deal. We knew that this bill was going to come through, so I loaded up on ethanol stocks.

Hadn't these stocks already reacted to the news?

This post was two weeks before the bill was introduced in Congress. The story was carried in some local Kansas City newspaper. The news had not yet been disseminated on national media. It was just that songw was such a great researcher that he found this story. Eventually, the news started getting picked up by mainstream media, and you could see the upward waves in prices as the news became more and more widely distributed.

Was this the first time you held a position for a while?

Yeah.

How long did you hold the ethanol stocks?

I held them for the full move. I sold the day the bill went to Congress. I crushed it. Three of the ethanol stocks I bought went up over 1000% in 10 trading days. I think I made more money on this one combined trade in two weeks than I had made on all my trades up to that point. That was the first time I saw the power of a sector move with a hard catalyst and a well-defined date. I realized these were the types of trades you could put on with high conviction and achieve large jumps in your account.

So these stocks topped when the bill went to Congress.

It's amazing how catalysts are over the second the public believes it is the beginning.

Did this trade change the way you trade?

It did. It was the first time this sector-trading concept clicked for me. Before then, I was trading these one-off stocks, without any idea why I was buying the stock other than because of some zigs and zags on the chart. I saw this crystal-clear catalyst and the price move that resulted. It changed my career. It is how I trade everything now. I like to buy a whole sector of stocks at the same time. When I get into a sector, I use a shotgun approach. I buy everything in the space—every stock, every related stock. Initially, I buy smaller positions, and then I start researching the idea intensively. I read filings on all the companies. Once I get conviction on the trade, I start pyramiding my positions by hundreds or even thousands of times. Initially, I might have a position as small as a thousand dollars in a stock so that I am watching it. However, once I am in love with the idea, I'll bet millions on it.

Do you still participate in this chat room?

No, I left it about five years ago.

Why?

I don't like other people's input anymore. I don't want my ideas filtered through someone else's lens. Also, a chat room is the trader's water cooler.

Besides looking for a catalyst and focusing on sector trades, how else has your trading approach changed from the earlier years?

At this point, I don't just sit here and look at a company. I will visit the company. If they make a consumer product, I will buy it and see if I like it. If I don't like the product, I won't trade the company.

Can you give me an example?

A few years ago, I started hearing about 3D printing, so I spent $10,000 and bought four 3D printers. I taught myself CAD so that I could print out things that I wanted. I printed out pegs for a turtle house I designed.

[Neumann has a large pet turtle that roams (ever so slowly) his backyard.] I wanted to know which 3D printer was the best and why. I not only listened to shareholder calls, but I attended 3D printing conferences. Learning enough about 3D printing to understand what these companies were doing and being surrounded by 3D printers helped me get positioned in these stocks before they took off. I turn myself into an expert in each of the sectors I invest in.

Once you decide you like a sector, how do you decide where to get in?

In the case of 3D printing, the stocks had already started moving up, so there were no downtrend line breakouts to use as entry signals.

What do you do then?

There I had to use a 30-day downtrend or a 30-day flat line.

So you are talking about breakouts from shorter-term consolidations.

Exactly.

How do you decide where to get out?

It all depends. It depends on the significance of the catalyst and the strength of the sector. I don't have any preset formulas or rules where I get out. For example, I don't get out when I'm ahead 10% or anything like that.

Using 3D printers as an example, how did you decide where to get out of those stocks?

The leader in the space, 3D Systems, had gone from $10 to almost $100 in just over a year. I was no longer one of the only guys at shareholder meetings. There was lots of talk about 3D printing stocks in the chat rooms and CNBC. Once everyone is talking about it, I no longer have an advantage. By that point, if I am not already out, I want to be looking for a place to get out.

Did you wait for the market to break down, or did you just get out?

Analogous to the downtrend line that I draw to help me decide where to get into stocks, I draw an uptrend line to help me get out. When the sector leaders broke their uptrend lines, even though some of the smaller stocks held on, I started getting out of everything.

One other thing I should mention is that the 3D printing experience led me into what turned out to be my most profitable trade ever. I found a 3D printing company that was doing bioprinting. The company, Organovo, would take cells from a person, grow them into a huge number, and place them into a 3D printer to form them into different shapes. When cells are placed into different 3D shapes, they react differently than when they are in a flat plane. The goal was to use this technique to determine what kind of drugs might work best for a specific person. I started buying the company as soon as I heard about it, which was about two months after they were listed on the OTC. The market cap at the time was probably only about $40 million. As I was making money in the 3D printing stocks, literally, every day, I would buy more Organovo stock, as my conviction level grew.

I compare trading to a puzzle that needs to be filled in. The number of pieces in the puzzle were growing—other 3D printing stocks were moving higher, which was a big part of the puzzle for me, and volume in the stock was rising. I visited the CEO, who was also the founder, and I could see his sheer enthusiasm about the company. I met the original angel investor. I got to see their 3D bioprinter in action. Then they uplisted to the NASDAQ and did a concurrent share filing raise, which knocked the price of the stock down about 30%. But from my perspective, the uplisting provided the ultimate buying opportunity, and I went all in. At my peak, I probably owned 3% or 4% of the company. At the time, Organovo was at $3.50, and within a year, it went to $12, which is where I liquidated most of my position. That was the year I made $10 million.

What happened to Organovo after you got out?

It went slightly higher before it started going down. Now it's back to around $1.

So after a massive rally, it went all the way back down. Was that true of the 3D printing sector as a whole?

Yes, the stocks got smashed. They ended up going all the way back down again as well.

Any other trades that stand out in your mind?

For a lot of my best trades, the stocks don't even exist anymore.

Can you give me an example?

One day back in 2009, I noticed that this one-penny stock called Spongetech traded 200 million shares in one day. I checked the insider trading filings and discovered insiders had recently bought 750 million shares at 7/10 of one cent—an amount equal to half of all the outstanding shares! I checked into what the company did and found that they made a sponge with the soap built into it. I thought to myself, "OK, this is mildly interesting." I ordered the product and tried it, and I actually liked it. However, the biggest thing for me was the filing that showed that insiders had bought half the outstanding shares. So I bought something like six or seven million shares.

Where did you get in?

I got in between one and two cents. The company then went on a massive advertising campaign. They sponsored a program on HBO about football called *Hard Knocks*. Every time you saw a player, they had a Spongetech logo on their jersey. They sponsored the Home Run Derby and had this huge Spongetech banner. They sponsored the US Open women's tennis tournament, and they had this visual of the Spongetech logo at center court that you could only see on TV. These guys were everywhere. They started selling in Walgreens and CVS. I decided to stay with my position and wait to see how big this company could get.

One day, after the stock had gone up to ten cents, I was at the bar with a few of my friends, and they were talking about Spongetech. They were cultish about it, and these are not stock trading friends. They had found the stock too, maybe through all the sports advertising. The stock price just kept on going up.

I travel every summer, and that summer, I decided to hold onto the Spongetech position during my travels. It was the only position I had on. Every penny up, I would sell 100,000 shares. While I was on safari in Kenya, I received a text from my buddy telling me that Spongetech had gone up to 25 cents. At 25 cents, the company's market capitalization was nearing $400 million, and all they did was make a sponge with soap. I was in a panic.

Since you had been selling on the way up, how much of the position did you still have left?

I still had over half the position—several million shares. I was in a tent camp in Kenya, and I didn't have a computer or phone access.

How were you able to get text messages if you had no phone access?

I had a BlackBerry, and you could get text messages from other BlackBerry users. There might have been some way to make an international call, but I had no idea how to do it. So I bribed the lady at the reception desk to use their dial-up computer, which was so slow that it took me several minutes to get each trade through. By the time I got my last order in, the stock price had climbed to 28 cents. After I was back in my tent, my buddy sent me a frantic text saying, "Spongetech is down to five cents! What do I do?"

The same day!

Yes, literally five minutes after I got back to my tent.

What did you tell your friend?

I had texted him that I was selling my position while I was getting out. When he texted me back later saying that the stock price was down to five cents, I was at a loss for words.

Had you been following the stock while you were traveling?

Periodically. I was pretty comfortable with the position.

When was the last time you had checked on the price before you received your friend's text?

It was probably several days earlier.

So if you didn't get the text, or if you had been several minutes slower in getting your orders through, you would have given back almost all your profits on the remaining position.

Yes, that was probably a $700,000 text message.

What had caused the abrupt, enormous crash in the stock price?

To me, it seemed to be like a play straight out of *Reminiscences of a Stock Operator*. [This classic book on speculation, whose protagonist is widely assumed to be Jesse Livermore, is set in the financial backdrop of an age replete with bucket shops and market manipulation.] The insiders owned 750 million shares. Two months earlier, they couldn't even have sold 100 million shares at one penny. However, if they could generate tons of publicity and get the price way above 10 cents so that 10 cents looked good, then they could sell the entire 750 million shares at 10 cents easily. I'm sure what happened that day is that the insiders started selling out their position, and as prices began to collapse, they kept on selling until they couldn't sell any more.

[In 2010, the SEC charged Spongetech and its executives with "a massive pump-and-dump scheme that deceived investors into believing they were buying stock in a highly successful company." Spongetech had also defrauded Madison Square Garden and a host of professional sports teams, leaving them holding the bag for millions of dollars of unpaid sponsorship and advertising bills.]

Do you also trade from the short side?

I never go short.

How then did you manage to make over $1 million in 2008 trading only from the long side?

I feel like traveling has helped my trading career. Taking summers off has been beneficial to my trading because summer always seems like a really tough time for the markets. When I came back in the fall of 2008, the world was falling apart. I was fresh and ready to go. My account was at all-time highs. I had all sorts of new stocks to watch. I was ready to catch a move, whereas people who had been trading during the summer were completely demoralized, and their accounts had been beaten down.

I nibbled at some financial stocks, which had declined particularly sharply, trying to pick a bottom, but I was continually stopped out. I knew that at some point, I was going to make a move. Then one day, you could see something was different in the financial stocks. There were 10 minutes left in the day, and I loaded up on a whole basket of financial stocks.

Why?

I saw the stocks breaking through their steep downtrend lines on high-volume. Someone was buying, so I joined in. I bought loads of equities, and I levered up by buying a ton of two-week-out options on financial stocks. After the market closed, I remember driving to play tennis with my friend, and I heard a story on the radio about TARP. [The Troubled Asset Relief Program allowed the US government to buy up to $700 billion worth of illiquid assets from financial institutions.] It was the first time I had heard the term. I knew things were going to be crazy. The next morning, all the stocks I had bought were up big; some were up as much as 50% from where I had bought them. Within five minutes of the opening, I took profits on all the positions I had bought the previous day. I made nearly $900,000 that day. I had held these positions maybe a total of 15 minutes of market time—10 minutes the previous day, and five minutes that morning. [Neumann had not caught the market bottom, but only a short-term relative low. The market continued to move lower in subsequent months, so it was quite fortunate that he took quick profits.]

Initially, you started out trading penny stocks. What kind of stocks do you focus on now that you are trading tens of millions?

I still focus on small-cap stocks. My sweet spot is stocks in the $200 million–$500 million capitalization range.

Why is that?

I think that it is much easier for a company in that size range to have a big price move.

Given your much larger account size, do you ever still trade penny stocks—I mean that literally: stocks trading under $1?

Sure, sometimes, they are my best trades.

Isn't liquidity a problem?

Well, I break up my orders into smaller trades. I also scale into positions over time, sometimes buying more every day.

How about getting out?

If I pick the right trade, and the stock is moving sharply higher, excitement builds, and there tends to be a substantial increase in liquidity. By the time I take profits, there is usually good liquidity in the stock.

Can you give me a recent example of such a penny stock trade?

About two months before CBD became legal at the federal level (it was sort of gray-line legal within individual states until the farm bill passed), I went to a local liquor store, which is the biggest beverage store in Texas. I asked the manager of the non-alcohol beverage section, "Do you have anything with CBD in it." This guy stopped in his tracks and said, "We have one product, and this product has changed my life like nothing else before." He was 60 years old and had suffered from arm pain issues. He would not let me leave the conversation for 15 or 20 minutes. I heard his name paged on the intercom, but he wasn't paying any attention to it. He just kept telling me how much he loved this water. He got me excited about the product. It was four dollars for a small bottle, and I bought a case.

I got home and looked up the company. It was a two-cent stock, and it was right at the cusp of a two-year downtrend line. Given how excited the manager at the store was about the product and with a small bottle selling for four dollars, I figured the sales could be outstanding. I also had my primary chart buy signal—a breakout from a long-term downtrend line. I bought a couple of percent of the company. I tried the product, and it seemed to be working for me.

What ailment did you have?

I had herniated a disc a few years before, and I was taking Aleve every day.

So this CBD water worked for you?

It did, but it's hard to know if it was the water or just a placebo effect. I started going to the store every day. I wanted to see who was buying the product.

Did the manager think it was a bit odd that you were hanging out at the store every day?

After the first day, I told him why I was there. I told him that I was interested in the stock and that I had bought a bunch of other CBD stocks as well. He thought that was cool. I got to know the manager pretty well. I noticed the clerks were all drinking the water.

The stock started running and went up 1,000% from where I had bought it only a few weeks earlier. The stock hit 25 cents. I went into the store for my daily visit, and the manager rushed up to me. His face was white, and he said, "We just pulled all the product. They found something floating in the water." I said, "OK. Are you going to get it back in?" He said, "We pulled all the product from our main warehouse. We don't know if we'll ever carry it again."

I drove home as fast as I could. I got home, and sure enough, the case I had bought the day before had this brown stuff floating in it. Up to that point, I thought I would be holding onto this stock for a long time. I started selling as fast as I could. There was unlimited liquidity in the market. The CEO had just given an interview that morning in which he said that if the company got their sales above $1 million for the year, Coca-Cola might be interested in buying them out. The stock probably traded 100 million shares that day. I had three or four million shares at that point, and I was able to sell my entire position at the dead top without moving the stock price at all.

So you had advance notice of the product being pulled by their main distributor.

Yeah. I wouldn't call it inside information, but it was the type of information you get if you are out there looking for it.

What about the other CBD stocks you had bought? Since the problem was specific to this one company, were the other CBD companies impacted as well?

They were affected because I sold out of everything. I was probably the single biggest retail holder in these stocks.

I stayed interested in the space, though. I went to California for a month and turned myself into an expert on CBD and THC stocks. I went to every publicly traded retail and dispensary chain. There was one retail chain called MedMen that had a billion-dollar capitalization. I spent 45 minutes in one of their stores. There were 20 employees. One other customer came in while I was there, and he bought a single joint. I was thinking to myself, "These employees are probably making $15 or $20 an hour. The store is on prime real estate, which must be expensive to rent. They don't make the product they sell, and they're hardly doing any business. How can this company be worth a billion dollars?" I didn't go short because I don't short stocks, but I had been nibbling on the stock, and after that store visit, I sold my small position. I also did a blog post on the stock.

What eventually happened to the stock?

It went down from over six dollars to about two dollars in a few months.

In almost all the examples we discussed, it seems you focus on new product categories. Is that indeed an integral part of your investment approach?

I like to try new products early on. Sometimes, I can envision applications for a new product before they even exist. I don't remember the year, but I had bought this biometric scanner that plugged into my laptop and allowed me to log in with my thumbprint. I remember holding this dongle in one hand and my iPhone in the other and thinking, "This is so obvious. Why doesn't my phone have this capability?" Years later, I started watching AuthenTec, a biometric sensors technology company. When I got my downtrend breakout signal, I bought some. As it moved higher, I kept adding to my position. Then AuthenTec signed a deal with Samsung. My reaction was, "Oh my God. It's all systems go!" I had never seen a trade that was so obvious. I went all in. I had more than one-third of my account in this one stock.

Literally, more than one-third of your account in one stock!

Oh yeah. I still do that sometimes. At this point, my average price was much lower. I was just pyramiding, filling out the tail end of my position. About two weeks after the Samsung deal was announced, Apple bought the company. That was the only time in my career when a stock I held was bought out.

When you have more than one-third of your entire account in one stock, how do you protect yourself?

If the stock is not acting right, I scale out the same way I scaled in.

What do you mean by not acting right?

If the stock starts moving down instead of up, or liquidity is declining, or big orders are getting hit on the ask instead of the bid. By the time I buy several percent of a company, I have a pretty good idea of how the stock acts. If the stock starts acting differently, I start reducing my position.

———

A long conversation ensued about cryptocurrencies and Neumann's positioning in this space. To recap succinctly, he got long very early on based on a chart breakout and held a core position throughout the entire giant upmove that culminated in late 2017. Our discussion turned to why he decided to get out when he did.

———

Did something change atmosphere-wise when you decided to get out?

Yeah. I call it my golf course indicator. I usually never talk markets with my golf buddies. I showed up for the first tee, and this 60-year-old who has never speculated in stocks asked me about Litecoin. To me, that was a clear sign that the masses knew about this trade. By that point, I had been in this trade for over a year. I thought it was time for me to start looking to get out.

If you get stopped out of a trade, will you look to reenter it if conditions are right?

It's easy for me to buy it again. I have no qualms about buying higher.

Did any books influence the way you trade?

It probably took more than a year of trading before I read my first financial book.

Which book?

Reminiscences of a Stock Operator.

Did that book influence your trading, and if so, how?

It reinforced what I was already doing—most importantly, placing large bets when you had the right set up, and keeping bets small when you didn't. My winning percentage on trades is way less than 50%, but I still do well because I can recognize the one or two times a year when all the pieces of the puzzle are in place, and I need to bet big on a trade.

What else did you get out of *Reminiscences*?

There is an anecdote in the book about a time when Jesse Livermore had a giant position, and there was a newspaper story publicizing that fact. The stock gapped up sharply the following day based on that news, and Livermore took advantage of the increased liquidity to get out of his entire position. When I am holding a penny stock or small-cap stock, I think of that episode to remind myself that I need to take advantage of those times when there is increased liquidity to take profits on my position.

How would you define your trading methodology?

I look at trading like a puzzle; I have to get the four corners in first.

What are the four corners?

The first corner is technical analysis; you have to have the right chart pattern. The second corner is a clean share structure.

What do you mean by that?

The stock has few or no options or warrants, and preferably, there are fewer than 200 million shares.

What are the other two corners?

Being in the right sector and having a catalyst or story that will make the stock or sector move up. Once the four corners are in place, you can then fill in the pieces.

What would those include?

Details on filings, checking into what management has done before, trying the product, and pyramiding your position correctly.

What are the trading rules you live by?

What's next? Always look for the next big opportunity. Understand when you get out of a position that's not acting right, you can always get right back in. Look for 10 to 1 return/risk trading opportunities.

What personal traits do you have that you believe have helped make you successful?

One of the best interviews I've seen was with David Tepper after the financial crisis. [David Tepper is the founder of Appaloosa Management, a highly successful hedge fund.] Tepper made the analogy that he was like a wildebeest in a great migration, and he wanted to be that first wildebeest that came into the valley and could have all the fresh, green grass he could eat. Sometimes there would be a lion waiting if you are that early on, and it was a lot safer being in the middle of the pack, but then you wouldn't get that fresh, green grass either. That comment really stuck with me.

Was that because it described you?

It described how I wanted to be in the market. I wanted to be first. Even if I got smacked around sometimes, it was OK, as long as I could be ahead of everyone else for whatever theme was next.

What other traits have helped you succeed?

I am quick to see when I made a mistake, and I immediately pivot and correct it. I learn from each mistake. The second I realize I am wrong and get out of the stock, it's over. I don't even remember the trade a minute later. It happened. It's gone. I've accepted it.

———

Early. It came to me in my sleep one night while I was working on Neumann's chapter. I hadn't realized it while I was interviewing Neumann, nor in the initial days of listening to my interview recordings and working on this chapter. A common theme that underlies Neumann's spectacularly successful trading career and a recurrent source of his edge is that he is early. When NASDAQ transitioned from quoting prices in fractions to decimals, Neumann was there to take advantage of the temporary trading opportunity created as different brokers permitted orders with different decimal placement.

In the trading style Neumann subsequently adopted, he enters his trades at the very point of breakouts from long downtrend lines—the earliest possible technical signal of a trend transition. Of course, this type of entry point often results in buying multiple false breakouts before a valid breakout occurs. But here again, Neumann is early—he gets out immediately if the breakout doesn't follow through, thereby assuring a near-breakeven outcome, even on premature trade entries.

Neumann is always looking to get in at the very early stages of new product sectors, such as 3D printing. Many of these emerging industries go through a cycle of an initial upward price wave, as hype over a new product sector generates excessive buying that is unwarranted by the nascent fundamentals, and then experience a near-complete price decline once reality sets in. Sometimes these companies will recover, sometimes not. Either way, however, Neumann seems to be there to catch the upward price movement stage.

In talks I give on the subject of lessons of the Market Wizards, I often refer to the perspective of being attracted to trading because "it is an easy way to make a lot of money," as an illustration of a wrongheaded approach. Ironically, that perspective precisely describes Neumann's motivation to start trading—and it worked! I still think that most people who pursue trading as a get-rich-quick endeavor will fail, but after interviewing Neumann, I have to concede there are some stark exceptions to this rule.

Buying trendline breakouts or anticipated, imminent trendline breakouts is an essential component of Neumann's success. Yes, by itself, buying trendline breakouts is far from a prescription for trading success. I would even argue that given the increasingly wide popularity of chart analysis, false trendline breakouts are so frequent that, over the long run, this technical signal is more likely to lead to net losses than net gains, let alone spectacular gains. Nevertheless, if you see Neumann's trade entries (after the interview, Neumann flipped through a series of charts on his monitor, showing me where he got into various trades), you can't help but be struck by how incredibly great these trade entries look. Chart after chart, his entry points were near the absolute low following a prolonged decline and right before a massive, near-vertical rally. The trade entries look uncanny—almost as if Neumann had an advance copy of the following month's prices.

So how was Neumann able to use a type of technical signal of such questionable efficacy with such incredible effectiveness? The key is that the trendline breakout is only one component of his overall strategy. By itself, buying trendline breakouts is a loser's game. However, knowing *which* breakouts to buy is what makes Neumann's trading approach so effective. Neumann's core trades share many, if not all, of the following characteristics:

⚡ The stock has seen a large decline or an extended sideways movement near lows.

⚡ The company has a service or product that suggests considerable upside potential.

⚡ There is a catalyst to suggest the prospect for an imminent price rally.

⚡ The stock is part of a sector that Neumann has defined as being primed for a substantial upward price move.

⚡ He is familiar with the product and has usually tried it himself.

⚡ The stock is showing some signs of life—either a sudden upmove after an extended period of decline or sideways price movement, or an abrupt spike in volume after a lengthy period of relative inactivity, or both.

When most, if not all, of these elements are in place, Neumann is primed to look for his breakout. So what looks like a simple trade of buying a downtrend line breakout—one of the most basic technical signals that can be imagined—is a far more complex trade taking into account a gamut of factors that have to be appropriately lined up.

There is another essential factor that explains how Neumann can be so successful using the mundane approach of trend breakouts for trade signals, and it has nothing to do with trade entry. Neumann buys a stock right at the moment he thinks it is ready to go (for example, at the cusp of a critical breakout where he is taking out the last portion of a large sell order). If after Neumann buys the stock, it fails to follow through on the upside, let alone begins to drift back down, Neumann will exit the trade immediately. Because he enters a trade at a point at which there is likely to be at least some minor follow-through, even if the trade ends up being wrong, Neumann can typically get out not far from breakeven. So Neumann's phenomenal track record is not merely a matter of a superior trade entry strategy—although he certainly has one—but also his unflinching ability to exit trades without hesitation when they are not behaving as he expected them to. His exit strategy is steeped in risk control, whether he thinks of it in these terms or not.

It is fascinating to compare Neumann's technical entry signal with Peter Brandt's (see Chapter 1). Neumann only wants to buy breakouts from downtrend lines because they will provide a better entry price (when the signal is valid), and he is willing to accept the greater number of false signals to get this better price. Brandt uses the exact opposite approach: He avoids trendline breakouts because he considers them unreliable. He only wants to buy breakouts from horizontal consolidations because their greater reliability allows for the placement of a protective stop that is both meaningful and close. The two traders have opposite perspectives about technical trade entry signals, yet both are very successful—a classic illustration of the principle that there is no single correct trading methodology.

Whereas Neumann and Brandt provide a study of contrasts in terms of trade entry timing, it is noteworthy that Neumann's trade exit timing is the embodiment of the contrarian trading philosophy expressed by Jason Shapiro (see Chapter 2): "I try to find out what everyone is doing, and I do the opposite because when everyone is in the same trade, they lose money." This sentence provides a good description of how Neumann exits trades. In virtually all the major trades discussed in this interview, Neumann exited when the trade became popularized. Consider the following examples:

⚡ He sold out of his ethanol stocks the day the bill to increase the ethanol content in gasoline went to Congress—a point of peak media coverage.

⚡ He liquidated his 3D printing stocks once they become popular enough to be the subject CNBC coverage and widespread chat room conversations.

⚡ He started scaling out of his Spongetech position once it became the topic of bar conversation among friends who were not stock investors.

⚡ He liquidated his cryptocurrency holdings based on his "golf course indicator."

You need to stick to your methodology and trading plan. Beware of being enamored by an unplanned trade. Neumann's biggest loss (in percentage terms) came early in his career when he deviated from the market-making strategy that was generating steady returns to impulsively buy a stock that was soaring based on a good story. That one trade wiped out 30% of his account in one day.

It is striking how many of Neumann's most successful trades were dead wrong from a long-term perspective. 3D printer stocks and Organovo surrendered their entire advance, ultimately declining to levels even lower than where Neumann had first bought them. Spongetech proved to be a scam and became worthless. The point is that what matters is not what a stock does long term, but instead what it does while you are holding it. Neumann's entry and exit techniques protected him from any substantial loss, while still allowing him to experience windfall gains. Successful trading is a matter of skillful money management (expressed via entry and exit methodologies), not prediction.

A lot of Neumann's trades seem like pure luck. For example, his getting out of the CBD water stock near the absolute high because the store clerk happened to tell him about the impurity problem. But think about it: Neumann put himself in the position to be lucky. It was only because of his on-the-ground research and his continual monitoring of local store sales that he was in the store to get that valuable news. The BlackBerry message he received while on safari in Kenya on the day Spongetech made its all-time high was a bit of extraordinary luck. But it was only because

Neumann had the right instincts to immediately liquidate his position during the market buying hysteria that this message made a difference.

The Spongetech trade also provides a perfect illustration of a trading principle noted in *Hedge Fund Market Wizards*: "If you are on the right side of euphoria or panic, lighten up. Parabolic price moves in either direction tend to end abruptly and sharply. If you are fortunate enough to be on the right side of a market in which the price move turns near vertical, consider scaling out of the position while the trend is still moving in your direction. If you would be petrified to be on the other side of the market, that is probably a good sign that you should be lightning your position."[*]

Readers of Peter Lynch's book, *One Up on Wall Street*, should find parts of this interview resonate strongly with Lynch's central message. Specifically, Neumann's habit of trying out new products and visiting stores to see how products are selling are integral to his trading success and responsible for some of his best trades—getting out as well as getting in. Neumann is the living embodiment of Lynch's "invest in what you know" philosophy. Neumann also focuses on seeking trading opportunities that have the potential to be what Lynch termed "ten baggers"—investments that achieve a tenfold price increase.

Neumann steps on the gas when he has a particularly high conviction on a trade. For example, in the case of AunthenTek, he had between one-third to one-half of his entire account in this single position. This highly aggressive positioning in situations in which Neumann has firm conviction is a significant component of the tremendous compounding he has achieved. This particular aspect of Neumann's trading style, however, requires a strong note of caution and would be dangerous for most traders to attempt to follow. Extreme position concentration has worked for Neumann because of three factors. First, he has a high success rate on his high-conviction trades. Second, he scales into his positions so that by the time he has as much as one-third of his account in a single stock or single sector play, his average entry price is much lower, providing him with a substantial cushion if the stock starts falling. Third, and perhaps

---

[*] Jack D. Schwager, *Hedge Fund Market Wizards* (New Jersey, John Wiley & Sons, Inc., 2012), 497.

most importantly, he is very quick in scaling out or liquidating his position if the stock starts moving down or exhibits other signs of not acting as he anticipated. Unless a trader has similar skills, taking such large concentrated positions would be very risky and expose the trader to an account-ending loss.

CHRIS CAMILLO
Neither

FOR the entire history of market analysis, methodologies could be divided into either being fundamental or technical, or a combination of the two. Chris Camillo's approach is neither fundamental nor technical. His methodology would have been impossible until the modern era of combined processing power and social media. Camillo has effectively created an entirely new class of market analysis and trading—an approach he terms "social arbitrage."

Camillo's trading methodology developed as an outgrowth of observing social trends and cultural shifts in everyday life. To broaden his scope in spotting these trends, Camillo founded TickerTags, a company whose software allows monitoring and measuring social media mentions of words or word combinations (which he terms "tags") that are important to specific stocks. Camillo describes the perplexed responses he gets when he explains his methodology. "People will say to me, 'You mean you don't even look at PE; you don't look at management; you don't look at price action.'" My response is, "I don't look at anything other than my tags."

To use a visual metaphor, Camillo's trading career could be described as a pair of islands—one a rugged, desolate rocky outcropping, the other a lush tropical paradise—separated by a wide channel. Excluding his first trade as a young teen, which is described in detail in the interview, Camillo's initial foray into trading was an abject failure—years of multiple failed methodologies and a steady depletion of all his investment assets (which fortunately for Camillo were limited by what he could save off his moderate salary). After a decade-long hiatus, Camillo returned to trading in 2006 and, in stark contrast to his prior trading effort, experienced spectacular success. In the near-14 years since he resumed trading, Camillo has achieved a 68% average annual compounded return, turning his original $83,000 stake into $21 million, including net cash withdrawals.

I initially met with Camillo when he emailed me to request a meeting, seeking my advice on an unspecified matter. I replied that if he wanted to fly to Boulder to meet in person instead of a phone call, I would accommodate him. We met over a long brunch at the Buff, one of my favorite local spots. Although Camillo's primary vocation is trading, he has a long-running interest in film, dating back to when he wrote an unproduced screenplay in college. He currently produces a YouTube series called *Dumb Money*, which primarily consists of short videos in which Camillo and his friends invest in local businesses. Camillo explained that, at some point, when he figures out how to approach the project, he would like to do a movie about trading. He wanted to know if I would be willing to participate—in what specific way he had not yet determined—and if I had any thoughts about the idea. I told Camillo that I thought the concept would be challenging to execute because achieving an accurate depiction of trading and producing an engaging film seemed like incompatible goals. Camillo hasn't figured it out yet either, but he's thinking about it.

By the time Camillo and I met, I had decided to do another *Market Wizards* book, which was not the case in our first email communication. From his introductory email, it sounded like Camillo could be a possible candidate, so I asked him to send me his monthly statements if he had an interest in participating. When we met in Boulder, I had already decided I would interview Camillo for the book, and I was careful to avoid any discussion about his trading—a conversation I wanted to reserve totally for the actual interview.

When I scheduled the interview, I allowed for an eight-hour block of time because I knew from our first meeting that Camillo was a conversationalist, and there would be a lot of ground to cover. For efficiency, I scheduled the interview to coincide with a day I was in Austin (Camillo lives in Dallas). When I arrived at the Austin airport that morning, I discovered that my flight was canceled due to thunderstorms, as was every other flight until late that afternoon. My only recourse was to rent a car for a four-hour drive through steady rain and weather-induced traffic jams. Some trader interviews are a chore because the subject is tough to draw out, while in other interviews, the conversation flows smoothly. Given the stress of a canceled flight and an energy-sapping drive, I was fortunate that Camillo's interview fell into the latter category.

I interviewed Camillo in a covered section of his backyard, which provided shelter from the steady rainfall. We continued the interview over dinner at a club Camillo belonged to. To avoid the restaurant noise, which would have made the recordings of our conversation unintelligible, we were served dinner privately in the aboveground "wine cellar"—an accommodation for which I was profoundly thankful.

Where did you get your first awareness of markets?

My older brother was a stockbroker. You always look up to your older siblings. So, I guess that was my first impression that trading was a thing. But I really didn't get interested in it till I was 12 or 13 [he laughs loudly]. I was always aware of knowledge arbitrage, and in a way, I was doing it from when I was very young.

What do you mean by knowledge arbitrage?

I was obsessed with garage sales when I was a kid, starting when I was about 12 years old. I would spend every Wednesday and Thursday analyzing the garage sales in the newspaper. When I could, I would go to the houses before the garage sale to inquire about what merchandise they were selling. I was trying to find things that I could resell. I would identify buyers who were interested in a particular type of item. I had a guy I called the "Fan

Man," who was only interested in buying old fans. I had another guy who bought old watches.

How did you find people who were interested in one particular item?

I went to antique malls and flea markets to find people who were interested in one particular item and were willing to pay a premium for it. There was no eBay at the time.

How could you assess the quality of what you were buying? If you were buying an antique watch, how did you know that it wasn't a piece of junk?

I can't say precisely how I figured this out. Garage sales and estate sales are almost exclusively managed by older women, who have a high degree of knowledge about items such as apparel, furniture, china, and antiques, but they have a much lower degree of knowledge about things that are male-oriented, such as watches and old train sets. Anything that was male-oriented, they just put a number on it and got rid of it. The stuff that I was buying was mispriced because the sellers deemed it as not being worth anything. But I would find someone interested in that one particular item. I did this for years here in Dallas, and it became a real obsession. I got the bug for—I don't know what you would call it—treasure hunting or arbitraging knowledge.

As a young teen, how did you get to these garage sales?

I rode my bike and took buses.

How much money did you make doing this?

Some weekends, I didn't make anything. But on a good weekend, I could make $100 or $200, which was the world to me at the time. I also had a car detailing business. I was very entrepreneurial. I had a 30-year-old mind in a kid's body. I wasn't doing the stuff I should have been doing. I graduated in the bottom quarter of my high school class. I don't think that was because I wasn't as smart as the other kids, but rather because I had a hard time focusing on things that didn't interest me. School, at the time, didn't interest me; making money did. If it were today, I would probably have been diagnosed with ADD [attention deficit disorder] and put on meds. Back then, they didn't do that.

How did you go from garage sales arbitrage to trading?

Every Friday and Saturday before I went to my garage sales, I would stop at a 7-Eleven and buy a lemon-flavored Snapple iced tea. They always had two full refrigerators of Snapple. One morning, I went there, and they had consolidated all the Snapple drinks to one-half of one refrigerator. There was barely any Snapple left and none of my flavor. I asked the clerk what had happened. He explained they were now carrying a more limited Snapple selection because there were new competitors on the market, such as Arizona.

I came home that day and told my brother about it. I asked him, "Hey, is there any way I can make any money out of this?" He said, "Yeah, we can short Snapple by buying puts." He told me Snapple's earnings were a week away, and he explained how puts worked. I gave him $300. He bought Snapple puts for me, and a week later, Snapple announced they were building up inventory in the channel, which I didn't understand at the time. But the insight I had at the 7-Eleven was correct, and I tripled my money on the trade. It was a magical moment for me, and, from that point on, I was hooked.

How old were you then?

About 14.

Did you understand your brother's explanation of what puts were?

Oh yeah, I understood everything. What I didn't recognize at the time was how powerful the methodology I had discovered was. I didn't realize that the way I went about figuring out that Snapple trade would ultimately be the methodology I would carry forward in my investment career. That methodology, however, wouldn't come until many years later.

Here's what happened with my subsequent trading in high school and early college. It didn't go well. I was terrible. I would go from one methodology to another, depending on which book I had read last. For example, one of the books I read—I don't remember the name—was about the Hunt brothers cornering the silver market. For a while, I became obsessed with commodities. There was a store several miles from my house where you could buy silver. I went there and bought a 100-ounce silver bar. Every day, I would get the newspaper and chart the price of silver. It took me about five months to realize that I wasn't going to make any money in commodities [he laughs loudly].

Were there any market books that had a positive impact on your trading?

Over the years, I read a lot of market books, but only one had a significant impact on me: *One Up on Wall Street* by Peter Lynch.

Actually, your Snapple trade could be a poster child for the theme of that book.

It really could. The book resonated with me and had a major impact on my thinking about how I could successfully invest. It gave me the confidence that what I did in the Snapple trade wasn't just luck. If it weren't for reading Lynch's book, I would have thought, "You can't beat the smartest minds on Wall Street by just walking through a store." I wasn't interested in technical investing. I wasn't interested in fundamental investing. Although fundamental analysis made sense to me, it didn't connect with me. I thought it was boring. There were a lot of smart people doing fundamental analysis, and I knew I would never be willing to spend enough time at it to be better than everyone else.

How would you summarize the main lesson you got from Lynch's book?

For me, the central theme was the concept of looking for investments in your everyday life.

When did you open your account?

When I was in college, I opened an account at Fidelity. When the college got a Bloomberg terminal, no one knew how to use it. I read the manual and learned how to use the terminal. I did a lot of options trading in college because I didn't have much money, and I figured the only way I could generate any real return on my limited resources was by using options. I was trading out-of-the-money, high-risk options almost every time. I was going for the big 20X profits and losing money on virtually every trade.

How did you get the money to trade?

I still had my car detailing business on the weekends, and I was earning considerable money from it. I also got a full-time position at Fidelity as a mutual fund trader, which was a lot less exciting than it sounded. My job was answering phones and providing mutual fund quotes to customers.

You had a full-time job plus detailing cars! How did you have any time to study?

I have found that the busier I am, the better I do on everything. I also didn't have an interest in college; I just did what I needed to do to get through. I would regularly skip classes to go to the basement to use the one payphone to touch-tone trades. I would have to touch-tone in the option code, and then the computer program would read back the option symbol I had typed in. It was a very slow process. Sometimes it would take me 15 to 20 minutes to get one trade through.

I thought you were working at Fidelity full-time. How could you be placing these orders?

My job at Fidelity was after market hours.

How big was your trading account?

It was very small because I kept losing money on almost every trade [he laughs].

Did you have any winning trades?

I had some, but I don't remember what they were. All I know is that I lost every dollar that I invested.

So you were making money working and then losing it investing.

I was losing 100% of it.

Ironically, your first trade did so extraordinarily well, and then you lost consistently.

My first trade got me hooked, and then I spent years losing money in a variety of ways. I realized that I didn't have any superior method for trading using known techniques. At some point during all of this, I lost interest in investing.

I am not surprised, given the results. Obviously, at some point, you regained your interest in markets. When did you get back into trading, and what was the catalyst?

It was quite a while later—maybe 10 years—before I started trading again. At the time, I was working for a market research firm and doing well, but my financial needs were more extensive than the income my job could deliver. So, at some point, I got back into trading. I didn't have a lot of money at the time—I think I started with around $80,000 in my account.

Given how unsuccessful you had been in your previous trading attempts, what made you think this was a way to make money?

I knew there was opportunity there, but I just had not figured it out yet. I don't know what made me go back to my original methodology. It was probably subconscious, but I just naturally went there. Also, it probably helped that I was in the market research industry. I was running the entire panel department for the largest panel company in the world. [A market research panel company selects a panel from its large population of participating respondents to match the target audience needed for a survey.]

I had visibility into a tremendous amount of research. I realized market research was not as accurate as you would like it to be. People don't do what they say they are going to do. For example, when the iPhone was coming out, you might ask people the question, "Would you buy a phone without a keyboard?" And people would say, "No, I would never buy a phone without a keyboard." I saw so much of this disconnect between what people said and what they did that I lost complete faith in market research as an industry. It was also really slow.

It sounds like it's more an issue of accuracy rather than slowness.

It was slow as well. When a firm looks to generate research, they would have to come up with the thesis of the study, hire a third-party company to formulate the questions, which would take weeks, and then the questions would go to a panel company. By the time you're done, you are six or seven weeks in trying to analyze results. I knew it was inefficient. When I started trading again, I went back to my original methodology of investing based on what I observed. At the time, I didn't know if I was just being lucky or was really onto something. But, in the course of a few years, almost every trade I made was profitable.

Can you give me an example of some of those trades?

It was Peter Lynch type stuff. Some examples would be the Cheesecake Factory or P.F. Chang's. If you are a trader on Wall Street, you don't see Cheesecake Factory or P.F. Chang's first hand. You can read about it, but you don't understand what those restaurant chains were to Middle America. One of the enormous advantages I had was that by living in Texas, I was able to see firsthand what phenomenal investments they were. They were game-changers. For the first time, you had multi-hour waits in the middle of the week to get into a restaurant chain. These were people who had never had Chinese food.

And they still hadn't. Was it a matter of seeing the long lines at these restaurants?

It wasn't so much that as it was realizing that Wall Street had blinders on to certain things because of a geographic bias, or other bias. People sometimes say, "I bet your methodology works well on small companies, but it could never work on large companies." That's untrue. I traded Apple when the original iPhone came out because of a bias that very few people realized existed.

The original iPhone was initially released only on AT&T. At the time, the AT&T network in Manhattan was notoriously terrible. It was virtually unusable. No one talked about that fact, but it was a primary reason why the iPhone had slower adoption in the first year after its release within the financial community than in the rest of the world. On top of that, the financial industry was tied hook, line, and sinker to the BlackBerry because they needed it for corporate communications. I saw those biases early on. I had friends in New York, and the first thing they said about the iPhone was, "We can't use the iPhone here because it's on AT&T."

I'll never forget the first day the iPhone came out. I know exactly where I was when the first person showed it to me. I was at a party, and I saw the reaction of 25 people. I knew right then and there that it was going to be big, and I wasn't an Apple person. I had never even owned an Apple product in my life.

I shocked myself by how well I did in that first year after I went back to trading, and, quite honestly, I didn't know if it was just a matter of my being lucky. At the time, I signed up for Covestor, which was a portfolio tracking service. For a while, I was the top trader out of about 30,000 accounts on Covestor. That was when I knew I was really onto something. I'll never forget telling my friend at work, "At some point, I'm going to be making more money on my brokerage account than I am from this job." At my peak salary, I was making just over $200,000 a year. At the time, my account was only about $100,000, but the growth was pretty rapid. I remember wondering whether I would be able to build the account to $1 million. It didn't take that long until the account reached $1 million, and I was making more from my trading than from my job. That was the day I quit my job.

Did you leave so that you could trade full-time?

Yes, and that was dangerous for me. It is something I have struggled with ever since. Looking back, I think a big part of my success when I went back to trading was my ability to look past the noise and be patient. I wasn't in the industry. It wasn't my job, and I wasn't under any pressure to trade. I could go six months without a trade, and I didn't have to answer to anybody. My biggest mistakes over the years have always been a consequence of trading too much. If I just stuck to my highest conviction trades, I believe my account would be tenfold what it is today. My methodology works best when I identify a significant piece of off-radar information that allows me to have a tremendous amount of conviction going into a trade. And that doesn't happen very often. It's very difficult to say, "I'm going to wait for a high-conviction trade and not do anything for the next three months."

Can you elaborate on your methodology for identifying those high-conviction trades?

I call what I do "social arbitrage." What the word "social" means to me is that it is something not financial. My trading is dependent on my ability to identify meaningful off-radar information early—information that is either not recognized or is underappreciated by the investment public. In some ways, my focus was the inverse of what it was during my garage sale years. In my purchases at garage sales, I was focused on male-oriented items that female garage sale organizers had mispriced. I quickly realized that a lot of the biases on Wall Street provided opportunities for me to identify information that was either female-oriented, or youth-oriented, or rural-oriented. I don't want to say that my methodology is totally dependent on those areas, but in my earlier years, it focused on those areas. I immersed myself in fashion and pop culture—things that are entirely off the radar screen of the typical Wall Street trader or fund manager.

How did you spot trading opportunities?

I would term it as retraining your brain. You are still living your normal life, but you are observing in a very different way. Anytime I uncovered anything that was potentially meaningful, I would follow up with more research. For example, when Wendy's announced their pretzel bacon cheeseburger back in 2013, I went out to observe as much as I could. I spoke to the managers at a dozen different Wendy's locations. I asked them how many years they had been at Wendy's and how this item compared with other past seasonal items. And every time the answer I got was the same: "We've never seen anything like this before." I spoke to the customers about what they thought.

But you are only surveying consumer sentiment in Dallas. How do you know it's at all representative of what's happening in the country as a whole?

What is amazing about Dallas is that it may just be one of the most representative markets in the country. I also looked at different online chat sites where people talk about fast food. I know that sounds crazy, but these sites exist. It was a great trade that was totally missed by Wall Street. Every fast-food chain has a seasonal item they introduce, usually in the spring. Typically, these items come in and go away, and it's no big deal. This item, however, was so large that it moved the needle for the entire company. Because that type of impact had not happened before, it wasn't on the radar of people who follow the stock.

Out of the many trades you've made in your career, do any stand out as particularly painful?

Ironically, one of my most regretful trades was also one of my largest winners. Many years ago, it was a brutal winter, and I had identified massive consumer adoption of Under Armour's ColdGear that was being completely ignored by the street. Their ColdGear was underwear designed to keep you warm in cold weather.

I cross country ski, and I remember buying long underwear by brands such as Patagonia as far back as the 1970s. What was different about ColdGear?

Under Armour made it for the masses. They had a wider distribution of this type of product than anyone ever had.

How did you spot the consumer trend?

I spotted that trend off of social media. I have a large number of proprietary word groups that I monitor every evening. At the time, I was monitoring a word combination that included ColdGear, Under Armour, and some other words. I measure the conversational volume of the word groups I follow, and if I see the volume is abnormally high, that is the first signal for me that something is up. I spend only about four hours a day on trade research and analysis, but when I find something like the Under Armour trade, I will spend 14 or 15 hours a day for days or even weeks on due diligence.

What specifically do you mean by due diligence?

I will try to accumulate every bit of data I can that is related to my trade. I start with a hypothesis. In this particular case, my hypothesis was that Under Armour was experiencing exceptional sales of their ColdGear products. Then I have to test my hypothesis. I interviewed store managers and consumers. I went online and scoured every piece of information related to my assumption. I had full corroboration by virtually every piece of information I checked. It was one of the largest trades I ever made. When I have a high-conviction trade, I can get to the point where I have 95% plus confidence in the trade. But even with that high level of confidence, it doesn't necessarily mean I will make money on the trade. There are always external factors at play.

Why was this one of your most regretful trades?

Because several days before Under Armour reported earnings, Lululemon came out with their earnings, and it was a disaster.

Were Under Armour and Lululemon correlated?

At the time, they were correlated enough so that after Lululemon saw one of its most substantial breaks following its earnings, Under Armour got crushed as well.

I guess that is a perfect example of what you would call an external factor.

Yes. Then a relatively respected research firm came out with a bearish report on Under Armour, anticipating a negative earnings report. Meanwhile, I was holding one of my largest positions ever. A week before, I had 98% conviction; after these events, my conviction level had fallen to maybe 60%.

So, what did you do?

I sold off about two-thirds of my position just out of fear and self-doubt.

How large was your position?

I was risking about 8%–10% of my equity. But my position was expressed in options, so if the stock closed below the option strike prices, I could lose the entire amount. It was a big trade for me. I didn't want to lose that in one day.

Do you typically use options to express your positions?

I will use options when there is adequate liquidity, and the option price is reasonable.

In what percent of trades are those conditions fulfilled?

Roughly 50%.

I guess you use options to leverage your trades?

Yes.

Do you use out-of-the-money, at-the-money, or in-the-money options?

It has changed over my trading career. I used to use more out-of-the-money options. Now that my portfolio has grown over the years, I tend to use at-the-money or in-the-money options. But if it is a very high-conviction trade, I will occasionally invest in out-of-the-money options as well.

What percent of your account equity might you commit to a single trade?

On a high-conviction trade, I could put in as much as 5% to 15%, knowing that I could lose the entire amount, even if the stock doesn't decline by much.

How far out do you go in your option positions?

I attempt to determine what the information dissemination event will be. Usually, it is an earnings report. These days, as Wall Street is getting smarter about identifying off-radar information sooner through credit card or other data, a lot of the information that I trade on will become known before earnings. So, sometimes, I will buy options that expire before the earnings date to save money on the option premium. In those cases, I actually hope that the market will see what I see before earnings.

What happened to the remainder of your Under Armour position?

The Under Armour earnings came out, and they were right in line with what I initially expected. The ColdGear sales were phenomenal, and I don't remember exactly how much the stock went up, but it was probably close to 20%. I ended up making a ton of money on the trade, even after the losses I took on the two-thirds of the position I had liquidated previously. If only I had kept that position.

But you ended up making a lot of money. Why is that trade so painful?

Because I let myself be swayed out of most of my position when I was absolutely right. I regret that trade so much.

How did that change you?

It showed me that this game is all about confidence. I should not let extraneous factors impact my confidence. I know what I should be doing, but doing it is a different thing. I used to have this thought about the market that, "They must know something that I don't know." That is a thought I have continually tried to shake off. After the Under Armour trade, I walked away saying to myself, "Don't ever, ever get shaken out of a trade by thinking they know something that you don't."

Were there subsequent trades where that lesson came to bear?

Absolutely. A great example was Netflix a couple of years ago when they released the show *Stranger Things*. Netflix is one of the most covered companies in the world, closely followed by the brightest minds on Wall Street. Every time there is a new show on Netflix, I monitor the depth of interest in the show by measuring the conversational volume. The way Wall Street approaches the stock is to focus on viewership. There is a firm that provides Nielsen-type ratings for Netflix. The problem with that approach is that every top Netflix show has roughly the same amount of people watching it. So that statistic doesn't tell you anything.

When Netflix released *Stranger Things*, everyone knew it was a hit show—that by itself wasn't any real information. Also, a hit show on Netflix doesn't mean anything because they have hit shows with some regularity. The real question was whether *Stranger Things* was an anomaly. I measured the volume of people speaking the words *Stranger Things*, and then I compared it with the top five shows they had produced in the prior five years. I discovered that for all those other hit shows, conversational volume peaked in the first week and then went back down to the prior level. *Stranger Things* did something different: It hit that peak in the first week but then plateaued at that level week after week. When you combined all the mentions during the first 60 days after the show's release, the total was triple the second-highest amount for a past hit show.

What was particularly interesting about this trade was that almost every single analyst on the street was predicting a bad earnings quarter for Netflix. Here I was a few years after the Under Armour trade, and all these negative reports about Netflix were coming out left and right. It may still have made me nervous, but I didn't let it impact my actions. I had invested a large amount of money in Netflix, and I kept the full position. I even wrote an article on Netflix because I wanted it time-stamped that I called this trade with high conviction.

The earnings came out, and Netflix not only knocked it out of the park, but they attributed the strong earnings to the impact of *Stranger Things*. Although everyone knew that *Stranger Things* was a hit show, they didn't realize it was different from all the other hit shows in the past. But I knew it was different. It was one of my most profitable trades for the year.

Do any other trades stand out as providing a particularly important lesson?

Not long after the 2008 election, Michelle Obama wore a yellow J.Crew dress on Jay Leno's *Tonight Show*. I watched that episode. This event was one of the most defining moments for J.Crew in a decade. After that show, Michelle Obama was on the cover of almost every tabloid and fashion magazine. Immediately after that, the African American demographic completely embraced J.Crew as a brand. I totally missed that trade.

But you saw it at the time. You recognized the trade.

I didn't recognize it. I saw it, but I didn't observe it. Missing the trade was so impactful for me that I went on eBay and bought the dress. I have the dress in my closet; I could show it to you.

Why did you buy the dress? Was it to stare you in the face as a reminder of that missed trade?

Yes. I wanted it to remind me of how much opportunity is out there that I am missing every day. Missing that trade made me realize that for every trade that I found using this methodology, I was missing dozens.

How did that change you?

I knew I had to figure out a better way to apply my methodology. I needed to capture more data. I had to figure out how to broaden the funnel. I was doing really well with this methodology, and I thought, "If I am missing 10X and maybe even 100X more trades, how big could this get?"

Why do you think you missed that trade?

My methodology is so easy that, theoretically, anybody could do it. At the same time, it is so hard. When you see a big movement in a stock price, there is a reason why that price change happened. In many cases, the price moved because there is some inflection point in demand for that company's services or products. Was there a way to identify that change early? I knew those opportunities existed, but I couldn't figure out how to capture more of them. The opportunities I was catching were very random and based on my physicality—where I was, and what I saw at that moment in time.

One of my best friends had twins, and his wife had a post on Facebook. Paraphrasing, the post said, "My twins were silent for the first time in their lives. I thought something tragic had happened in my house. I ran up to the playroom and found them staring at the TV, watching the show *Chuggington*. This show is my savior." Then other mothers started posting about how their kids were obsessed with the show. Let's say you are a portfolio manager, and you see this post from your friend's wife, are you going to do anything? It is probably something you read for a few seconds and then move on to the next thing. I was proud of myself for stopping and thinking, "What is *Chuggington*?" I googled *Chuggington* and found that it was a program produced by a small company in Europe that fortunately happened to be publicly traded. I realized they would probably get some big license deals because of the show's popularity in the US. I invested in the company, and about four months later, that stock was up 50%.

That day I was on my game. But even on that day, I don't know how many other similar opportunities were there that I missed. So I spent the next few years obsessively thinking about how I could scale the methodology. I felt that if I could pull it off, I could either trade it as a hedge fund, or sell it to Wall Street, or both. I ultimately ended up doing both.

How did you solve the problem of missing the majority of trade opportunities that were theoretically identifiable using your methodology?

Going on Twitter and Facebook to manually look for things that I thought were happening was very inefficient. I thought, "What if instead, I could structure all the theoretical words and word combinations that would represent anything that would be meaningful to any publicly traded company?" Those terms would include the name of every significant publicly traded company, every CEO, every product, every brand, every technology, every cultural movement, and every government regulation that could affect a company. Essentially, I needed to figure out the name of anything that could impact a company in any way that someone might speak or write about. I called these word combinations "ticker tags."

It seems like an overwhelming amount of work to compile all these potentially meaningful word combinations. How could you possibly do all that work?

I had a partner who was a brilliant computer scientist, and we began by hiring 40 students from local colleges to curate these ticker tags. They curated a quarter of a million tags. The idea was to combine these ticker tags with unstructured data licensed from social media firms, such as Twitter and Facebook, so we could measure the relative frequency with which those tags were being mentioned across these social networks in real time. For example, I could tell you how many people were talking about getting an iPhone during the three weeks before a current iPhone release versus corresponding periods for previous iPhone releases.

How did you pay for this venture?

I put up $1 million of my trading profits to launch the company, TickerTags, and we also raised a few million dollars.

Wouldn't the value of these tags be dependent on the skill of the people who were putting them together? How did you know these 40 students were doing the task correctly?

I coached them on how to curate tags for a company. Each student had a list of companies. For each company on their list, they were instructed to research the company, research quarterly earnings reports, find news articles about the company, all with an end goal of identifying the price drivers for that company. They would tag any word associated with anything that could move the needle for the company. For example, "pretzel bacon cheeseburger" would be a tag for Wendy's.

We eventually got to over one million tags mapped to over 2,000 companies. We could detect conversational anomalies and understand whether there was more or less interest in a granular topic than a particular benchmark, whether that benchmark was internal to the company—a comparison to a previous year—or whether the benchmark was a competing product. Anytime conversational volume would pick up around a granular subject, our system would identify it. I believed that this was the end game for me—the culmination of everything I had worked for in my methodology.

I thought we had built what could be the most impactful institutional data product for Wall Street.

Can you give me an example of how TickerTags helped you identify a trade that you would otherwise have missed before?

Through TickerTags, we can now discover products very early on. A perfect product example is La Croix. Are you familiar with La Croix?

My wife and I practically buy it by the truckload.

Very early on, we were able to spot the conversational acceleration in people talking about La Croix, and not just La Croix, but bottled water in general as a market segment. Years before Wall Street realized this was a thing, we were able to identify the change in consumer behavior. I was a very early investor in National Beverage Corporation, which is this weird company in Florida that manufacturers La Croix, and La Croix accounts for the majority of their revenue. So National Beverage Corporation was almost a pure play on La Croix.

Everything I do is about early detection of change. That's it. I always knew that if we could develop something to detect change early, that was all you needed on Wall Street. What is the earliest point you can identify change? It's always going to be when people are talking about something. We were able to recognize the social shift away from soda and toward sparkling water early, and La Croix just happened to be the brand sitting there when that cultural shift occurred. I live for that. National Beverage was the most beautiful pure trade on this methodology—early detection of a cultural change that was going to have a positive impact on a specific company and a negative effect on other companies.

The information timeline begins with social communication—people talking with each other online or offline. Then it makes its way to the non-financial press. After that, the financial media picks it up. As the last step, it hits company earnings statements.

Wall Street now has access to data they never had before, such as credit card transactions. Credit card data shows what people are buying before the earnings come out. That's my competition as a trader. I can't rely on credit card data, which, by the way, I subscribe to.

Which is earlier, the social chatter or the credit card data?

That is precisely the point. How can you go even earlier than transactional data? The only way to get earlier information is to pay attention to conversation trends. I often have people say, "So, you're trying to predict the future in people's behavior." That's incorrect. I'm not trying to predict the future; I am trying to accurately and quickly depict the present. I'm not trying to predict what people will do, but rather identify what they are doing right now. What are they interested in right now? What are they buying right now? People talk about something when it is happening or immediately before it happens. In my world, that is the earliest point at which you can detect change.

Why then do you subscribe to transactional data when you already have the earlier signal provided by social information?

I subscribe to transactional data because I want to understand when the information I have is being disseminated.

Oh, so you use the transactional data as your exit.

Yes, when I believe it indicates the information has already been sufficiently disseminated.

Do you have any examples of where an increase in online chatter led to a shorting opportunity?

Sure. I love cultural shifts because Wall Street is always late catching on. There was a cultural shift of women going from traditional bras to wireless bras or wearing no bra at all. Very early on, I was able to detect that women were talking more and more about going "braless" or wearing "bralettes," which is how they referred to wireless bras. If you look at Victoria's Secret, they are famous for the traditional wired, push-up bra, which is their brand image. I knew this trend was going to be destructive to their brand. It was so obvious if you were monitoring the conversational frequency of the terms "braless" and "bralette." Wall Street didn't see it at all.

I assume you bought puts to take advantage of the trade idea.

Yes, I bought short-term puts before each of two consecutive earnings reports, and both trades worked out very well.

Any other shorting examples?

Yes, here is one of my all-time favorite trades. I'm sure you remember when the E. coli scare hit Chipotle.

I sure do.

There was a tremendous amount of work done on Wall Street to determine the impact of the E. coli scare on foot traffic at Chipotle. Before this E. coli scare, Chipotle had become famous for having long lines at lunchtime. Chipotle was such a trendy brand that it was common for people to tweet about having lunch there. They would also frequently tweet about how they were waiting in line at Chipotle. I was able to gauge real-time foot traffic by monitoring word combinations, such as "Chipotle" plus "lunch," and "Chipotle" plus "line," in online conversations. Almost overnight, the mentions of these word combinations dropped by about 50%.

When the E. coli news came out, it was on all the evening news channels. Didn't the stock take an immediate dive?

The stock took an immediate dive, but not remotely close to the decline it ultimately experienced. The general market perception was that the E. coli scare wouldn't have a long-lasting impact. No one anticipated the extraordinary collapse in foot traffic that would ultimately result from this event. But I could tell that the foot traffic was staying down because, for the next year, the word mentions with Chipotle never recovered.

When did you go short?

It was soon after the event, but for the next year, I traded in and out of Chipotle around news dissemination events, such as earnings reports.

Oh, another great shorting example was SeaWorld in the aftermath of the release of the documentary *Blackfish*.

Yes, I saw it. It was excellent. [The movie is a documentary about the physical and psychological harm experienced by killer whales in captivity told with a focus on one SeaWorld orca responsible for the deaths of three people, including a veteran trainer.]

The movie triggered a massive, global online hate campaign against SeaWorld. We see negative things happen to brands all the time, and they can usually recover relatively quickly. The typical scenario is that something bad happens, the company does some brand repair, and then weeks or months later, everybody forgets about it. SeaWorld was one of those rare situations where the level of negative conversation spiked, and then just kept building. Unlike many other negative events that happen to companies, this one didn't die out. SeaWorld's market cap dropped by over 40% during the next year and a half. I shorted the stock repeatedly during that period, trading in and out around information dissemination events, such as earnings calls, because I knew the situation wasn't improving, and the market refused to believe it.

Was this a matter of looking for mentions of SeaWorld?

No, this was a situation where I was interpreting the sentiment of the conversation, which was extraordinarily negative. Nearly 100% of all the social conversation around SeaWorld after the movie was released was negative, and it didn't go neutral for years. I usually don't trade on sentiment, but this was one of those rare circumstances where the sentiment was extraordinarily one-sided.

What percent of your trades are on the short side?

About 20%. I am neutral and opportunistic, but for whatever reason, about 80% of the insights I uncover are on the long side. It could be that when you are looking for anomalies in conversational volume, more often than not, they will involve something positive rather than negative.

Why did you decide to sell TickerTags?

A few years ago, we received a call from Twitter, informing us that our data rates were going to increase in the coming years, and the amount of increase was very substantial. We had to decide whether to raise another $5 million in venture capital or sell the company, and we decided to sell the company. I built TickerTags, not because I thought it was a good idea that other people would like, but because it was something I knew that I needed to have. So, here we are today, TickerTags is no longer my company, and I get to be a client.

I assume you get a free subscription.

I am still a consultant to the company. I'm helping them to refine the platform because I am knee-deep into it. I appreciate the platform more than any other client.

Do you get paid for being a consultant?

I get a free subscription to TickerTags, which is a very expensive platform. The subscriptions are only available to hedge funds and banks.

Aren't you concerned that having this tool available to hedge funds and proprietary trading operations will compromise its effectiveness?

No, because I think it will be a very long time before hedge funds are going to have the confidence in this tool that I have. In fact, while we were developing TickerTags, I would often share my trade ideas with hedge funds.

Did you share the ideas after you put on the trades?

I would speak freely about my trades with hedge funds, even if I was only partially positioned.

Weren't you concerned that sharing the information would move the trade before you fully got in?

No, because I knew these guys wouldn't move on the information. This type of methodology is so foreign to them that their lack of comfort and confidence in this approach would lead them to move much more slowly on the trade than I would, if they made the trade at all.

I used to ask myself, why isn't Wall Street digging in deeper into my methodology? I never understood it until I started TickerTags. After it launched, I was in New York every other week for two years straight. I met with almost every top hedge fund. These managers were some of the smartest people I have ever met. Their world is really noisy. They have a hundred different ways to look at things. They are so entrenched in doing things a certain way that for them to adopt what I do would be radical and extreme. They can't look at something like conversational volume impacting a specific stock because there is no history there. They want to see high correlation to trust the data.

I can't say that every time conversational volume peaked in the way it did for Netflix, the stock moved. It was a one-of-a-kind event. You have to understand and interpret this data. You have to be willing to trust it. Hedge fund managers want something repeatable and systematic. They wanted to know how often this approach would generate tradable information with high conviction. I couldn't give them a hard answer. It could be a handful of times a year; it could be 25 times a year. They want things that are repeatable and work for thousands of tickers. They have a lack of comfort with the variability in how this data is applied, but I don't.

Unless the methodology is your own, you won't trust it. I don't know what percent of systems sold to the public have any value. But, I always tell people that even if 90% plus of the systems sold make money with reasonable risk—a drastic overstatement I'm sure—I would bet that over 90% of the people who purchased those systems would still lose money. Why? Because every system or method will have its losing periods, and if you don't have confidence in the approach, which you won't if the methodology is not your own, you will abandon it. You're coming to hedge funds with a strategy they have never used, so they can never have your conviction. It even took you many years to get to that point.

Not just many years; it took me over a decade to get to the point where I had high conviction in my methodology.

When you get a volume spike in one of your tags, couldn't it just as well be bearish as bullish?

I look at the context of the conversation. It doesn't take long to determine the narrative. I will never trade on data alone. Every trade I do has a thesis with a narrative associated with it.

I will use a trade I am in right now as an example. About two months ago, I noticed a conversational spike in e.l.f., a manufacturer of low-priced cosmetics, that hadn't been doing too well in the past few years. That alone didn't tell me anything. Was there a spike because people liked a product or because they were complaining about a product?

Some further checking revealed the spike could be traced to a video made by a makeup tutorial artist named Jeffree Star, who has 15 million followers on YouTube. Jeffree had made a video where on half his face, he used an e.l.f.

product that is sold at Walgreens and Target and costs about $8, and on the other half of his face, he used a top-selling product that costs $60. He said that the $8 product was as good as the $60 product. He instantaneously changed the consumer perception of the e.l.f. brand from being viewed as a cheap drugstore product to being considered a quality product. The stock moved up more than 50% in two months. The odd thing is that I bet that most analysts who cover e.l.f. have no idea who Jeffree Star is.

Are there cases where you used the same word combination for both bullish and bearish trades?

Sure, Smith & Wesson is a good example. The combination of the words "gun" plus "class" is a good indication of the degree to which people are buying guns.

"Gun" and "class"?

Yes, class. Interesting, right? When people go out and purchase a gun for the first time, they start searching for gun classes. Another word combination that is a good indicator of gun sales is "gun" plus "ban." So anytime I saw a spike in the number of people concerned about guns being banned and also people looking for gun classes, I would view it as an early sign that gun sales were increasing. I used these word combinations as a buy signal for American Outdoors Brand Corporation, the maker of Smith & Wesson, multiple times. I also used it as a bearish signal when Trump came into office. There was a notable drop in people talking about gun bans and gun classes, and sure enough, the gun market fell apart, and gun stocks got killed.

Another example where I was able to trade both sides of the market using the same word combination was Beacon Roofing, which is one of the largest roofing distributors in the country. One of the things that cause Beacon Roofing's sales to go up is when there is a larger-than-normal hail season. Hail damage is difficult to detect because even if there are more hailstorms, if the storms are not located in highly populated areas with lots of roofs, they will not make a big dent in the roofing business.

No pun intended.

Yes, exactly [he laughs at his unintended pun]. The insurance industry puts out a report on estimated roofing damage claims, but that report is released many months after the fact. I will look at the word combination of "roof," "hail," and "damage." Every March–May period there is a seasonal spike in this word combination. A couple of years ago, I noticed a seasonal spike that was triple the size of any previous seasonal spike. There were three such abnormally high spikes in a row. I realized it was a severe hail season, and I took a long position in Beacon Roofing based on that assumption. As I expected, Beacon Roofing subsequently came out with a very bullish earnings report. Conversely, last season, the same word combination volume was exceptionally low during March–May, and the price of Beacon Roofing subsequently collapsed by nearly 50%.

You said earlier that there were over a million tags on TickerTags. Clearly, you can't follow more than a small sliver of these tags. How do you decide which tags to follow, and how do you avoid still missing most opportunities?

There is no way I can look at all the granular tags. Instead, I use what I call "umbrella tags." These tags are word combinations that allow me to detect early on when any topic is erupting on social media and give me insight into what other tags I should be looking at.

Can you give me an example of an umbrella tag?

The word combination "obsessed" plus "new" plus "game" will alert me when there is any new game that is sparking an upsurge in online conversation. So that umbrella tag would clue me in as to what specific game tag I need to start following at that moment, even if I had never heard of the game before.

How is that word combination different from any of the other word combinations we talked about, such as "gun" and "class," or "roof," "hail," and "damage"? What makes it a so-called "umbrella tag"?

An umbrella tag is going to pick up on anything in a category. For example, if toys are a category, I may have hundreds or even thousands of related words that I may occasionally look at. But if I look at the word "toy" and an emotional word, such as "obsessed," connected to it, I will be able to identify if anything is happening in the toy sector that is an anomaly that day.

So an umbrella tag is a word combination that can signal something happening anywhere in an entire sector rather than something specific to one particular stock?

Exactly. Some umbrella tags are even more general than a sector and are intended to capture anything that is trending.

What is an example of a very general umbrella tag?

The phrase "I can't find" followed by anything. I'm pretty tight-lipped about the exact umbrella tags I use, especially those that are broad in coverage.

What is an example of a trade that was signaled by a general umbrella tag?

A few years ago, a general umbrella tag uncovered a spike in mentions of "Elmer's glue." At first, this spike seemed somewhat perplexing. Why Elmer's glue? Some further checking revealed that the mentions of Elmer's glue were associated with DIY slime [do-it-yourself slime]. At the time, there was a big trend of kids playing with slime. The main ingredient in slime is Elmer's glue, and Elmer's glue was selling out everywhere.

Who makes Elmer's glue?

Newell Brands.

How big a part of their product line is Elmer's glue?

That's what's interesting. Elmer's glue was a small piece of Newell Brands, but Newell Brands was a very slow-growing company. Looking at how big the trend in slime was, I assumed that sales of Elmer's glue would increase by a minimum of 50%, and possibly as much as 100%. That type of increase would significantly move the needle for the company because their growth was only about 1.5% per year. Sure enough, earnings were up 17% that quarter, primarily because of the increased sales of Elmer's glue. I am so proud of that trade because no one else following Newell Brands would have thought to focus on sales of Elmer's glue.

Can you describe your trading process from getting in to getting out?

Whenever I come across a piece of information that I think the market doesn't know or is not paying attention to, I have to determine whether it can move the needle for the company. Sometimes the company is so big, and the information is so limited in scope, that it doesn't make any difference. If I believe the information could potentially be significant, I then have to determine to what degree it has already been disseminated to the investment public. If it's already market knowledge, then I have to assume it is reflected in the price. If the information is both significant and not yet disseminated, I then have to research whether there might be any extraneous factors that could meaningfully impact the company during the time window of my trade. Is there any impending lawsuit, or management change, or new product line, or anything that could trump the information I am trading on? Once I have excluded all the factors that could nullify the relevance of the information, I then conclude there is what I term an "information imbalance."

What is interesting about this methodology is that I apply it completely blind to other fundamentals in the company and the price action. I don't care if the company is overvalued or undervalued. I assume that the stock is trading relatively efficiently on the information that is out there. Then once this new information is added to the picture, the stock should adjust accordingly.

The last step is to define the trade window so that I can determine the appropriate option to purchase. For example, if I were trading Disney based on the expectation that a new movie would be a larger-than-expected hit, I would buy options that expire beyond the opening weekend. I want to select options that expire as soon after the expected information dissemination as possible to keep my option premium expenditures as low as possible. Typically, the option expiration will revolve around an earnings report, but it could also be determined by a product release or the availability of transactional data that can be used to anticipate earnings. If there is a reasonable expectation for information parity before the release of earnings, there is a distinct advantage to purchasing options that expire before earnings, since their prices won't need to embed the extra volatility surrounding an earnings release.

OK, you have described the entry process for a trade. What about the exit?

I have only one piece of information that the market is not seeing or appreciating, but there are lots of things that could drive the stock price.

As an analogy, my methodology is like playing roulette and betting on red because you know five black numbers have been removed from the wheel. It's not that I know an investment is going to work out; it's a knowledge edge. The second the information I am trading on hits the street, whether it's through analysis by a sell-side firm, or a media story, or the company itself reporting it, I call that "information parity," and my trade is over. I must sell immediately when information parity happens. I only invest when there is an information imbalance, and I must sell when there is information parity.

Is that true whether or not you're making money on the trade?

Whether a trade has a profit or a loss at information parity is entirely irrelevant. Either way, I have to follow my methodology.

It sounds like you almost don't need to know what the price is.

I don't even want to know what the price is.

When did you start your hedge fund, and why did you close it?

As the TickerTags project was nearing completion, I thought I should open a hedge fund because that was what everyone was saying I should do. They looked at my returns and told me that if I could do the same thing on a larger scale, I could have an incredible hedge fund.

I would have told you the same thing.

The concept was that TickerTags would be the engine for the hedge fund. I spent a year and a half meeting with family offices, and I lined up 23 investors, mostly in the Dallas area. I had commitments for almost $10 million. I spent about $250,000 setting up the fund. Starting a hedge fund seemed really interesting because it was what the other side of the business did, and I was never part of that world.

What was your hedge fund called?

SIA, which stood for Social Information Arbitrage. We launched the hedge fund around the same time TickerTags was in beta mode.

Weren't you hesitant about sharing the same methodology through TickerTags that you were planning to use for your hedge fund?

Not at all because I thought the value of TickerTags would far exceed the value of my little hedge fund. The problem was that when I took my first week of meetings with hedge funds to market TickerTags as a data product, they loved the concept, but every fund I met with told me not to come back as long as I was still running my hedge fund. They said that they could not take the risk I might front-run the data for my own fund before they saw it. So I was naïve to think that I could do both. Long story short, the hedge fund was open for only 60 days, and then I had to shut it down.

So you closed your hedge fund right after opening it because it impeded the TickerTags venture?

Right or wrong, that was the decision that I made.

Did you make any trades for the hedge fund before you realized you had to close it?

I made two trades. The first trade was in a small toy company called Jakks Pacific. The trade was based on a doll called Snow Glow Elsa, which was affiliated with the Disney movie *Frozen*. The doll was released right before the holiday season. It was not only the hottest toy of that holiday season; it was the hottest selling holiday toy in seven or eight years.

Since this doll was associated with a Disney movie, wouldn't many other people have been aware of it?

Not necessarily since there were a lot of other merchandise items related to the same Disney movie. It's funny how people always seem to congregate around one hot item.

Since this doll was a new product, what kind of tag would have caught it?

We had tags for every company. The researchers update each company every quarter and add new tags whenever they are meaningful. So Snow Glow Elsa was a tag. By using all the hot-selling holiday toys during the past five or six years as benchmarks, we could compare the conversational volume of this toy versus the others. We knew this toy was going to be an absolute blockbuster, and it was. It was a very high conviction trade that met the critical criteria: the market didn't appreciate the extent of how hot this toy was going to be, and it moved the needle for the company.

Since it was a small company, it probably moved the needle in a big way.

Huge. I was proud of this trade—my first trade in my own hedge fund. I couldn't even sleep the night before earnings. Sure enough, the next day, the company blows out earnings expectations. Pre-market, the stock is trading up 30%. I'm on top of the world. All I want to do is impress my investors, all of whom are local people I know. Just before the open, the stock drops 30% in ten minutes in the pre-market and then opens near unchanged. Over the next two hours, the stock goes down 25% on one of the heaviest trading days in the company's history, and I don't have a clue as to what is happening. It made no sense to me.

Up to that point, the company didn't have a single thing going for it. Now it had the biggest toy product in the world, and the price was collapsing. I didn't find out until two months later what had happened. The company had a rocky road in the prior two or three years. Their largest shareholder, a fund that owned 11% of the company, had sold off their entire position that day. Jakks Pacific was not an actively traded stock, and this fund had apparently decided that they would use the first day with good liquidity and strength to get out of their entire position.

Wouldn't you have sold your position after the earnings were released, since, in your words, it would be a point of "information parity"?

I had my full position in slightly out-of-the-money options. Since the market opened near even and moved lower, there was no opportunity for me to liquidate my position.

So your options lost 100% of their premium. What percent of your fund equity did you lose on that trade?

It was probably about 4%. My second trade for the fund ended up making about the same amount. So, when I closed the fund, it was at about even. I was the only person who lost money in my fund because of the quarter of a million dollars I had spent to structure the fund.

At the time you lost your money in that first trade, you didn't yet know you would be closing your fund. Did losing on your first trade bother you?

It bothered me tremendously. I learned that I didn't have what it takes to run other people's money.

So that loss bothered you more than losing your own money on a trade.

It killed me. I could have lost ten times that amount in my account, and it wouldn't have bothered me as much. I rarely take a loss on a high-conviction trade, and this was as high conviction as it gets. If I had the opportunity again, I would make that trade ten times over.

The approach you use is entirely different from every other trader I have ever interviewed. In what ways do you consider yourself different from most other traders?

I could never be a good fundamental or technical trader because I don't enjoy those methodologies. The four hours I spend every night doing my analysis is something that I love. I never know when I'm going to hit on that thing that will take me down the path to my next big trade. It's the same feeling I had as a kid going to garage sales. Every night I start the process, and I don't know what I'm going to find. I enjoy doing my nightly analysis; that's why I think I'm good at it.

The things I do are so different from other traders. You would have a hard time finding someone who is more risk-tolerant than I am. I never use stop losses. Most traders will say, "Never add to a losing position." If I am in a losing position and nothing has changed in the information dissemination, I will double down. I don't care about price action. Other traders want a methodology that is systematic and regular; I am as far removed from systematic and regular as it is possible to be.

What personal traits do you believe were instrumental in your success? Which of those traits were innate, and which were learned?

If I were a kid today, I think I would be diagnosed with ADD. I feel my ability to focus on subject matter that is of interest to me is my number one strength. The type of analysis that I do requires an immense amount of work for something that often doesn't have any immediate payoff. I could go for months without finding a high-conviction trade.

Is ADD the right term? Isn't ADD the inability to focus?

I disagree. ADD is the inability to focus except for those things you have an innate interest in, in which case, it works exactly the opposite.

Any other important traits?

Patience. I know some trading opportunity will pop up at some point, but I don't know when it's going to be or what company it will be. I know that if I keep on doing what I do every day, it could be tomorrow, or it could be four months from now, I will hit something. I just need to have the patience to wait for that trade.

Are you naturally a patient person?

Quite the opposite. I had virtually no patience when I started trading. Patience is something that I have slowly developed over the past 15 years. Today, I am a much more patient trader. The type of strategy I use requires extraordinary patience. Ideally, with my methodology, I should be making a trade only once every couple of months, and it is hard to have the patience to trade that infrequently after doing all the daily work I do. It's still a struggle for me.

What is your advice to someone who wants to be a trader?

Don't try to change who you are to match some perception you might have about what professional traders do on Wall Street. Don't try to learn mathematics if you're not a natural mathematician. Don't try to learn financial analysis if you have no background in it. There is probably something in your background—some area of knowledge or intense interest—where you are willing to spend an inordinate amount of time to develop deep expertise. If that's what you do, then you can outsmart the generalist, and most market participants are generalists. You have to find a niche where you can excel. I would ask a new trader: What is your niche? Where is your expertise? What are you willing to spend four hours a day researching in your off time because it's your passion? Investing is one of the only industries in the world where you can take your interest and monetize it, and that's very exciting to me.

To succeed, traders must find their own market approach. Probably no one I have ever interviewed exemplified this principle more than Camillo. Camillo not only developed his own approach, he virtually invented an entirely different trading methodology. Neither fundamental nor technical analysis appealed to Camillo, so he came up with a third market analysis category: social arbitrage—profiting by spotting a societal shift or trend that will impact a stock and has not yet been reflected by the stock price. Initially, Camillo uncovered these opportunities through everyday observation. Eventually, after developing the TickerTags software, social media became his primary tool for trade identification.

OK, I know many readers are probably thinking, "This idea of using social media as a trading tool sounds appealing, but what good does it do me when I can't get access to TickerTags?" (TickerTags is only available to institutional clients.) That objection misses the more general point. TickerTags may be a particularly efficient way of tapping into social and cultural trends, but it is not the only way. Camillo was extremely successful in using this general approach for about a decade before TickerTags ever existed. The key lesson is that being observant and highly attuned to new behavioral trends, both in your everyday life and in social media, can be a source for uncovering trading opportunities. For example, consider trades such as Cheesecake Factory and P.F. Chang's, which Camillo identified by observing Middle America's reaction to these chains—a response he knew Wall Street would be blind to. Observation of consumer response to a product can even identify trading opportunities in the largest companies, as was the case for Camillo's long position in Apple based on his seeing how people reacted to the first iPhone.

Question: What trading mistake did Camillo make in Jakks Pacific, the first trade for his hedge fund, in which his long call positions expired worthless? Think about it before reading on.

Answer: Trick question. He didn't make any mistake, and that is the point. Camillo followed his methodology precisely, and he placed a high-conviction trade—the type of trade that had a demonstrated history of strong net success. In this particular instance, a completely unforeseeable event—the total liquidation of a position by the company's largest shareholder—caused the profit on the trade to be reversed in an instant. Sometimes, even the best-planned trade can fail. Such a trade will be a losing trade, but it is not a bad trade. On the contrary, if Camillo repeatedly takes such trades, he will come out way ahead, and it is impossible to tell a priori which of those trades will end up losing. The lesson is: Don't confuse a losing trade with a bad trade—they are not necessarily the same thing. Losing trades can be good trades, and, similarly, winning trades can be bad trades.

Don't ever listen to anybody when you are in a position. Stick to your own approach and avoid being influenced by contradictory opinions. Camillo's most regretful trade was one in which he allowed himself to be swayed by conflicting market opinions into liquidating two-thirds of his Under Armour call position at a loss, only to then see his original trade premise fully validated. Camillo learned his lesson, and when a similar situation arose when he was long Netflix, he ignored the conflicting opinions. In my experience as well, it is amazing how catastrophic listening to other opinions can be.

Patience to wait for the right trade opportunity has been cited as a valuable trait by multiple traders I have interviewed. It is also one of the most challenging qualities to acquire. Camillo believes that he would have done far better if he restricted his market activity to his high-conviction trades. He states, "My biggest mistakes over the years have always been a consequence of trading too much." Camillo's problem is that the high-conviction trades he favors may come along only once every couple of months or even less frequently. He finds it difficult to spend four hours a day searching for and researching trades and then waiting for months to place a trade. But Camillo is mindful of the importance of being more patient and believes his improvement in this regard over the years has enhanced his trading success.

Not all trades are the same. As is the case for Camillo, many traders may have trades that vary in their perceived probability of success. There is a middle ground between taking all prospective trades generated by a trader's specific methodology and taking only perceived high-probability trades.

Alternatively, a trader can vary the position size, taking larger positions on higher-probability trades and smaller positions on lower probability trades.

Confidence is one of the best indicators of future trading success. The Market Wizards tend to be highly confident in their ability to continue to win in the markets, and Camillo certainly fits this description. He exudes confidence in his methodology and firmly believes it will continue to provide him with a clear edge in the markets. As well as he has done so far, he expects to do even better in the future. One way traders can ascertain how likely they are to succeed in the markets is to gauge their level of confidence. Traders should ask themselves: "Am I confident that my trading methodology and process will make me a winner in the markets?" If the answer is anything less than an emphatic "yes," they should stringently limit their risk capital until they achieve a higher level of confidence in their approach.

Camillo made his first trade when he was 14. I have found that many of the highly successful traders I have interviewed developed their interest in trading and markets at an early age. Traders who fit this profile probably have a better-than-average chance for success.

Successful traders love what they do. Camillo succeeded because he found a way of approaching the markets that resonated with his natural interests and passions—indeed, his methodology even echoed his childhood entrepreneurial pursuits. Both fundamental and technical analysis left him cold, and if he had pursued those traditional paths, he most likely would have failed.

MARSTEN PARKER

Don't Quit Your Day Job

When I interviewed Ed Seykota for my book, *Market Wizards*,* I asked him, "What are the trading rules you live by?" Two of the rules he mentioned were:

1. Follow the rules without question.

2. Know when to break the rules.

These lines came to mind when I interviewed Marsten Parker because his trading story is a testament to the truth inherent in Seykota's reply, notwithstanding its superficial facetious appearance.

When I first looked at Parker's performance statistics, my initial response was that I probably would not include him in this book. Although his track record was certainly good, neither his return nor his return/risk statistics were close to the spectacular levels achieved by most of the other traders I had already interviewed or was scheduled to interview. But then I noted that Parker's track record was 22 years long, a substantially longer period

---

* Jack D. Schwager, *Market Wizards* (New Jersey, John Wiley and Sons, Inc., 2012), 151–174.

than most of the other traders I had decided to include—an important consideration that should not be ignored. I reconsidered.

Parker's average annual compounded return during the past 20 years was 20.0%, more than triple the 5.7% return of the S&P 500 total return index during the corresponding period.* His return/risk numbers were solid: an adjusted Sortino ratio of 1.05 and a monthly Gain to Pain ratio of 1.24, approximately triple the corresponding S&P index levels.** I realized that I was becoming overcritical in my selection process, spoiled by some of the extraordinary results posted by other traders I had found. Ninety-nine percent plus of professional equity managers would be thrilled to have a 20-year record of trouncing the S&P 500 by similar margins.

There was another factor that was instrumental in my decision to include Parker. He was the only purely systematic trader I had found whose performance was sufficiently superior to even merit consideration for inclusion. Perhaps the lopsided overrepresentation of discretionary versus systematic traders I found in my search for exceptional performance is not representative of the total trader population, but I suspect it is. Ever since the release of my first *Market Wizards* book in 1989, I had found that standout individual traders tended to be discretionary, and this bias seems to have become even more pronounced over the years. There may be many systematic traders who are profitable, but few that outperform benchmarks by wide margins over long periods. I felt it was desirable to include a strictly systematic trader who had successfully earned a living by trading.

In contrast to most of the successful traders I've interviewed, Parker had no early interest in the markets. His passion was music, not trading. His original life goal was to be a professional violinist. He attended the Mannes School of Music in New York, but, while there, he realized that he was not

---

* I excluded the first two years of Parker's track record in the return and return/risk calculations because this period included discretionary trading, which is not representative of the systematic methodology he adopted and used for the rest of his trading career. In addition, this period also included trades in which he followed the trades of another trader. The return and return/risk statistics would have been even better if these two years had been included.

** For an explanation of these performance statistics, see Appendix 2.

good enough to succeed as a professional classical musician. Although music would remain an essential part of his life—he is the concertmaster for a community orchestra in Newton, Massachusetts—it would be a dead end career-wise.

The path that eventually led Parker to trading began with another early passion: computer programming. His initial interest was sparked in ninth grade in the pre-PC era. Parker's school had a Data General Nova computer, which provided his first exposure to programming. His interest in programming was rekindled in college through access to a computer lab and abetted by a free DEC VT-180 PC his mother had arranged for him to receive. This hobby led to a programming career and, eventually, systematic trading.

Parker's trading career could be divided into three distinct phases: an initial 14-year period of consistent profitability; a subsequent three-year period that very nearly drove him to quit trading permanently; and the most recent four-year period when he achieved his best return/risk numbers ever.

I interviewed Parker in his home office. One of his two cats had a fondness for jumping on the desk. I kept a wary eye on her, concerned she might step on the stop button of my recorder, causing an unintended paws pause. Parker recorded every trade he ever made, and his custom-built software program allows him to generate year-by-year profit/loss charts, segmented by trading system and by long and short trades. He continually used these programs to generate performance charts as we walked through his trading career in the interview.

How did you go from being a violinist seeking a career as a professional musician to becoming a trader?

In high school, there were two things I was really into—one was violin, and the other was computer programming. I tried to get into Juilliard but didn't make it. So I went to Mannes School of Music, which was my fallback choice, and I was probably one of the worst players there. Although I kept trying, I realized I wasn't going to be a star. I thought about switching colleges to major in computer programming, but, by that point, I was already in my junior year, and I thought I might as well finish my degree.

What prior experience did you have with computers?

My first exposure to computers was in ninth grade. They had a refrigerator-sized computer at my high school, and we were required to do some BASIC programming for algebra class. I thought it was a lot of fun, so I kept going back to the computer room. You typed your program on a Teletype. If you wanted to save your program, you had to print it out on a roll of paper this long [he spreads his hands out wide apart]. I carried around a box with little rolls of paper tape, which was my software library. Then I shifted my focus to the violin, and I didn't do much with computers for the rest of high school.

I got back into computers when I was in college. Mannes had an arrangement that allowed students to take courses at Marymount Manhattan College. I discovered Marymount had a computer lab with Apple IIs, and I spent a lot of time there playing around with them. My mother worked at an advertising agency, and her most important client was Digital. She mentioned my interest in computers to one of their vice presidents, and he said, "I have a spare one; I'll send it to him." After that computer arrived at my apartment in New York, I knew that programming, rather than music, was what I wanted to do.

What did you do after you graduated?

After I graduated, I moved back to Boston. I had no idea what I was going to do. I ended up taking a job in a computer software store. It was the early 1980s when the PC was just in its early days.

Did you have any idea of what you wanted to do with your life? I am assuming that being a salesman in the computer store wasn't it.

No, at that point, I was floundering. I was spending a lot of time writing programs.

What kind of programs?

I programmed some fun stuff like games. I also wrote a program to do my accounting. I did this programming on a primitive computer that had only 64K of memory. I remember spending $1,000 for a 10 MB hard drive.

How long did you stay at the computer store job?

I was there for only a few months. By pure chance, I met the president of a small software company called Cortex at a party. The company had about 20 employees, and he offered to get me an interview with their tech guys.

Had you tried to get a programming job after you graduated college before taking the computer store job?

No, because I had assumed I couldn't get a job as a programmer since I was just an amateur.

What happened at the interview?

I brought along some of the programs I had written for myself. They looked at the code and said, "Oh, you have some talent. We'll give you a try." They hired me at a low salary, similar to an intern level. But they gave me two raises in the first year to get me up to a level so that I would stay. I stayed there for five years.

Why did you leave?

Cortex developed software for DEC VAX minicomputers, and I wanted to work more on PCs, so I took a job at Softbridge, a company with about 100 employees that was more PC-focused. I stayed with them for three years until 1991. When we found out that our entire group was going to be laid off, our group leader made contact with a small startup called Segue Software, which had a contract with Lotus to port their spreadsheet software to Unix. Four of us formed a group called Software Quality Management. We were subcontractors to Segue, who were contractors to Lotus. They hired us to be the QA [quality assurance] group for the project.

In those days, most software testing was done manually, which was a very time-consuming and error-prone process. We created software that automated the testing using a methodology that we were able to patent.

Ultimately, Segue agreed to buy our technology in exchange for stock, and our group was merged into Segue. An interesting side note is that Jim Simons of Renaissance was the principal investor in Segue and was involved in the merger negotiations, which resulted in our getting stock in Segue in exchange for our technology.

At the time, did you know who Simons was?

Someone told me he was a rich guy who was a commodity trader. I didn't even know what a commodity trader was. I remember that we had a strict no smoking policy, and Simons was the one exception.

How did you make the transition from programming to trading?

There was a brief time in 1995 when we had the leading QA software, which coincided with a time when virtually any technology company could go public. Segue IPO'd in 1996 (ticker symbol: SEGU). The stock opened at $23 and then, in just over a month, rallied to a high over $40. At the high, my stake in Segue was worth about $6 million. I couldn't sell any stock, though, because we were still in the six-month lock-up period when employees aren't allowed to sell their stock. Shortly afterward, there was a correction in NASDAQ stocks, and some large customers delayed their buy orders, forcing us to issue an earnings warning. In two months, Segue fell from its high just over $40 to $10. I eventually sold out of my stock during 1997 and 1998 at an average price of about $13. I left Segue at the end of 1997 to trade.

You left to trade. How did you get interested in the market?

I got interested after my company went public. I owned about 150,000 shares, so I was very motivated to watch the stock price every day.

I understand that with virtually your entire wealth tied up in the IPO shares that you started monitoring the price of the stock. But how did you go from there to the idea that you could trade for a living?

That didn't happen right away. One of the board members of the local orchestra I played for was a CPA. The first thing I did was to go to him for advice. He referred me to a financial planner who gave me the usual financial planner's spiel about how the stock market goes up 11% per year and will do that forever. He explained how I could pay him 2% per year to put my money in mutual funds that also charged 2% per year. That plan didn't make a lot of sense to me. I started going to the bookstore, browsing through the investment section, and buying trading books. One of the first books I bought was *Trading for a Living* by Alexander Elder. I saw the title and thought, "Oh, people trade for a living. What a concept!"

When you left your job, did you have any idea about how you were going to trade?

It was all very clueless. I didn't have a plan. I just had this vague intuition that I could learn how to trade because I was interested in it. I thought it would be fun. I also liked the idea of having more time to spend with my family and practice the violin. It was just an experiment. I assumed I could always get another job.

I also developed a correspondence with Gary B. Smith, who was writing a column called Technician's Take for TheStreet.com. His method was an adaptation of William O'Neil's CANSLIM method, minus all the fundamental inputs and using much closer profit targets.* Gary described the strategy in several of his articles. It was the first time I had come across a detailed description of a systematic approach to trading, and it appealed to me. So I started emailing him and soon became his trading partner.

In February 1998, I decided to start trading using his method, which was partially discretionary and partially mechanical. The exits were fully defined. Once you were in a position, you would place a bracket exit order with a target that was 5% higher and a stop that was 7% lower (assuming a long position). The strategy would take both longs and shorts, and the main criterion was unusual volume. We both subscribed to *Investor's Business Daily*, and they published a table of stocks that had unusually high volume on the previous day—basically, stocks with a high ratio of the previous day's volume to the past 20-day average daily volume.

---

* Readers can find a description of O'Neil's CANSLIM method in William J. O'Neil, *How to Make Money in Stocks* (New York, McGraw Hill, 2009). O'Neil was also one of the interview subjects in *Market Wizards* (ibid., 221–238), and he described the CANSLIM method in his interview.

What would qualify as a high ratio?

Volume that was two times or more the recent average. We would look up all the stocks in that table and filter out stocks whose relative strength was less than 80 [stocks that had not outperformed at least 80% of other stocks during the past 52 weeks]. So basically, we were looking for strong-performing stocks that had unusually high volume on the previous day. These two conditions would narrow down the list of stocks considered for a trade to about 20 or 30. Here is where the discretionary part would come in. We would review the charts of those stocks, looking for stocks that had recent breakouts to new highs from prior consolidation periods.

You mentioned that you traded both longs and shorts. Were the sell signal conditions just the reverse of the buy signals?

No. The preconditions were the same as the longs—we were still surveying only strong-performing stocks that had abnormal volume. The difference was that for shorts, we were looking for stocks that had a sharp breakdown from recent highs, as opposed to a breakout to new lows.

I assume what you just described was Gary Smith's method. What did you bring to the table?

Initially, I didn't contribute much. I was mainly following his trades. But after we had traded together for a month for two, I said, "Why don't we try to test this method?" So I brought backtesting to the table. As we went along, to me, the process of looking at charts and deciding which trade to take seemed arbitrary. I wanted to test things. I didn't feel comfortable assuming some pattern worked just because somebody said so. I wanted to be able to quantify it.

What was Gary's response when you suggested testing the methodology?

He liked the idea. My idea for testing probably came up during a drawdown. That's what always motivates people to do testing [he laughs]. The first thing I did was to test different target exits and stop levels. This computer testing was my first step down the path towards naïve, over-optimized system development. It was very exciting to backtest and find out what would have worked best. At that point, I didn't have a clue about the dangers of curve fitting and data mining. I naïvely assumed that what had worked best in the past would continue to work best in the future.

Did anything useful come out of that initial testing?

I realized that using stops was detrimental to the system.

So how did you get out of positions if your profit target wasn't hit?

I would use a stop, but it was only activated on the close.

Oh, so you didn't eliminate stops, you eliminated intraday stops.

That's right. I found that by using intraday stops, I was getting stopped out a lot on meaningless intraday volatility.

Were there any other significant changes that resulted from your initial backtesting efforts?

The most significant impact was that once I got involved in building backtesting software, I became obsessed with it. At heart, I am more of a software developer than a trader. By mid-1999, I had become skeptical that there was any connection between how nice a chart pattern looked and the probability of a successful trade. I wanted to delegate chart evaluation to my software. Gary's trading identity, however, was built around how good he was at looking at charts. By that time, he had started a subscription service called *Chartman*, and he was putting out trading recommendations every day. So, although we stayed in touch, we each went our own way.

Had you developed a specific system that you were trading?

I didn't make an abrupt, full transition to mechanical trading. Through most of 1999, I was developing the software and continually tweaking my trading rules, while still allowing some discretion. By the end of November, I was up about 20% year to date, all of the profits coming from short trades. I got cocky and increased both the size and frequency of my short trades in December, just in time to catch an upside surge in stocks. During that last month, I ended up giving back almost all my profits for the year. My long trades, meanwhile, actually lost money in 1999—a rare feat. That experience permanently soured me on being a semi-discretionary trader, and I resolved to trade 100% mechanically from that point on.

Was the system still based on the trading method you learned from Gary?

Pretty much. My first independent backtesting discovery that I used profitably was the observation that the further a stock dropped on the first day, the more likely it was to continue falling. It was a finding I didn't want to believe because, instinctively, I thought the larger the initial drop, the more the stock was oversold. At first, I didn't even test for unusually large declines on the first breakdown day. I had restricted my test to a range of declines between 2% and 6%. Then I thought, "Why not go all the way?" I found that if there was a 20% drop on the first day, there was a very high probability of a continued price decline.

I'm curious, is that particular characteristic still valid in the markets?

No, although, initially, that pattern worked very well. From 2000 to 2012, I made more than half my profits from the short side using that strategy. But then in 2013, it stopped working.

We'll get there. In your first system, were there as many shorts as longs?

No, because since the system needed a more significant break on the downside for short entries than upmove for long entries, there were only about half as many short trades.

My methodology as it was evolving then, which I now understand is somewhat flawed, was to run a system until it had a drawdown, then backtest and find different parameters that wouldn't have had that drawdown, and switch to those parameters. [A *parameter* is a value that can be freely assigned in a trading system to vary the timing of signals. For example, if a system required a specified percentage price decline on a given day to generate a sell signal, the percentage would be a parameter value. The same system would generate different signals for different parameter values.]

Besides trading a fixed set of parameters until you had a significant drawdown, what was the specific system you were trading in 2000 when you first adopted a fully systematic approach?

I kept every system that I ever traded. [Parker searches his computer to find the exact system he traded in 2000.] In 2000, all the system profits came from the short side. Here are the complete rules for the short signals for the system I traded throughout 2000:

⚡ The average daily volume had to be at least 250,000 shares.

⚡ The price per share had to be at least $10 and no more than $150.

⚡ The breakdown day's volume had to be at least 15% greater than the highest volume during the past 20 days.

⚡ The price had to drop at least 5% after having been within 5% of a 20-day high or 10% after having been within 10% of a 20-day high.

⚡ The price break had to be at least $1.50 per share.

⚡ I would exit the trade either at a 12% profit target or a $3 stop—that's a very arbitrary stop [he says this in a surprised and amused tone, seeing this rule for the first time in many years]. There was an additional exit rule to liquidate the position on any up day with a higher volume than the previous day.

How long did you trade this system before making any significant change?

It was only about a year. Although the system did very well in 2000—in fact, it was my best calendar year ever—it had about a 20% drawdown in early 2001. I thought, "Well, that doesn't work anymore. I guess I'll have to quit." It looks like I stopped trading for over a month. [He points to the equity curve chart on his screen, which goes flat in March 2001.] I had been entering trades on the opening of the following day. The most significant change I made was to run the system about 20 minutes before the close so that I could enter trades on the close of the same day as the signal. I had developed an understanding that the pace of the markets was speeding up.

I used the same basic system, executing on the close, from March 2001 through 2004. Then in early 2005, I had another drawdown, and I couldn't find any parameters for my system that would have avoided that loss. I realized that even entering on the close was not quick enough and that I had to detect the signals earlier in the day. I came up with the innovation of using a stock's volume as of each minute of the day to project its daily volume. For those stocks that had projections for an abnormally high volume day, I would then use the same formula I had been using to generate trade signals. So starting at 9:35 a.m. and each minute after that, if based on its projected daily volume a given stock fulfilled the conditions for a trade, I would buy or short it then.

And did that change help?

I made the change in May 2005. Not only was the revised system immediately profitable, but the 24-month period between October 2005 and October 2007 was the most profitable period of my entire trading career.

What happened to the system version that executed on the close?

It never recovered. In 2014, as part of a presentation I gave, I generated an equity chart of the original system with executions on the close going back to the mid-1990s through the then-current year. It looked like the system executing on the close hit a brick wall in early 2005. In the decade before, it had made steady profits; after early 2005, it steadily lost money. In my entire history of testing trading systems, I have never seen such a sharp turning point. It wasn't just a matter of having the wrong parameters; the system with executions on the close just stopped working.

So you are saying that during the same period you were experiencing the best performance of your trading career, the same system executing on the close, instead of throughout the day, would have lost money. Transacting during the day made that much difference?

Yes. I typically had over a thousand trades per year, so the expected profit per trade was pretty low. Little things could make a big difference.

So the entire profitability of the system was dependent on executing intraday rather than waiting for the close. Did it give you any hesitation that the system was so tenuous that if you executed a few hours later it would have been a losing strategy?

No, because I try to think about why a system is working and what the edge is. I had observed that trading was speeding up. High-frequency trading had entered into the picture. Mutual funds had mostly transitioned from human execution to executing algorithmically throughout the day. It made sense that executing quicker could make a big difference. In those days, I would say, "The only edge is being early."

How long did this basic system with intraday executions continue to work?

In August 2011, the stock market had a massive decline. Although I had a significant loss in my long positions, it was offset by the gain in my short positions. That is how the strategy is supposed to work—that is, if the market has a major move, one side should compensate for the other. In 2012, however, I noticed that the short side was not doing its job. It didn't have a major drawdown, but it wasn't protecting against losses on the long side the way it should have. Late 2012 marked the beginning of an extended drawdown in my short strategy. That was effectively the end of my short strategy working.

Of course, now we are talking with the benefit of hindsight. When did you eventually decide the system was no longer working, and what did you do?

I've always struggled with how to distinguish between a routine drawdown and a system that has stopped working. The system had done well for many years, so I was reluctant to abandon it right away just because I had a feeling that something wasn't right. 2013 was a year when anybody should have made money on the long side. The stock indexes went straight up with virtually no significant drawdowns. My long positions underperformed the index, and my short positions got destroyed. It was my first losing year.

Well, with the stock index going straight up, the steady losses in your short positions are explainable.

Yes, but in other past years when the index had gone up, my short positions were closer to even. If you backtest long mean-reversion strategies for 2013, you will find they did great. [Mean-reversion systems sell on strength and buy on weakness based on the assumption that prices will pull back to some period average.] It was the period when people introduced the term BTFD (buy the fucking dip). What was happening was that the same signals used for my short trades became popular buy signals.

Deciding whether a system is in a temporary drawdown or has stopped working is the primary dilemma of the system trader. How do you deal with that? When you made these structural revisions to your system, such as moving from entering trades on the close to executing minute-by-minute intraday based on volume projections, what triggered the decision to make the change?

Sometimes it was just because I thought of it. I would think of an idea, test it, and say, "Whoa, that's much better," and then I would change my system to trade it. Generally, though, I'm much more motivated to brainstorm and test new ideas when I am in a drawdown.

Did the ongoing drawdown in 2013 trigger a similar search for new ideas?

It did. I decided to search the internet for new ideas. I found this trading site called Stockbee. I hung out in that forum and started sharing my trading history, as well as opening up about my recent problems. Someone suggested I might want to take a look at mean reversion.

Mean reversion, of course, is the exact opposite of what you were doing.

Yes, more or less. I had always assumed that mean reversion was the equivalent of catching a falling knife and wouldn't work. I had never tested the approach. Digging deeper, I found books by Keith Fitschen, Larry Connors, and Howard Bandy, which discussed mean-reversion strategies. I started testing some of those strategies and got excellent results.

What is the basic concept underlying the mean-reversion system you ended up using?

For the long mean-reversion system, the underlying requirement was that the stock had to be in an uptrend because you don't want to buy a stock that keeps going down and down. Then the following condition was that the stock had to be down a certain percentage from its recent high within a given time frame. If these two conditions were met, then I would enter a buy order a specified amount lower, with the exact amount lower based on the stock's average daily volatility.

Wouldn't the success of the system be very dependent on picking the correct parameter values?

No. Actually, the system is profitable for a broad range of parameters. The more extreme the parameters you use for entry, the fewer the trades, but the higher the expected profit per trade. Conversely, if you use more moderate parameters for entry, there are a lot more trades, but the expected win per trade is marginal. So you try to pick parameter values that are somewhere between these alternatives.

How do you exit your mean-reversion trades?

For a mean-reversion long trade, you enter on a limit order as the market is dropping, and you wait for a day with a higher close to exit the position. The hidden secret of mean-reversion systems is that, initially, trades usually show open losses as of the close, and they need to be held overnight to be profitable. You are not waiting for a big rebound. You are just trying to capture a bunch of small wins.

What if the trade goes against you? Do you have a stop?

There is no stop. If you use any stop—even a very wide one like 20%—it kills the results.

That's the inherent difficulty with mean-reversion trades. If you are going long, it implies that you are taking the position because the market has fallen too much, too quickly. If you then use a stop-loss order, and it is activated, by definition, you would be getting out at an even more extreme point, which would make the rules somewhat self-contradictory.

That's right. The more the rubber band is stretched, the higher the probability of the trade. That's why you can't use a stop.

Then how do you limit your risk? What if the market keeps on dropping each day without an intervening up day?

I use a five-day time stop. If a higher close doesn't occur within five days, I will liquidate the position. I now also keep the size of each position small enough so that even a total loss would not cause a 10% account drawdown, though I didn't do so at first.

Okay, so that's it. I felt something was missing. I knew there had to be some other rule to avoid a completely open-ended loss. So either you get your up day, or you liquidate your position after five days.

That's right. Also, I exclude biotech stocks from the universe of possible shorts because they have the possibility of multiplying in price in response to drug trial results or FDA decisions.

Are short mean-reversion trades the mirror image of long mean-reversion trades?

No, they are not.

What is the primary distinction between long and short mean-reversion trades, and why did you make that distinction?

Many people I know say, "I can't find a good short mean-reversion system." That is because they are trying to create a short mean-reversion system that is a mirror image of a long mean-reversion system. In other words, they are trying to design a system that will short a stock on a rebound in a downtrend. That just doesn't work. My short mean-reversion system is only looking to sell stocks that are in an uptrend.

So both your long and short mean-reversion trades are focused only on stocks that are in long-term uptrends. But then, if a market is already in an uptrend, how do you define a mean-reversion short trade?

Typically, these signals occur as part of a blow-off top in a major uptrend without any intervening correction. You are looking for a particularly prominent short-term upmove—namely, a large percentage price rise in a short period.

When did you switch from the momentum systems you were using to mean-reversion systems?

Although the mean-reversion strategies tested well, I was reluctant to make a complete switch. Instead, at the end of 2013, I decided to trade my classic momentum strategies, even though they were showing signs of failing, with half of my account, and the new long and short mean-reversion strategies I had just developed with the other half. During 2014, my original systems were about flat, while the new mean-reversion systems were up about 40%. My overall account, though, was up only 20% because I was trading the new systems with only half of my account. I felt angry that my cautious approach to phasing in the new systems had caused me to leave those extra profits on the table.

At the end of 2014, I decided my classic systems had lost their edge and that I would trade only the new mean-reversion systems going forward into 2015. And I was determined not to miss out this time, so I foolishly decided to allocate 120% of capital to them. The new systems did very well for the first four months of the year, gaining over 25%. My cumulative profits even hit a new high in May 2015. However, the rest of the year was a disaster.

That is when I discovered the tail risk inherent in mean reversion. First, there was a hit on the short side when I was shorting Chinese ADRs, and they just kept on going up. Then I took another hit after Hillary Clinton came out with a tweet about regulating drug prices, and the biotech sector fell apart. My mean-reversion system kept on buying these stocks, and they kept on going down. I not only gave back all my profits from earlier in the year, but I also finished 2015 with a net loss of about 10%. It was the worst drawdown of my entire trading career.

I didn't fully appreciate the extent to which losing trades can cluster together in time. It was the "eats like a bird, shits like an elephant" phenomenon. I knew about this possibility, and I had modeled my systems to account for it. I had analyzed in great detail how my systems would have done during every prior market correction since the 1980s. However, what emerged in 2015 that had not occurred in the prior data were sudden, large price moves in specific market segments (first China, then biotech) that subsequently persisted for longer than I had seen before.

To make matters worse, during this entire drawdown, I turned off my usual position size recalculation based on the daily account value and instead kept using the peak value. I had observed that mean-reversion systems often bounced back quickly from drawdowns, and I figured the system would recover faster with larger positions.

I had not yet discovered that, in contrast to my classic long and short momentum strategies, long and short mean-reversion systems don't naturally hedge each other. In mean-reversion systems, when the market is tanking, you don't get sell signals. So, you need to hedge a long mean-reversion system with a short momentum system.

At the end of 2015, I decided to put my original classic systems back into the mix. Almost immediately after making this change, I took a 10% loss in the first two weeks of 2016 when both long strategies tanked and neither short strategy compensated. I was now down 45% from the peak. At that point, it was all I could take, and I stopped trading. I had no confidence left. I just thought, "I can't do this anymore."

How did you regain your confidence?

I think it was just a matter of time passing. After a couple of months, I thought, "I can't quit. I have invested a lot into this. I know what I'm doing." I came up with a different, somewhat more conservative approach, and I have done pretty well since then.

It was also the first time I ever wrote a trading plan. I did it mainly for my wife to convince her that it was a good idea to resume trading rather than to do something else.

What was in the trading plan?

The most important rule was the inclusion of a system stop. Specifically, if I lost 10% from my starting level or 15% from an equity high after I was ahead at least 5%, I would stop trading.

Was that the first time you used a system stop?

No, I always had a 20% system stop. I hit those stops in 2001 and 2005, and I stopped trading both times.

How long were these hiatuses?

Until I did more backtesting, made some tweaks, and felt I was ready to start trading again.

Are we talking about days, weeks, or months?

In 2001, it was a couple of weeks. In 2005, it was a month or two. The more extended trading break in 2005 was mostly a consequence of my concluding that I needed to switch to a system of scanning for signals every minute during the day—a change that required time for new software development.

So a system stop was not something new. It was just that you were risking half the equity drawdown as before.

That's right.

When you resumed trading in March 2016, were you using only the long and short mean-reversion systems?

Initially, I was.

So adding back your classical systems only lasted for a few months?

It only lasted for a few weeks.

Since you were trading only the mean-reversion systems, what prevented the same type of drawdown you had experienced in 2015 when you were using only those systems?

I made several changes. I eliminated allowing the total position value to ever exceed 100%, even if it was only temporarily intraday. I switched from fixed-shares to fixed-percent-of-equity position sizing. Finally, I eliminated biotech stocks from both sides, after seeing how prone they were to extreme price moves.

What was the next significant change you made, and why?

I traded only my mean-reversion systems from March 2016 through December 2017. Although they did well during that period, ever since I had deactivated my classic momentum systems, I was looking for something to replace them. I like the idea of having a quad-system approach where you have long and short versions of both momentum and mean-reversion systems. If you are trading multiple systems that are well differentiated and diversify each other, the combination can be superior to the best individual system.

I noticed that a lot of the people on Stockbee focused on trading IPOs. That gave me the idea of limiting the trading universe to recent IPOs in backtesting momentum systems. I discovered that IPOs have some unique properties. I found that a very simple trend-following system based on buying new highs worked very well on recent IPOs, even though it didn't work at all on the general universe of stocks.

Was there also a short version of the IPO momentum system?

There was, but it didn't trade too often, and it didn't have much net impact. Also, this year [2019], I added a short momentum strategy that uses a mean-reversion entry.

So, are you now trading five systems?

I was for a while, but a few months ago, I deactivated the long mean-reversion system because of a risk-control rule I had added. I now will turn off a system if its equity curve goes below its 200-day moving average, which is what happened to the long mean-reversion system. It was the first time I used the concept of trading a system's equity curve as a signal to shut it off. The long mean-reversion system is currently in a 32% drawdown, but I only have a small loss in it this year because I am not trading it now.

When would you turn the system back on?

In some cases, I might reactivate a system if its equity curve went back above the 200-day moving average. However, the length and depth of the current drawdown make this system no longer attractive to ever trade again.

So you apply this approach for deactivating systems separately to each of your short and long strategies and only trade those systems that are on the right side of the 200-day moving average.

Right.

Doesn't that imply that you may sometimes find yourself trading only long or only short strategies?

Since I only recently started monitoring the system equity curves for deactivation signals, this year's long mean-reversion system decline below its 200-day moving average was the only time such an event has occurred. After concluding that this system was no longer usable, I recently spent several days brainstorming and testing other ways to structure a long mean-reversion strategy. I found and activated what I believe will be an effective replacement. Frankly, I am more likely to do new research than to reactivate a system that has stopped itself out.

What is your take on optimization? [*Optimization* refers to the process of finding the best-performing parameters for a given system. The underlying premise of optimization is that the parameters that worked best in the past have a higher probability of superior performance in the future. The validity of this premise, however, is open to question.]

You have to find the balance between looking for something that works better, while, at the same time, avoiding over-optimization. Early on, I didn't understand any of this. I would add any parameters I wanted, test over any range of values, even down to using decimal points, and then choose the parameter values that had the best past performance. I knew that was probably the wrong thing to do, but I didn't know what else to do. Eventually, I realized that frequent optimization doesn't help returns and that chasing the best recent parameters is an illusion.

What do you do differently now?

I have a bias in building a strategy to make it as simple as possible, using as few rules as possible, testing only a few parameter values that seem to be in a reasonable range. For example, if one of my parameters was the profit target, I might test values between 6% and 12% at 1% intervals. What I like is when the results don't differ too much between different parameter values because that means the system is robust. What's even better is when I can altogether remove a parameterized rule from a system. When I develop a new strategy now, I may not even run my optimization program.

What do you know now that you wish you knew when you started?

That's funny; I don't think I know that much even now. I feel in many ways, I am as clueless as I ever was [he laughs]. In one sense, my answer is "nothing" because if I knew everything I do now, I might never have tried trading in the first place. As my mother, who grew up very poor, didn't go to college and still had a very successful business career likes to say: "I succeeded because I didn't know that I couldn't."

Given that qualification, here are some insights that would have been helpful to know earlier on:

1. It's more effective to build a diverse collection of simple systems than to keep adding rules and re-optimizing a single system.

2. It's wise to include an on/off switch (e.g., an equity curve moving below its moving average) in each strategy, *even if it reduces profits in a backtest*. This rule can significantly limit losses if a system stops working, as can and will happen. The more strategies you run, the easier it is emotionally to turn one off. In this sense, this rule reinforces the importance of rule #1.

3. The tail-risk in a mean-reversion strategy is more likely to come from a cluster of medium-sized losing trades rather than from the potential for a huge loss in an individual trade. Allow for the possibility that the serial correlation of losses is probably understated in any backtest.

4. It is possible to succeed quickly, continue to do well for 15 years, and then have a near-career-ending drawdown. Therefore, it is advisable to maintain another income source, if possible.

5. Good things come from sharing your story and knowledge with others—something I was afraid to do for many years.

What advice would you give to someone who wanted to be a trader?

Don't quit your day job. Try to develop an appreciation for how much randomness there is in the market. Test everything. Don't assume something works or doesn't work just because someone says so. Maintain an ever-present spirit of experimentation.

Perhaps the most critical factor in Parker's long-term success is his willingness to substantively change or even entirely abandon systems when it appears they may have lost their efficacy. He made such major course shifts multiple times in his career, skirting disaster in the process. It is striking that some of the systems that Parker traded profitably for many years stopped working, and never recovered. If Parker didn't have the flexibility to radically alter his trading approach—even to the extent of switching from momentum systems to their exact opposite: mean-reversion systems—he would never have survived, let alone prospered as a trader.

A frequent recommendation given to systematic traders is to follow the rules of the system unwaveringly. This advice is sound for a system with a definitive edge and effective risk controls. In such cases, second-guessing system signals will frequently have a deleterious impact. It is in this context that Ed Seykota's first maxim cited at the start of this chapter—follow the rules without question—is intended to apply. And, indeed, Parker followed this prescription in designing a trading process that was 100% mechanical.

The problem, however, is that systems can work for a time but then entirely lose their edge, or even become consistent net losers. This uncomfortable reality implies that the ability to terminate or radically change systems is an essential ingredient to longer-term success as a systematic trader. It is this observation that Seykota's second assertion—know when to break the rules—is meant to address. Again, Parker adhered to this principle by changing his systems, sometimes radically, multiple times—actions that proved critical to his longer-term success.

One of the toughest dilemmas that face systematic traders is deciding whether an ongoing losing period for a system represents a temporary phase that will be followed by a recovery to new equity highs, or whether the system no longer works. There is no simple prescription for how to decide between these two opposite interpretations. However, the lesson systematic traders should draw from this chapter is that sometimes abandoning a system is the right decision. It is one of those rare instances where discipline in trading—in this case, following the system absolutely—may not be a good thing.

The trading strategy revisions that Parker made that were critical to sustaining profitability were all substantive. Examples include changing from entering orders on the close to entering intraday, switching from momentum to mean-reversion systems, and developing new systems that worked on IPOs, even though they didn't work more broadly. These types of structural changes are quite different from alterations such as changing parameter values, which are more cosmetic adjustments. Although Parker frequently changed the parameter values in his systems so that a recent drawdown would have been mitigated or eliminated if the revised parameter values had been used, he now recognizes that these changes made little difference in future profitability. Continually revising parameters to maximize past results (a process called *optimization*) can even have detrimental ramifications.

Traders who develop trading systems should be wary of the pitfalls inherent in optimization. The danger is not that optimization is likely to lead to worse trading results (although it may), but rather that it will give traders highly distorted expectations regarding the efficacy of the systems they test. In a worst-case, the overstated results that are implicit in optimization could lead system developers to select and trade a system that hindsight-free testing procedures would have revealed to have a negative expected return. Another danger is that over-optimization (fine-tuning a system to maximize past performance) can lead to designing systems that are too curve-fitted to the past to work well in the future.

Parker initially was oblivious of these pitfalls. With experience, he became aware of the distortions inherent in optimized results and the drawbacks of over-optimization. Regarding the deviation between optimized and actual results, Parker said, "Throughout my career, the systems I've used have generally shown annual returns of 50%–100% with maximum drawdowns of less than 10% in backtesting. Then in actual application, I get returns closer to about 20%, and that is what I expect." Parker now also severely limits the degree of optimization he uses, and, sometimes, he may not even run his optimization program when designing a new strategy.

Based on multiple empirical tests I have conducted in the past, my own key conclusions about optimization, which I believe are also consistent with Parker's views, can be summarized as follows:*

1. Any system—repeat, any system—can be made to be very profitable through optimization (that is in regards to past performance). If you ever find a system that can't be optimized to show good profits in the past, congratulations, you have just discovered a money machine (by doing the opposite, unless transaction costs are excessive). Therefore, incredible past performance for a system that has been optimized may be nice to look at, but it doesn't mean very much.

2. Optimization will always, repeat always, overstate the potential future performance of a system—usually by a wide margin (say, three trailer trucks' worth). Therefore, optimized results should never, repeat never, be used to evaluate a system's merit.

3. For many, if not most systems, optimization will improve *future* performance only marginally, if at all.

---

*   The following discussion of optimization is adapted from Jack D. Schwager, *A Complete Guide to the Futures Market* (New Jersey, John Wiley and Sons, Inc., 2017), 309–310.

4. If optimization has any value, it is usually in defining the broad boundaries for the ranges from which parameter values in the system should be chosen. Fine-tuning optimization is, at best, a waste of time and, at worst, self-delusion.

5. Given the above considerations, sophisticated and complex optimization procedures are a waste of time. The simplest optimization procedure will provide as much meaningful information (assuming that there is any useful information to be derived).

In summary, contrary to widespread belief, there is some reasonable question as to whether optimization will yield meaningfully better results over the long run than randomly picking the parameter values to be traded from reasonable value ranges. Lest there be any confusion, let me explicitly state that this statement is not intended to imply that optimization is never of any value. Optimization can be useful in defining the suboptimal extreme ranges that should be excluded from the selection of parameter values. Also, for some systems, optimization may provide some edge in parameter selection, even after suboptimal extreme ranges are excluded. However, I do mean to imply that the degree of improvement offered by optimization is far less than generally perceived. Traders would probably save considerable money by first proving any assumptions they are making about optimization rather than taking such assumptions on blind faith.

Risk management is as much an essential ingredient for success for systematic traders as it is for discretionary traders. Over the years, Parker adopted multiple risk control rules as part of his process. These rules include:

1. **Trading Stop**—Parker will stop trading if his account equity declines by a specified percentage. Initially, Parker used a 20% equity drawdown as a trigger to stop trading. In 2016, after contemplating quitting trading, he resumed trading but reduced this stop point to 10% (increasing this cut-out point to 15% once the account was ahead by 5%). A trading stop is a very effective risk management tool. It allows traders to determine the approximate maximum amount they can lose (assuming they have the discipline to adhere to their own rule). Traders can thereby define their worst-case outcome at the outset. By keeping this trading

cessation loss point small, traders can restrict losses to levels within their financial comfort zone.

An account-equity-based stop point can also allow traders multiple opportunities to succeed. Too many traders do not employ any account risk constraint, making them vulnerable to being knocked out of the game permanently by one large loss. Always keep your account risk small enough so that you have the opportunity to come back for another try with a clean slate if your initial trading foray is unsuccessful. The kitty in poker provides a useful analogy. If you have been dealt a lousy hand, you want to limit your loss to the kitty contribution rather than going all-in. You want to assure that you have the opportunity to try again with another hand.

2. **System Stop**—Parker will use trend-following applied to a system's equity curve to signal when a system should be deactivated. Specifically, Parker will stop trading a system if its equity curve falls below its 200-day moving average and wait to resume trading the system until its equity curve rises back above the 200-day moving average. There is nothing magical about the specific trend-following signal Parker uses. The critical concept is the idea of applying technical analysis to the equity curve as a risk-control method. This risk control strategy is not just applicable to systems but can also be implemented at the portfolio level for both systematic and discretionary traders.

Whether *trading the equity curve* of a system or portfolio is net beneficial will depend on the specific system or methodology employed. But traders should at least explore whether this approach would be net beneficial to them. Even in those instances where deactivating and activating a system (or portfolio) based on trend signals reduces total return, it can still reduce risk (e.g., mitigate drawdowns). The key consideration should be whether the approach increases return/risk. If it does, any reduction in return can be offset by increasing trade size, while still providing lower risk. Traders can find tools for applying technical analysis to their equity curves by linking or uploading their account data at FundSeeder.com. (Full disclosure: I have a financial interest in FundSeeder.)

3. **Position Sizing Adjustments**—In 2015, Parker learned the hard way of the dangers of increasing position size to make up for a prior missed opportunity. Trading size needs to be based on daily net account value and calculated using a consistent formula. Otherwise, while you might occasionally get lucky with an oversized win, you risk amplifying a cumulative drawdown.

Trading for a living is hard. Parker almost quit trading in early 2016, only eight months after having set new highs in cumulative profits and despite still being more than $5 million ahead. If you are trading for a living, it is not enough for your cumulative profits to continue rising. They have to continually keep climbing by more than the sum of taxes and cumulative withdrawals for living expenses. Parker's visceral experience with the difficulty of this task leads him to advise aspirants seeking to trade for a living to keep their day job as long as feasible.

MICHAEL KEAN

Complementary Strategies

MICHAEL Kean started investing in stocks as a hobby when he was a university student in New Zealand. After four years of working at financial service firms in jobs unrelated to investing or trading, he left New Zealand for London, hoping he would find a position closer to his interests in one of the world's leading financial centers. Kean never did get that market-related job. Undeterred, however, two years after arriving in London, he launched his asset management company, Steel Road Capital, managing a few small accounts for friends and family, as a side project to his day job. He eventually gave up the day job to focus full-time on portfolio management. Kean still operates as a one-man shop. Although he has outperformed the vast majority of hedge funds, Kean's assets under management remain quite small ($8 million), and he does not have any aspirations to manage large sums.

Over the years, Kean developed a unique management approach that combines long equity investment with short-term event trading, primarily on the short side of biotech stocks. In his short positions, Kean focuses on situations where less sophisticated buyers are more likely to be on the other side of the trade. These trades typically involve small-cap stocks witnessing fundamentally unwarranted rallies in response to news or an impending catalyst event.

The inverse correlation between the investment and trading components of his portfolio has allowed Kean to generate returns substantially outpacing equity indexes, while at the same time keeping his maximum drawdown under 20%. In the ten years since starting his management company, Kean has achieved a 29% average annual compounded return (before management fees), nearly triple the 11% S&P 500 return during the same period. His monthly Gain to Pain ratio (see Appendix 2 for definition) is also nearly triple the corresponding S&P figure: 2.86 versus 0.96.

Although living in London for a decade, Kean has retained a strong New Zealand accent, which, at times, left me befuddled as to what he had just said, forcing me to ask him to repeat himself. Sample: When he was talking about the advantages of using a managed account structure over a fund structure, I heard, "it saved me a lot of Edmund." "A lot of what?" I asked in confusion. It turned out he had said, "admin." At another point, when talking about a drug trial for a treatment for age-related macular degeneration (AMD), Kean kept referring to what sounded like "riskier injections," a phrase that made no sense to me. Finally, I had to stop him. "What do you mean by riskier injections?" I asked. After he repeated the phrase a couple of times, I realized, he had been saying "rescue injections." One more: During the interview, Kean kept using the term "closing grain" in talking about a stock's price movement. It seemed clear from the context that he was referring to a stock closing higher, and since I didn't want to interrupt him yet again to ask him what word he was saying, I let it go. It was only when I was listening to the interview recordings in writing this chapter that it finally dawned on me that he had been saying, "closing green." Kean took my difficulty with his accent in good humor, laughing at some of the misunderstandings. After our meeting, he sent an email, "If you have any issues deciphering my New Zealand accent, don't hesitate to reach out!"

Daljit Dhaliwal, a phenomenal trader (see Chapter 5) and an investor with Kean, offered this comment, "Michael is unique because he combines two very different approaches: long equities on one side and a unique short strategy on the other. His ability to do both shows how adaptable he is as a person, and adaptability is critical in the game of speculation."

As a native New Zealander, where did you get your interest in markets? I assume it's probably not a big thing in New Zealand.

Well, it's funny you should say that. Actually, the New Zealand stock market was a big thing in the 1980s, and then it was very quiet for a long time. The story I heard from my mom and dad when I was growing up is that they were able to afford the deposit on the farm they now own because of a stock market windfall. During the 1980s, there was a massive stock market boom in New Zealand. The catalyst for the bull market was that New Zealand transitioned from one of the most closed economies in the world to one of the most open in a few years. Tariffs, subsidies, and taxes were all substantially reduced.

I assume that was due to a change in government?

Yes, the Labour Party came in and shook things up.

Wouldn't the Labour Party be left of center?

They were.

And they pushed for opening the economy?

Funny, isn't it?

Well, I guess we have the exact opposite oddity in the US now, with Republicans supporting Trump's trade wars and massive deficits.

There was also a great deal of financial deregulation. As a result of all of these policy changes, a lot of money found its way into the New Zealand stock market.

Was it external or internal money?

I assume it was both, but it was a classic retail-driven boom. Everyone was in on it, and mom and dad were just like everyone else. They put all their savings into the stock market. They sold all their stock holdings in early 1987 to buy farmland, something they always wanted to do. They sold their stock then because they had bought their house with the assistance of a government subsidy that required they hold the property for five years. As soon as the five years were up, they were free to sell their home and buy a farm. They were very lucky. If the requirement had been six years instead of five, the story would have ended very differently. Your Black Monday was our Black Tuesday. The 1987 crash in the US was the event that popped the New Zealand stock market bubble. Within six months, the stock market was down 50%. It didn't recover to the old highs for over 20 years.

What percent profits did your parents make on their investment?

I don't know, but the New Zealand market went up sixfold, and they sold within a half-year of the high. So, I would guess they at least tripled their money.

So, the fact that your parents made enough money in the stock market to buy a farm, albeit by luck, registered with you. How old were you at the time they sold their stock and bought the farm?

I was only about five years old. But it was a story that was passed on as I was growing up, and that story stuck with me. My dad has a different perspective on his stock market windfall. He insists it was pure skill.

How did your interest in markets and trading develop beyond the family story?

My interest in markets developed when I was attending university. I had a group of friends who were always talking about the stock market. There were eight of us, and we ended up setting up an investment club. We each chipped in a grand for a pooled investment account. Initially, it was like a typical share club where we had meetings, and everybody had some input. But, eventually, only two of us, myself and one of the other members, ended up doing all the work, and everyone else just went along with our stock selections. After we graduated, my friend got an investment banking job, and he had to stop participating. So from 2004 on, I managed the portfolio on my own. The share club continued through 2010.

How was the performance?

Until 2008, it was average at best. Then in 2008, we lost 50% in six months. However, I realized that stocks were insanely cheap. I convinced some of the investors to double down, and the portfolio was up 88% in 2009.

Why did the share club end in 2010?

I wanted to convert it from a share club constitution into a formal investment structure. I used the strong 2009 performance to convince some of the club investors to invest with me in a managed account structure.

How much time were you devoting to the investment side?

I spent as much time as I could. I was working in London at the time, and I was fortunate to have a job with a very flexible work-at-home policy. I would get up very early every day to do my salaried work in the morning, and then I would trade the US markets in the afternoon. It was a unique situation that allowed me to almost be a full-time trader and still pay the rent.

Why did you leave New Zealand for London?

It's common for New Zealanders in their 20s to head over to London for a few years.

Did you move to London intending to find a market-related job?

Yes, London is a world financial center, so I thought it would be a good opportunity to work for a bank or a fund manager—something more in line with my interests.

Did you have any trouble finding a job in London?

I landed in London in September 2008! [He laughs as he says this because his arrival coincided with the financial meltdown.] I still remember exiting the Tube [London subway] and picking up the free newspapers they hand out. Every day, the headline was about how many people had been laid off in the City the day before. The figure was always in the tens of thousands.

How did you find a job in that type of environment?

I was able to get a three-month contracting job doing spreadsheet work. The three months ended up being extended to four years—at which point, I quit to devote full time to trading.

What strategy did you use when you started trading managed accounts?

Initially, I started by combining buy-and-hold investing with macro trading. I never had much success with the macro trading part. I didn't like it because you are trading huge markets, and there is always going to be someone out there who knows more than you do. My first significant success was shorting pump-and-dump stocks on the OTC. These were stocks that would go from 50 cents to $5 or $10 on virtually nothing and then collapse in a day. I found these research services and blogs that covered penny stocks. Most of them were focused on the pump, but I was interested in the services that focused on shorting these stocks.

I understand how these stocks can have a big run-up and then go back to virtually zero. But, to me, the difficulty seems to be in gauging how far they can go. If a worthless stock can go from 50 cents to $5, it can just as easily go to $10. So how do you get short without taking a huge risk?

Pump-and-dump stocks are unique in their price action compared with regular stocks. The typical pattern would be for the stock to start at a price like 50 cents and then go up every day by 20 or 30 cents. The critical catalyst was when the stock couldn't close up for the day; that would signal the pump was struggling, and the move was over.

Are you literally saying that these stocks would go up in stair-step fashion every day, until the first day they didn't, and then they would go straight down?

Yes, after the first down day, they could be down 60%–70% the next day. It was such a great strategy because these stocks always moved up in a gradual, controlled fashion. You never had the wild parabolic upmoves you can sometimes get in real stocks.

And that always worked? Did you ever go short after the first down day, and then have the stock go back to new highs?

I never had a significant loss in selling a pump-and-dump stock. But, you would only get one of these opportunities once a quarter or so.

How long did you use this strategy?

I traded it about a year or two.

Since it was such a consistent winner, how come you didn't use it longer?

Getting the short availability was very hard, and the strategy was not scalable. Also, the frauds were so brazen that the SEC eventually became more active in halting trading in these stocks.

Given that you only had a handful of these trades per year for two years or less, it sounds like the pump-and-dump shorting strategy was only a minor part of your portfolio. What was the basis of the bulk of your trades?

My real niche outside of my core buy-and-hold investing has been trading biotech stocks, which probably accounted for about 60% of my profits over time.

What was the strategy that you were using?

Biotech stocks are excellent trading vehicles. They have critical catalysts, such as clinical results for phase 2 and phase 3 trials, which are make-or-break events for small biotechs. The variability of the valuation of these companies, depending on the outcome of these trials, can provide great trading opportunities.

Biotech is a highly specialized area. How could you trade around such events, given that you didn't have any background in biology or medicine?

There are patterns in how these stocks behave that can be traded profitably without being an expert in the field. For example, in a healthy market, you can buy small-cap biotechs two or three months before a critical catalyst, such as the release of the results from a phase 3 trial. I would buy these stocks before the hype started, before brokers started issuing upgrades on the stock, and before retail clients started buying on the prospect that the stocks could skyrocket if the trial results were successful. And, I would sell the stock before the trial results were announced. Some stocks would double just on the expectation of the release of trial results.

Did you have situations where these stocks trended down instead of up going into the trial result announcement?

That could and did happen when the general market had a correction. However, the major pitfall in the strategy was that you needed to know when the trial results would be announced. Most small-cap bio stocks—I am talking about companies in the $100–$400 million range—generally have low-quality assets. If they are in a phase 3 trial and still have that low of a market cap, it suggests it is unlikely they are onto something. All the big pharma companies pick over companies when they are in phase 1 and phase 2, and the fact that they have chosen not to be involved with a company in a phase 3 trial has negative implications.

Were there situations where you couldn't narrow down when the trial results were going to be released?

I either avoided stocks where I didn't have any idea when the results would be released, or I got out much earlier than I normally would to minimize the possibility of still being in the stock when the results were announced.

Did you ever get caught still holding a stock when the trial results were announced?

There were a couple of times when the trial results came out entirely unexpectedly, and I was still in the position.

What happens in a case like that?

You lose 60% or 70% on the stock.

Do you still use that strategy?

Just a little bit. It's a pretty minor strategy for me now. Drug pricing in the States is a big issue, and biotech has been an underperforming sector.

What other types of strategies do you use?

Occasionally, I will bet on trial results in a biotech company.

What would prompt you to bet on the direction of the trial results?

There are circumstances where the odds for failure are very high, even if you don't know anything about the drug itself. For example, there has never been a biotech company with a market cap under $300 million that has had a cancer drug pass in a phase 3 trial.

Is that because if the drug had promise, big pharma would have bought them out?

That or the market cap would be $1 billion instead of $300 million.

Could you sometimes be long a stock in the period before the trial results were released and then switch to short going into the result announcement?

Yes, but you have to be careful about the short side because there could always be a surprise. I will typically use puts for these trades rather than shorts.

Are there other strategies you use to trade biotech besides the two we have just discussed?

Most of the trades I do in biotech are short-term trades—intraday to a few days—and most of them are on the short side.

What drives those trades?

Of course, the main news items in biotech relate to clinical trial results, but there is also an entire realm of other news items that impact biotech stocks. It could be news from the FDA; it could be the release of additional data from a phase 3 trial; it could be some corporate announcement. The company might issue a press announcement, and the stock could be up 20% to 30%. My job is to decipher whether that news was expected and whether it has any meaning or is just a spin job. Biotech is a funny industry; it can attract horribly promotional management.

Can you give me an example of that type of trade?

A good example is Avinger (AVGR) earlier this year [2019]. They released positive phase 3 data, and the next day the stock rallied nearly 40% from the previous day's close. However, when you examined the press release, it turned out that it was follow-up data to the original data released two years earlier. So, it wasn't news. Moreover, the fundamentals of the company were negative, with weak sales and large debt. I went short and was out within two days, by which time the stock had given back its entire gain and then some.

Last year [2018] was your first losing year. What went wrong?

I was down 4%, which was precisely in line with the S&P performance. My longs did way worse than the S&P, but my shorts bailed me out.

Why did your longs do so poorly?

I was overexposed in Chinese stocks, which took a big hit on the trade war. JD.com was my biggest loser.

What kind of company are they?

They are the Chinese equivalent of Amazon. I originally purchased the stock around $20 in 2016 when it was trading at a cheap valuation. The stock went all the way up to $50 by early 2018. I took profits on some of the stock at higher prices, but I still held onto about two-thirds of the position. By 2018, a couple of things had changed fundamentally. The company was no longer gaining market share, and other Chinese stocks were beginning to break down. Those were red flags, but the real warning sign came when JD.com announced a deal in which Google would invest in the company and promote its products on Google's shopping platform. The stock gapped higher on the news, opening near the highs of the day, and then closed sharply lower. I should have been out before that day on the changing fundamentals, but the worst mistake was ignoring that day's price action. As someone who trades for a living, I should have known better. Over the next few months, the stock went back down to $20.

And you held it all the way down?

[He laughs] I held it all the way down.

Had you ever made that type of mistake before?

Yes, when I first started.

Why do you think you made that mistake again with JD.com?

Part of it was that I had fallen in love with the position. Also, I had been doing very well on my short-term trades, so I justified that I could hold on to the position.

What happened when the stock went back down to $20?

At $20, the stock valuation was ridiculously low again, so I added back the portion of the position I had sold at higher levels. [Update: By spring 2020, JD.com had fully recovered and moved to new all-time highs.]

Is all your short-term trading in biotech?

The majority is, but about 20% of my short-term trades are in other sectors. As an example, I recently shorted Beyond Meat (BYND) after McDonald's announced they were going to experiment using their product in some of their Canadian restaurants. The market jumped from a closing price of $138 to a preopening price well above $160 on the news.

Why did you go short?

The reasoning was similar to the biotech short we discussed. It was great that McDonald's announced they would test their product, but Beyond Meat had been issuing these types of announcements ever since they listed the stock, and McDonald's was the only major chain left that they hadn't made a deal with. So this news was entirely to be expected.

So, you're saying that the news was already priced into the stock.

I think the stock was pricing in a lot more than that. After listing earlier this year [2019], the stock saw a parabolic move from $45 to $240 in a couple of months. The rally was so extreme because the stock had a small float, and there was a short squeeze. Once the news came out that the founders were selling a portion of their holdings, the stock collapsed back to under $140 in less than two weeks. So, another reason why I went short was that it was already a broken stock when the news about McDonald's came out. I wouldn't have stepped in front of that news if the stock was still in its roaring up phase; I was only willing to go short because the character of the stock was completely changed.

When you go short into a bullish news rally like that, how much are you willing to risk on the trade?

For a trade like that, I would use a stop that allows the stock to move roughly 10% against me. On a non-biotech position, I'll risk only about 30 basis points of the portfolio and size the position accordingly. On biotech stocks, which are more my bread-and-butter type of trades, I may risk closer to 1% of the portfolio on a single trade and, sometimes, even as high as 2% or 3% if I have a particularly good setup on the trade.

Is there a structure as to how you combine your different strategies into a portfolio?

Generally, I will have roughly 60% of the portfolio in long positions—a percentage that can vary up or down, depending on how cheap or expensive I think the general market is—with the remaining portfolio utilized for short-term trading and the occasional longer-term biotech short. To use an analogy to the typical 60/40 long equity/long bond portfolio, where the bond position is used for diversification, in my 60/40 portfolio, short-term trading provides the diversification.

What percent of your short-term trading is from the short side?

About 70%.

How do you select the stocks in the long position portion of your portfolio?

My long book can be broken into two parts: large-cap stocks, which I buy when they are getting hammered on what I consider indiscriminate selling, and small-cap stocks with high revenue growth.

Can you give me an example of a large-cap stock you bought because of indiscriminate selling?

One long I currently hold is Bayer, which acquired Monsanto a little over a year ago. Shortly after their acquisition, Monsanto was hit by a massive lawsuit based on claims that their weed killer caused cancer. It is trading at a 40%–50% discount to average historical valuation levels. You could argue that the market is pricing in €30–€40 billion of potential legal liabilities. The way I see it, assuming a €30–€40 billion liability is pretty outrageous. Other than for tobacco, there has never been any settlement larger than €10 billion. I expect that the Monsanto settlement will be closer to €5–€10 billion.

How do you choose your small-cap holdings?

Typically, I am looking for companies that are growing very fast—at least 20% to 30% revenue growth per year—but haven't reached scale yet. So, they are companies that are probably losing money at the moment, but if they execute correctly, they will have reasonable earnings-per-share within two or three years and a prospect for the stock doubling or tripling in that time. I like these types of fast-growing stocks because if they hit their targets and start earning money, there is a catalyst to move the stock price higher.

What is your risk management process?

In a recession, the market will typically go down 20%–30%. Assuming my 60% long portfolio does no better than the market, it will lose approximately 12%–18%. I would expect my short-term trading and short positions to cover that loss.

So, a key element of your risk management is your portfolio construction. How about risk management in individual positions?

On my catalyst short positions where I'm looking for a company to fail on an upcoming trial, I might risk 1%–2%. At the moment, I'm risking more than that on one trade because I'm up over 20% year to date. On a typical short-term trade, like the Beyond Meat trade we discussed, I will risk 30 basis points.

What was your most painful trade?

It was a trade I did in 2012, which was early in my career when I didn't have the type of risk management controls I do now. It was a technology stock called Broad Vision (BVSN) that went up fourfold in just over a month. Even management was saying they didn't know why the stock was up so much. Although it was a real company, the stock price moved just like one of the pump-and-dump stocks, and I traded it the same way. The stock had gone from $8 to over $30 in just over one month, and I shorted it the first time it broke down. But unlike the pump-and-dump stocks, which just kept on going down once their uptrend broke, this stock reversed back sharply to the upside. It nearly doubled on me within a few days, resulting in about a 10% loss of my portfolio value. I couldn't handle it anymore and capitulated.

What eventually happened to the stock?

It got as high as $56 and then went all the way back down to $8.

After that, did you ever have a large loss on a single trade?

I never had another material loss in the trading portion of my portfolio. My big losses have always come from my longs.

I assume that is because you don't have stops on your investment longs since you count on the trading portion of your portfolio, which is primarily short-biased, to provide a hedge on your longs.

That's correct.

Have there been any situations where you had a long position with a substantial loss, and you decided to take it because you were wrong on the trade?

In 2014, I was up 35% for the year with only a month to go, so it felt like I had earned the right to take more risk [he laughs at the recollection]. Unfortunately for me, the next trade idea that popped up was triggered by the price slide in the oil and gas sector, which was getting completely smoked at the time. I started loading up on—it's ridiculous when I look back on it now—Russian stocks and MLPs, which are pipeline distribution companies. The stocks had gone down 70%, and I thought they wouldn't go down any further, except they did.

And these were part of your long portfolio, so there were no stops.

That's right.

At what point did you decide to get out because you were wrong?

I got out two weeks later when I was down 7% on these stocks. If I had stayed with those positions for a couple more weeks, I would have gotten out with only a small loss. But I had no business being in those positions.

Was that because these stocks were outside your normal sphere?

That's right. They had nothing to do with my expertise. It was just reckless trading. Instead of waiting for a good set up, like a biotech short, I went crazy buying these stocks, which I knew nothing about, just because they were down a lot.

Was that the only time you strayed from your approach this way?

Yes, since then, I've been disciplined about sticking to my types of trades.

What do you know now that you wish you knew when you started?

You want to be underconfident rather than overconfident. When I was a new trader, I would do some research on a stock and think I knew more than everyone else. Now, I am the complete opposite. I assume I am the dumb one and trade accordingly. At best, my success rate is going to be 50%–70%. So I'm always looking for reasons why I shouldn't be in the trade if it's not working.

Do you do anything differently when you are in a losing phase?

I still keep trading, but I reduce my risk per trade. If I would typically take a 1% risk on a good set up, I'll cut it down to 30 basis points.

What advice would you give to someone who wants to be a trader?

⚡ You need to be persistent. Realize that it is a long road to develop a decent edge.

⚡ You need to know your edge and develop your trading process around that edge.

⚡ You need to be great at learning from your mistakes. Analyze every mistake you make until you learn something from it and then incorporate what you learn into your process.

⚡ You need to love trading so that you can get through the tough times.

It is ironic that trades that appear highly risky—e.g., short biotech stock positions held into clinical trial announcements, and shorts implemented after overnight price gaps triggered by corporate announcements—are a core component of Kean's risk mitigation strategy.

Appropriate risk management encompasses two tiers: the individual trade level—limiting the loss on any single trade—and the portfolio level. At the portfolio level, there are again two components. First, analogous to individual trades, there are rules to limit the loss for the portfolio as a whole. Such rules might include a defined process for reducing exposure as a loss drawdown deepens, or a specified percentage loss at which trading is halted. The second element of risk management at the portfolio level pertains to the portfolio composition. Positions that are highly correlated would be limited to the extent feasible. Ideally, the portfolio would include positions that are uncorrelated and, even better, inversely correlated with each other.

The concept of building a portfolio of uncorrelated and inversely correlated positions lies at the heart of Kean's trading philosophy. Any long-only equity portfolio faces the problem that most of the positions will be highly correlated. The majority of Kean's portfolio consists of a long equity component (approximately 60% on average, although this level can range depending on Kean's assessment of the prevailing potential return/risk of the overall equity market). Kean solves the problem of a long equity portfolio inherently consisting of highly correlated positions by combining this portion of his portfolio with a trading strategy that is, on balance, inversely correlated with long equities.

The trading portion of the portfolio consists mostly of very short-term trades and, to a lesser extent, longer-term short positions in the biotech sector. The inverse correlation derives from the fact that nearly three-quarters of the short-term trades, as well as the longer-term biotech positions, are shorts. Even the long positions in the trading portion of the portfolio are uncorrelated to the long equity investment holdings because they are day trades tied to company-specific events. By combining two inversely correlated segments, Kean is able to extract the long-term appreciation in equities without the typical downside exposure of long equity portfolios in bear markets.

Kean's unique method for hedging his long equity exposure, which relies heavily on shorting biotech stocks, is not applicable or advisable for most traders. However, it is not the specific method that Kean uses to reduce portfolio risk that is pertinent to readers. Instead, it is the concept of seeking uncorrelated and, preferably, inversely correlated positions that is important. Traders need to not only focus on their trades but also pay attention to how these trades combine in a portfolio.

Kean also applies risk management at the individual trade level, a practice that is particularly critical for short trades, which pose, theoretically, unlimited risk. Kean learned the importance of limiting the risk on individual trades early in his career when he shorted a stock in a parabolic upmove without a plan on what to do if he was wrong. The stock price nearly doubled on him in a matter of days, resulting in a 10% hit to his portfolio—his worst loss ever. He never repeated this mistake. Kean will typically limit risk to 1% on his biotech trades, his area of expertise, and to only 30 basis points on non-biotech trades. Also, while Kean does not use protective stops on his long equity positions, large-cap holdings are only entered after a sizeable retracement, limiting further downside scope in these positions.

Usually, Kean is rigorous in taking only those trades that fit the criteria of one of his strategies. In late 2014, though, Kean let his discipline lapse. He was up 35% for the year, with only one month left. He felt he had earned the right to take more risk, given his profit cushion. The trade he took— buying a group of energy-related stocks because the sector was down sharply—had nothing to do with his standard methodology. Within two weeks, he had surrendered 7% of his profits for the year. It is commonplace for traders to get sloppy when they are doing particularly well. Beware of letting a period of strong performance go to your head.

Important fundamental news that results in counter-to-expected price action can often represent a critical signal. The price action in JD.com after the announcement of a deal with Google—an initial upmove followed by a sharply lower close—provided a perfect example of this principle, as the stock moved sharply lower in the ensuing period.

PAVEL KREJČÍ

The Bellhop Who Beat the Pros

W<small>HO</small> is Pavel Krejčí?* (Apologies to Ayn Rand.) That is what I wondered when I saw his account consistently show up in the top 10 and often top five traders on the FundSeeder.com leaderboard. FundSeeder.com is a website that provides traders with free performance analytics and the ability to create verified track records by linking their brokerage accounts to the site. (Full disclosure: As a founding partner, I have a financial interest in FundSeeder.)

Every time I looked, Krejčí's equity curve showed a steadily rising trend, virtually quarter after quarter. The return stream was Madoff-like, except, in this case, I knew the numbers were real because Krejčí's account was "verified." (As a linked account, his returns were received directly from a prominent brokerage firm.) Finally, I called Krejčí to get the story behind his incredible performance. Here is what I discovered.

Krejčí lives in the Czech Republic. After graduating high school, he did a year of military service. He then worked as a bellhop in Prague for ten years. Midway through this job, Krejčí opened a restaurant, while

---

* Pronounced: Cray-chee.

still maintaining his bellhop job because he needed the money. During this period, he worked 14-hour days between his job and business. The restaurant failed after 10 months. "I couldn't manage people," Krejčí says in explaining his unsuccessful venture.

While still working as a bellhop, Krejčí opened a stock account with $20,000, hoping to establish a trading career. His first foray into trading did not go well. After losing 80% of his starting stake in six months, he closed his account at year-end 2005. Krejčí spent the next six months researching and developing a methodology. By mid-2006, he felt confident he was onto something. Krejčí opened another stock account with $27,000, which included money he borrowed from his brother. Within a little over a year, he had more than doubled his account and felt confident enough to quit his bellhop job.

Krejčí is a long-only equities trader with a 14-year track record that trounces 99% plus of long-only professional managers. I would bet that last sentence would be accurate using 99.9% instead of 99%, but I don't have the data to verify.

For the first 2-1/2 years after resuming trading (mid-2006 through 2008), Krejčí achieved an average annual compounded return of 48%. Even more impressive than his average annual return level during this period is the fact that he was up 13% in 2008 trading a long-only equity strategy—a year when the S&P 500 index was down 37%! Unfortunately, Krejčí only had annual statements available for these early years, so I could not include them in calculating his return/risk statistics.

For the subsequent 11-1/2 years, Krejčí's average annual compounded return was 35.0% (versus 13.6% for the S&P 500), with a maximum drawdown of only 13.2% based on daily data (7.0% using month-end data). His return/risk metrics were outstanding: an adjusted Sortino ratio of 3.6, a monthly Gain to Pain ratio of 6.7, and a daily Gain to Pain ratio of 0.81 (see Appendix 2 for the definitions and interpretation of these statistics). These return/risk statistics are between three to seven times the corresponding S&P 500 levels. Krejčí's outperformance versus the S&P 500 would have been substantially greater if his earlier years could have been included in these calculations. Krejčí's performance has also been remarkably consistent: He had positive returns in 93% of all quarters.

Krejčí has the distinction of having by far the smallest account of anyone ever included in a *Market Wizards* book. His trading account has generally ranged between $50,000 and $80,000. Krejčí trades only stocks with extremely high volume, so his methodology could easily be applied to a much larger portfolio. Given the liquidity of the stocks he trades and his exceptional performance, why is his account size so small? The answer is straightforward: Krejčí uses his trading profits to pay for living expenses. So, although his returns have been consistently excellent, he has never been able to build his account size.

I interviewed Krejčí during the 2020 pandemic, which ruled out travel and a personal meeting. So our "meeting" was via Zoom.

How was Krejčí able to achieve his exceptional performance using a long-only equity strategy? That was the main subject of our interview.

———————

I know you ended your education after high school. Did you consider going to university?

I was not a very good student. It's funny now, but I remember my high school economics teacher telling me, "Pavel, you will never do any job that has anything to do with economics." The high school grading system ranged between 1 and 5, with 1 being best and 5 being worst. I had a 3 in economics. I did even worse in math, in which I got a 4. I knew I wouldn't survive one day at a university. I don't think that education is that important in trading; a passion for learning how to trade is far more crucial.

What gave you the inspiration to start trading?

When I worked at the hotel, I saw many businessmen reading *The Wall Street Journal* or the *Financial Times*. I thought, "What a great job, just to sit there, read the newspaper, and make some calls to place trades." I thought that trading for a living would be a great life. Of course, I didn't have any experience, and I didn't know anything. In 2005, I opened a stock account to start trading.

Were you trading US stocks?

I traded US stocks from the very beginning.

What did you read to get some knowledge about the markets and trading?

I read some local books on technical analysis. I also read your *Market Wizards* book, which was translated to Czech.

What was your trading approach when you began?

I had no approach at all. If a stock looked like it was going up, I would buy it. I didn't use stops, which was my biggest problem.

How large was the account?

$20,000.

What happened with that account?

I lost half the money and stopped trading. I was bad at trading, but an even bigger problem was that I was using a local broker and paying $10 round turn for 100 shares. If you are paying those type of commission levels, it is impossible to make money day trading.

How long did you stop trading for?

I didn't trade for a little over half a year. I saved some money to add to the account and borrowed another $5,000 from my brother so I would have enough money to place at least three day-trades a day.

Did you develop a methodology in the interim?

Yes. It was similar to the same method that I still use today. The biggest difference was that, at that time, I didn't pay any attention to the volume or liquidity of the stocks I traded.

Were you still working as a bellhop during this time?

Yes. I waited until I had a full year of profitable trading before I quit my job, which I did near the end of 2007.

So, since then, have you supported yourself on your trading profits?

Yes, and I also made a little money at the beginning in sports betting. It was not hard to beat some bookies. But when they know what you are doing, they kick you out.

What sports were you betting on?

All sports. The sport didn't make any difference.

What was your betting method?

It's called sure betting; it's a type of arbitrage.

Since the bookies will take a cut, how can you have an arbitrage?

You bet on both sides. For example, let's say there is a match between Germany and England. I would simultaneously bet on Germany with England bookies and on England with German bookies.

Are you saying that the odds would be different in different countries, depending on who the favorite was?

Yes. Since most people bet on their national team, the bookies have to adjust their odds shortly before the match, decreasing the payoff on the national team and increasing the payoff on the foreign team. There is a short time window when arbitrage can occur—usually only a few seconds. You have to be quick to catch it. The profit on the bets was very small, but you couldn't lose. I did it for about a year and a half until they stopped taking my bets and closed my account.

How long did it take you to develop your trading methodology?

A little over one year. At the time, I was still working a full-time job. I was probably spending 16 hours a day between my job, stock research, and trading.

Did you try approaches you discarded?

In the beginning, I tried lots of things, including longer-term trading, but I found that it just wasn't my nature to hold trades.

So what did you find that worked for you?

I looked for stocks that moved a lot in one day. I looked at stock charts back to 1997, and I noticed that for many stocks there were four times a year when there was a particularly big daily move. At first, I wondered why that happened. Then I found out that these price moves were caused by earnings reports. I discovered similarities in the price action in stocks the day after earnings that held as far back as I had data, which was 1997.

Since you are trading just on earnings reports, I assume most of your trading is concentrated in a minority of trading days.

Yes, most of my trades occur in the approximate month-long period each quarter in which most earnings reports are released. Some earnings reports are released outside of these periods. So I would say my year breaks down as four months in which I make most of my trades, three months of lighter trading, and five months when I focus on research.

What kind of research do you do?

I review my previous trades to see how I could have done better. For example, I try to answer questions such as: Would I have done better if I held the trade longer?

You do that trade research manually?

Yes, manually. I would say my job is 95% analyst and 5% trader. I am not a frequent trader. I have to see a high-percentage opportunity before I take a trade.

How large is the universe of stocks that you follow?

About 200–300.

Do those stocks share some common characteristics?

They are stocks that have very high daily volume. On the days after earnings reports, which is when I trade, the average volume of the stocks is 5 to 10 million shares.

Since your trading size is minimal and liquidity is not an issue, why is high volume the most important characteristic?

Many years ago, I thought that I might one day be able to trade a much larger account. So I switched from trading any stock to just those stocks with high liquidity.

Was your motivation then that if you were successful and were able to attract assets to manage, you could continue to use the same methodology?

Exactly.

Do you take both long and short trades after earnings reports?

No, I will only be a buyer. I never go short.

What percent of your trades are made following bullish earnings reports as opposed to bearish earnings reports?

I would say that 80% of my trades and 90% of my profits are in stocks in uptrends with bullish reports.

Will you ever buy a stock that has a bullish report but is in a downtrend?

Yes, but such trades are infrequent. I may buy a stock that is in a downtrend if it is in a prevailing strong sector because then the stock trend is less important.

I assume the rationale for buying after a bullish earnings report is that the markets don't fully discount the report at the opening and that if you time your entry correctly, there is still a profit opportunity. But what would be the rationale for buying after a bearish earnings report?

Some stocks that are in downtrends and have a large short interest can be so oversold that they will have a positive reaction, even if the earnings report is bearish.

There are four combinations of report implication and stock trend:

1. **stock uptrend, bullish report**

2. **stock uptrend, bearish report**

3. **stock downtrend, bullish report**

4. **stock downtrend, bearish report**

You said that 90% of your profits come from category 1. Why then even bother with trades in the other three categories.

The category 1 trades also have the highest return-to-risk. The problem, however, is that among the stocks I follow, it is not always possible to find enough trades in which both the stock is in an uptrend and the report is bullish. So, it is necessary to supplement category 1 trades with less frequent trades from the other three categories.

What do you look for in deciding whether to take a trade in a stock after an earnings report?

I have charts for the post-earnings-reports price action going back about 15 years for all the stocks I trade. I look at how the stocks behaved after earnings when they were in uptrends versus sideways markets or downtrends. The best trades are when the general market is sideways to down, and the stock is in an uptrend and has a bullish report. That is when you can see the stock's independent strength rather than just a reflection of a rising market.

Are there other price patterns you look for?

Yes, the best situations are when the stock is an uptrend and there is a pullback before the earnings report because people are worried about what the report will say. If the report is then bullish, there will tend to be immediate strong buying from people who got out before the report.

Is there any other pattern that makes a stock a good candidate for a buy after an earnings report?

Yes, if the last earnings report was bearish, more longs will cover before the earnings report because they will be concerned about a repeat occurrence. If the earnings report is bullish, many of these liquidated longs will be buyers.

I can think of another reason why a prior bearish earnings report combined with an uptrend in the stock is a bullish indicator. Essentially, that combination implies that the stock was able to resume its uptrend after a prior bearish earnings report. The ability of the stock to shrug off bearish news is itself a bullish indicator.

Are there other types of things you look at in deciding whether you will take a trade after an earnings report?

I consider questions such as: How much did they beat earnings estimates by? How big is the short interest? What is the pre-open volume? What is the pre-open price move?

Does the decision of whether there is a trade depend on the stock having a specific minimum percentage price response to the earnings report?

Yes, that is exactly right.

Do you trade all stocks the same way, or are there differences in the way you trade different stocks?

I use the same type of analysis for all stocks. I will also have a protective stop on every trade I do.

How much would you risk on any particular trade?

I will place my stop about 4% to 5% below the entry price.

Do you enter the stop at the same time you enter your order?

I will place the stop order one second after I enter the trade.

Do you trade in the pre-open market following an earnings report release, or do you wait until the official opening?

I wait until the opening. But the pre-open market action in the stock is one of the most important things I watch. I also pay particular attention to the commentaries and the revised targets by the analysts following the stock. I keep a notebook of what all the analysts have said in the past about a stock. What were their past price targets? How have they changed their price targets? What are they saying now compared to what they said three years ago? How did the stock respond to analyst upgrades and downgrades in the past? There is a saying that the analysts are always wrong. Yes, that may be generally true, but the day after an earnings report, some of their upgrades and downgrades can be critical to the market price action.

Do you enter on the open?

I will get in anywhere between a few minutes to a half-hour after the opening. I will always put in my order during the first half-hour when the volume is greatest.

Why do you wait to get in until after the open as opposed to on the open?

Because at the open and right after the open, the bid-ask spreads can be extremely wide, and you can get a very bad fill. Also, I need to wait for the market to calm down before I can place my stop. If I buy and place my stop in the first few minutes of trading, there is a much higher chance of getting stopped out, even if the trade is correct.

Do you wait for a pullback to get in, or do you get in shortly after the open?

It depends on the historical pattern for the stock. Different stocks behave differently. Some stocks tend to have a pullback after the opening, while other stocks tend to move straight up. For example, in the situation we discussed before, stocks in which the previous earnings report was bearish, I will usually be a buyer very soon after the open because I expect the stock to move immediately.

How do you decide where to get out?

It depends on the price action. Sometimes there will be a huge price jump in the stock early in the day, especially for stocks with a large short interest, and I will take profits. But if there is no significant price response, I will usually wait until the close to get out.

Are there any trades that stand out as being particularly painful?

When I was starting out, there was one trade where I lost 30% of my equity. I bought a stock—I don't even remember the name. At first, it went up, but then it started going down. I kept thinking it would go up again, but it never did. I didn't have any stop on the trade.

How long did you hold the stock?

I held it for many weeks. It was my biggest mistake. After that trade, I never kept a stock overnight.

Was that also the point at which you started using stops on every trade?

Yes. If I didn't use stops, my percentage of winning trades would be higher, and my returns would probably be very similar, but my drawdowns would be much larger.

What percent of your trades are profitable?

About 65%.

Are your wins larger than your losers?

My average win is about 1.5 times as large as my average loss.

Besides not having a stop on the trade that caused the big loss, have you made other trading mistakes since then?

I would say my biggest mistake has been not being aggressive enough. The method I use could make more money if I wasn't such a very risk-averse person. If I had a 15% or 20% drawdown, I would be out of the business. Three losing trades in a row is very painful for me.

Roughly speaking, it seems that whatever you make each year you pull out of the account, and your trading account stays about the same size.

All the money I make in my trading, I spend on my living expenses. It is sad to see my account still at about the same size it was 10 years ago. But that is the reality.

What would happen if you had a year where you didn't make any money?

If I didn't make any money for one year, I could survive. If I didn't make any money for two years, I would have to quit. It would be the end of trading for me.

Are you happy with your life as a trader?

I am. It fits me well. I prefer to be on my own. I don't feel comfortable in large groups. I am happy fishing, taking walks in the forest, working on my garden, and trading. These are all activities I can do by myself. I know I am only an average person with an average education. Years ago, when I searched for what I could do, I knew I wanted to find something where the success or failure would depend only on me, not my colleagues, my boss, or anybody else. If I make money, that's great; if I lose money, it's my mistake. Trading is great in this way. You can't find many other activities where success or failure depends only on you.

Why do you believe you have been successful as a trader?

I don't know that I am a successful trader, but any success I have had is because I hate losing. I work extremely hard when I am losing. When I am losing, I can't focus on anything else besides figuring out how to improve what I am doing. In this way, my losing periods are actually beneficial to my future trading.

Perhaps the most important message in this interview is that it can be done. Given the tremendous growth in the quantification of trading in the past two decades, many individual traders and investors wonder whether it is still possible for them to succeed. Indeed, it is entirely reasonable to ask how a solo trader can compete against a plethora of management firms with scores of PhDs.

It is true that the majority of individual market participants will not succeed, in the sense of outperforming the relevant benchmark, such as a passive stock index investment—and by this gauge, neither will the majority of professional managers. However, Krejčí demonstrates that success and superior performance are still possible for the individual trader. Krejčí had no education beyond high school, no mentors, and minimal funds. Yet he developed a methodology that has achieved performance characteristics that far surpass those of well over 99% of long-only equity managers and hedge funds. He has also supported himself for 14 years off his trading profits.

Krejčí chose trading as a career path because he sought an endeavor in which he would be responsible for his success or failure. The operative word here is *responsibility*. Winning traders understand they are responsible for their outcomes. If they lose money, they will give you one of two explanations. Either they followed their methodology, and the losing trade was within the percentage of losing trades that is inevitable, or they made a mistake—a fault they will completely own. Losing traders, on the other hand, will always have some excuse for why they lost. They followed someone else's bad advice; the market was wrong; high-frequency traders distorted prices, etc. Politics aside, I would bet that President Trump would be an awful trader because he has never taken responsibility for any mistake or failure.

Krejčí provides one more example of a trader who ultimately succeeded because he found a methodology that fit his personality. He was uncomfortable holding positions overnight—"It wasn't my nature to hold trades," he says. By focusing on trading stocks only on the day after earnings reports, Krejčí was able to develop a strategy that could generate significant returns, at acceptable risk, on day trades. The lesson is that to succeed in the markets, you have to find a methodology that you are comfortable trading. If there is anything in your approach that is uncomfortable, you need to figure out how to change it.

One characteristic that has been common in so many of the traders I have interviewed is that they have a strong work commitment. To develop his trading methodology, Krejčí had to put in 16-hour days between his day job and market research. Even though his method results in virtually no trading opportunities in five months of the year, he will still devote full-time to the markets in those months, using those down months to continue his market research.

Krejčí attributes his long-term success to how he responds to losing periods. Whenever he is in a drawdown, he becomes obsessively focused on research that can lead to improvements in his methodology.

One critical element that has enabled Krejčí to achieve his exceptional return/risk performance is his restrictiveness in the trades he places. Krejčí will only take what he perceives to be high-percentage trades. Many traders could improve their performance by trading less—passing on the marginal trades and waiting for high-probability opportunities.

Although Krejčí's edge comes from his trade selection and the timing of entry and exit, it is risk management that has made it possible for him to continue to profit from his methodology. There are two ingredients in Krejčí's risk management. First, his approach avoids the risk of holding positions overnight. Second, he places a stop on every trade, thereby limiting his loss on any single trade. Krejčí explains that without stops, his percentage of winning trades would be higher, and his returns would be about the same, but his drawdowns would be deeper. Since larger drawdowns could easily have forced Krejčí to abandon trading, risk management has been instrumental to his long-term success.

CONCLUSION

46 Market Wizard Lessons

THIS chapter summarizes the key lessons to be gleaned across all the interviews in *Unknown Market Wizards*. While the 11 traders interviewed each approach the market in their own unique and individual way, the insights from these interviews nevertheless contain important general lessons for all traders.

Readers of other *Market Wizard* books will note that there is significant overlap with analogous summaries in those books. This observation should hardly be surprising since the advice of great traders reflects basic market truths that are invariant to methodology or time period. Some of the lessons that follow, however, are unique to *Unknown Market Wizards*—insofar as the ensuing summary is based solely on the interviews in this book.

1. There Is No Single True Path

After reading this book, it should be clear that there is no single formula for succeeding in the markets. The paths the traders interviewed traveled in achieving their exceptional performance were widely varied. The approaches ranged from fundamental to technical, to a combination of both, to neither. Trade holding periods ranged from minutes to months. Trading success is not about finding the *right* approach but instead finding the *right approach for you.* No one can tell you what that approach is; it is something you need to discover.

2. Find a Trading Method that is Compatible with Your Personality

Even an excellent methodology will yield poor results if it is not consistent with your beliefs and comfort zone. To succeed, traders must find their own market approach. Some examples:

⚡ Dhaliwal started out using technical methods. He felt uncomfortable with the approach because he didn't understand why it should work, and, consequently, he didn't have any confidence that it would continue to work in the future. Dhaliwal became enormously successful when he switched to using fundamentals—an approach where he felt he had a much clearer understanding of why prices moved from one level to another.

⚡ Neither fundamental nor technical analysis appealed to Camillo, so he came up with a third market analysis category, social arbitrage—profiting by spotting a societal shift or trend that will impact a stock and has not yet been reflected by the stock price.

⚡ Krejčí was uncomfortable holding positions overnight. He dealt with this strong personal aversion to overnight risk by developing a strategy that could generate significant returns, at acceptable risk, on day trades.

The lesson is that to succeed in the markets, you have to find a methodology that you are comfortable trading.

3. You May Have to Change Your Method Before You Find the Right One

Richard Bargh started out as a technical trader, switched to a fundamental approach, and ultimately discovered that combining his fundamental analysis with technical input worked best. If Parker didn't have the flexibility to radically alter his trading approach—even to the extent of switching from momentum systems to their exact opposite, mean-reversion systems—he would never have survived, let alone continued to profit, as a trader.

4. Keep a Trading Journal

Maintaining a trading journal is one of the most effective tools a trader can use to improve. A trading journal can provide two critical types of information: what the trader is doing right and what the trader is doing wrong. Several of the traders interviewed (Bargh, Sall, Dhaliwal) emphasized the critical role of keeping a detailed trading journal in their improvement as traders. Besides documenting the reasons for trades and associated right and wrong decisions, a journal can also be useful in recording emotional observations. For example, Bargh records his thoughts and feelings daily to identify weaknesses in his mindset and to track how his mindset changes over time.

5. Categorize Trades

Categorizing trades by type can be extremely useful in determining what works and what doesn't. Although systematic traders can test defined trade types retrospectively, discretionary traders must record the trade type and outcome as they occur. One thing Brandt regrets is that he didn't keep track of results by types of trade. For example, he believes that trades that were not on his weekly monitor list were poor performers on balance, but he really doesn't know if that assumption is true.

6. Know Your Edge

If you don't know what your edge is, you don't have one. Knowing your edge is critical to identifying which trades to focus on. For example, with the aid of his detailed trading journal, Dhaliwal was able to study the characteristics of his big wins. He discovered these trades shared multiple common denominators: the presence of an unexpected market event, harmony between his short-term and long-term views, and a tendency for the trade to work immediately. An awareness of the type of trades that accounted for the bulk of his gains—that is, understanding his edge—was an essential component of Dhaliwal's stellar performance. As Dhaliwal advises, "Stay in the sphere of your edge by playing your game and not someone else's."

7. Learn from Your Mistakes

Learning from mistakes is how traders improve. Perhaps the most valuable benefit of a trading journal is that it greatly facilitates the identification of trading errors. Reviewing such a journal periodically can remind the trader of past mistakes and, in so doing, reduce the repetition of the same mistakes. Sall used his journal to identify a mistake he was making after winning periods.

He noticed that he was continually taking subpar trades after highly profitable periods. He realized that because he came from a working-class background, these subpar trades were an act of self-sabotage to bring him "back down to earth." Once he recognized the problem, he was able to avoid repeating it.

As another example of a trader identifying a mistake through his trading journal, Dhaliwal noticed that emotional disharmony he was feeling could be traced to trades where he had a conflict between his short-term and long-term views. When he had a longer-term trade on but saw an opportunity for a short-term trade in the opposite direction, Dhaliwal would end up trading neither view effectively. Once he recognized the source of his trading error, he solved the problem by separating the two conflicting trades. He would leave the long-term trade on, and then trade the short-term opportunity separately.

8. The Power of Asymmetric Strategies

Most of the traders interviewed had track records characterized by large gains being far more frequent and much larger—sometimes tremendously greater—than large losses. These traders achieved their positively skewed return profiles by utilizing asymmetric trading strategies. The King of Asymmetry is Amrit Sall, who had 34 days with returns greater than 15% (three greater than 100%) and only one day with a double-digit loss (and that loss was caused by a computer glitch). Sall will wait for trades tied to events where he expects an immediate, significant price move and will exit the trade quickly if the anticipated market response fails to materialize. The average win on these trades will be far greater than the average loss.

As another example, Neumann focuses on identifying trading opportunities that have the potential to be what Peter Lynch termed "ten baggers"— investments that achieve a tenfold price increase. He uses trendline breakouts to enter the trade and will liquidate immediately if the stock price fails to follow through.

9. Risk Management Is Critical

I don't care how many times you've heard it, but when virtually every successful trader stresses how critical money management is, you better pay attention. Sure, money management is not as sexy as devising trade entry strategies, but it is essential to survival, let alone excelling. Several elements of risk management came up in the interviews:

⚡ **Individual position risk controls**—It is striking how many of the interviewed traders experienced their worst loss due to the lack of a protective stop. Dhaliwal's biggest loss—the trade he took in response to an erroneous *FT* story—was as large as it was because he didn't have a stop. Sall's worst loss, which occurred when his PC suddenly powered down at a critical moment, was also due to not having a stop. Kean learned the importance of limiting the risk on individual trades early in his career when he shorted a stock in a parabolic upmove without a plan on what to do if he was wrong. The stock price nearly doubled on him in a matter of days, resulting in a 10% hit to his portfolio—his worst loss ever. In all three cases, these experiences led the traders to use stops religiously. They never made the same mistake again. As another example of a trader transformation regarding risk control, Shapiro went from blowing up plus-half-million-dollar accounts twice to never entering a trade without a predetermined exit.

⚡ **Risk management at the portfolio level**—Limiting the loss on individual trades is critical, but it is not sufficient for adequate risk control. Traders also need to be concerned about correlation between their positions. If different positions are significantly correlated, then the portfolio risk may be unacceptably high, even if every position has stop protection, because different trades will tend to lose money together. Shapiro handles the problem of an excess of correlated positions in two ways: He reduces the sizes of individual positions, and he seeks to add trades that are inversely correlated to the existing portfolio.

The concept of building a portfolio of uncorrelated and inversely correlated positions also lies at the heart of Kean's trading philosophy. Any long-only equity portfolio faces the problem that most of the positions will be highly correlated. Approximately 60% of Kean's portfolio consists of a long equity component, which, by definition, will contain positions that are highly correlated with each other. Kean addresses this problem by combining this portion of his portfolio with a trading strategy that is, on balance, inversely correlated with long equities because the majority of these trades are shorts.

⚡ **Equity-based risk management**—Even when risk management is applied at both the individual position and portfolio levels, equity drawdowns can still exceed acceptable levels. Equity-based risk controls will either cut position sizes or cease trading altogether when equity drawdowns reach specific threshold levels. For example, Dhaliwal will cut his position size in half if a drawdown exceeds 5%, and cut it by half again if a drawdown exceeds 8%. If a drawdown reaches 15%, Dhaliwal will stop trading altogether until he feels ready to resume trading.

Equity-based risk controls can also be applied in dollar terms rather than percentage terms. Although the two are equivalent, a dollar-based risk point may be a more useful conceptualization, especially when starting to trade a new account. A risk control I recommend when starting a new trading account is to decide how much you are willing to lose before you stop trading. For example, if you open a $100,000 account, you might decide you are willing to risk $15,000 before you liquidate all positions and stop trading. There are three reasons why this type of risk action makes sense:

1. If you reach your account risk point, it means whatever you are doing is not working. So stopping trading and reevaluating your methodology makes sense.

2. If you are in a losing streak, taking a trading break and starting fresh when you feel ready and inspired to do so will usually be beneficial.

3. Perhaps most importantly, determining how much you are willing to lose before you start trading will keep you from losing all your risk capital in one failed attempt. This approach is also powerful because, at its core, it is an asymmetric strategy (the advantages of which were discussed in #8): You can lose only the dollar amount you set as your risk cutout level, but your upside is entirely open-ended.

10. Choose Meaningful Stop Points

Dhaliwal makes the critical point that protective stops should be placed at a level that disproves your trade hypothesis. Don't determine the stop by what you are willing to lose. If a meaningful stop point implies too much risk, it means that your position is too large. Reduce the position size so that you can place the stop at a price the market shouldn't go to if your trade idea is correct, while still restricting the implied loss at that stop point to an amount within your risk tolerance on the trade.

11. You Don't Have to Wait for a Stop to Be Hit

A stop is intended to limit your approximate maximum loss on a trade to some predetermined amount. However, as Bargh advises, you don't need to wait for a stop to be hit. The longer a trade has an open loss, the more seriously you should consider liquidation even though the stop point hasn't been hit. Bargh believes that the money saved exiting such trades before the stop point is reached will exceed the forgone profits on the trades that recover.

12. Brandt's Friday Close Rule

Brandt will liquidate any trade that is showing an open loss as of Friday's close. This rule is a specific example of the application of Bargh's concept of not waiting for stops to be hit on lagging trades (#11). Brandt's reasoning is that the Friday close is the most critical price of the week because it is the price at which all holders of positions commit to the risk of holding a position over the weekend. Brandt believes that an open loss on a position as of the Friday close has negative implications for the trade. Traders may wish to experiment applying (or tracking) Brandt's rule to see whether, on balance, the reduction of losses on affected trades exceeds forgone profits.

13. Don't Speculate with a Loss

Brandt's worst loss occurred when he was long crude oil at the start of the First Gulf War, and the market opened far below his intended stop point the next morning. When I asked him whether he might delay his exit in such circumstances, he replied, "If you speculate with a loss to get less of a loss, you end up with more of a loss." That indeed proved to be the case for this trade, as the market continued to sink further. I also have no doubt that Brandt's admonition is good advice in general.

14. Winning Traders Have a Specific Methodology

Good trading is the antithesis of a shoot-from-the-hip approach. All the traders interviewed had a precise methodology. Your methodology should be based on exploiting trades that benefit from your edge (#6) combined with appropriate risk management (#9).

15. Stick to Trades Defined by Your Methodology

It is common for traders to be tempted to take trades that are entirely outside their sphere of expertise. One such example occurred when Kean let his discipline lapse. One year when he was well ahead with only a month to go, Kean took a flier buying a group of energy-related stocks simply because the sector was down sharply. The trade had nothing to do with his standard methodology. This impulsive trade cost him 7% by the time he liquidated two weeks later. Avoid the temptation to take trades unrelated to your methodology.

16. Your Methodology May Need to Change

Markets change. Over time, even an effective methodology may need to be altered. For example, in his early years, Dhaliwal's most effective trading strategy was rapid entry in the direction of news headlines, seeking to capture the initial market reaction to the news. However, the development of algorithmic programs that could execute such trades faster than any human eventually made Dhaliwal's strategy unviable. He adapted his strategy to do virtually the opposite trade: fade the initial reactions to headlines. As his career progressed, he focused on in-depth fundamental research and longer-term trades.

Brandt is another example of a trader who had to modify his strategy. His trade entry was based on classical chart analysis patterns. However, many of the patterns that were once reliable ceased to be so. Brandt responded by significantly reducing the number of chart patterns he used for entry signals.

17. If You Are Uncomfortable with an Aspect of Your Methodology, Then Change It

If there is anything in your approach that is uncomfortable, you need to figure out how to change it. For example, Bargh felt unease with his exit strategy because there were instances when he would give back a substantial portion of large open profits on a trade. This sense of discomfort led Bargh to change his exit strategy in a way that avoided this problem.

18. How a Trade Idea Is Implemented Is Critical

One of Bargh's biggest winning trades ever was a bet that the Brexit vote would pass. The obvious trade that would profit from a surprise approval of the Brexit referendum was a short in the British pound. The problem with this direct way of expressing a bet on the passage of Brexit was that the British pound was swinging wildly as vote results came in for each region. The direct trade of shorting the British pound risked getting stopped out at a substantial loss if the timing of the trade was slightly off.

Bargh reasoned that if the Brexit vote passed, there would be a shift in market psychology to risk-off trades, such as long T-bonds. The advantage of long T-bonds versus short British pounds was that T-bonds were far less volatile, and hence the trade was less likely to get stopped out if correct, and would lose less if wrong. The indirect long T-bond position provided a far better return/risk position for expressing the trade idea. The lesson is that the direct way of implementing a market idea is not always the best approach.

19. Take Larger Positions on High-Conviction Trades

Don't take the same size position or risk on every trade. Taking much larger positions on high-conviction trades is an essential factor underlying the incredibly outsized returns achieved by some of the traders in this book. Sall, for example, will be aggressive in his position sizing for trades that he perceives combine large positive asymmetry with a high probability of success. Neumann steps on the gas when he has a particularly high conviction on a trade. In the case of AunthenTek, he had over one-third of his entire account in this single position.

To be clear, what is being advised is taking larger positions on high-conviction trades, not taking the huge positions (relative to equity) that traders such as Sall and Neumann will place when they see especially attractive market opportunities. Sall and Neumann are exceptionally skilled traders who have a high success rate on their strong-conviction trades and are quick to liquidate when a trade starts to move against them.

For most ordinary traders, taking huge positions, no matter how high their conviction level, is a risky proposition.

20. Don't Trade So Large that Fear Becomes a Dominant Factor

If you trade too large, fear will lead to poor trading decisions. In his early trading years, Bargh felt that he should be trading position size levels that exceeded his comfort level. As a consequence, he passed up many good trading opportunities. There is no contradiction between the advice here and the advice offered in the previous entry, which merely advised taking larger-than-normal positions on high-conviction trades. Even in that instance, the position should not be so large that fear interferes with the trade decision process.

21. If You Hope a Trade Will Work, Get Out

If you find yourself hoping your trade will work, that is a sure sign that you lack conviction. Early in his career, when Sall was taking trades based on technical signals, he found himself hoping trades would work. His unease with this feeling convinced him that technical trading was the wrong approach for him.

In another instance, Sall placed maximum positions in three highly correlated markets on a marginal trade idea. When the risk manager queried him as to what he was doing, Sall suddenly realized that he was *hoping* his triple-size position would work. Recalling this experience, Sall said, "The second I realized that I was hoping and not trading anymore, I immediately liquidated everything."

If you are hoping a trade will work, you are gambling and not trading.

22. Don't Trade Based on Someone Else's Recommendations

You need to trade based on your own methodology and your own decisions. Trades based on someone else's recommendation tend to end badly, even when the advice is correct. For example, Brandt lost money on a trade recommended by a floor trader for whom the trade worked very well. Brandt failed to appreciate the difference in holding periods between himself and the floor trader. Camillo's most regretful trade was when he liquidated two-thirds of what ultimately proved to be an excellent position at a loss because he was influenced by conflicting market opinions.

23. Distinguish Between Trade Outcomes and Trade Decisions

Many traders erroneously evaluate their trading based solely on outcomes. When asked to recount his worst trade, ironically, Bargh immediately described a dual-position trade that resulted in only a small loss. In this particular trade, Bargh experienced a quick, large loss but couldn't bring himself to liquidate the positions. He hesitated, and the trade partially recovered. Bargh used this pullback as an opportunity to liquidate his positions, exiting at only a moderate loss. Just after he liquidated, the market then moved violently against his original positions. Although Bargh's initial inability to exit the losing trade worked to his benefit, he realized that he had made an enormous trading error but had just been lucky. If the market hadn't experienced its short-lived pullback, his initial large loss could have turned into a disastrous one.

Bargh was able to distinguish between the outcome—a smaller loss—and the decision—an inability to act that could have resulted in an account-threatening loss. The point is that sometimes winning trades (or smaller losing ones, as was the case here) may be bad trades. Similarly, losing trades could be good trades if the trader adhered to a methodology that, on balance, is profitable with reasonable risk control.

24. The Return/Risk Ratio of a Trade Is Dynamic

Dhaliwal makes the point that trades are dynamic, and traders need to adjust their exit strategy accordingly. If a trader establishes both a profit target and a stop when a trade is initiated, and the trade moves 80% of the way towards the target, the return/risk at that point will be very different from what it was when the trade was implemented. In such a situation, the original exit plan no longer makes sense. If a trade moves significantly in your favor, consider tightening your stop, or taking partial profits, or both.

Brandt calls trades in which you have a profit and ride it all the way back to where you got in "popcorn trades." He avoids popcorn trades by a combination of taking profits and tightening stops—an approach that recognizes and responds to the dynamic nature of trades.

25. Human Emotions Are Detrimental to Trading

Human emotions and impulses will often lead traders to do the wrong thing. As Brandt said, "I am my own worst enemy." The next three sections detail different categories of emotion-based actions that adversely impact trading.

26. Guard Against Impulsive Trades

Impulsive trades are, by definition, emotional trades, and emotional trades tend to be losers. Beware of being enamored by an unplanned trade. Neumann's biggest loss (in percentage terms) came early in his career when he deviated from a strategy that was generating consistent returns to impulsively buy a stock that was rising rapidly based on a bullish story. That single trade resulted in a 30% loss in one day.

27. Trades Motivated by Greed Usually End Badly

Greed will cause traders to take marginal trades, or place positions that are too large, or both. Bargh's worst trading loss was a consequence of greed. In this particular instance, he initially took a large short position in the euro based on comments Mario Draghi made at a press conference. This initial position was entirely consistent with Bargh's methodology. However, Bargh then took a large long position in the Bund—a position highly correlated to his original trade, but one that had no justification, since Draghi's comments only pertained to the euro. Bargh admits that the doubling of his exposure by buying the Bund was entirely influenced by greed. Both positions then turned against Bargh. By the time he liquidated, Bargh was down 12% for the day—his worst daily loss ever—with most of the loss coming from the impulsively added long Bund position.

Traders need to be aware when a trade they are about to take is motivated by greed rather than an application of their methodology. Such trades will usually end badly.

28. Beware of a Compulsion to Make Money Back in the Same Market

When traders, particularly novice traders, lose money in a market, there is a reflexive instinct to try to make it back in the same market. This impulse, perhaps driven by a desire to seek revenge or to expiate the prior trading loss, leads to emotion-induced trading, and emotion-based trades are particularly prone to bad outcomes.

John Netto's experience on March 17, 2003, when President Bush issued an ultimatum to Saddam Hussein to leave Iraq, provides a classic example of the danger of trying to recover a loss in the same market. Initially, Netto went short the S&P 500 when it opened lower that day, anticipating a further slide. The market abruptly reversed, stopping Netto out at a large, single-trade loss. Had he stopped there, it would just have been an ordinary bad day. But, like a dog with a bone, Netto kept shorting the market. By the end of the day, he had gone short and been stopped out five times, nearly quintupling his original loss and wiping out his profits for the year.

29. The Real Damage of a Bad Trade

Many traders fail to realize that the greatest damage from a bad trade is often not the loss on the trade itself but, rather, the lost profits on subsequent good trades not taken because of the destabilizing effect of the bad trade. The day after Bargh experienced his worst loss due to the greed-induced trade detailed in #27, the Bank of England switched to a hiking bias. It was precisely the type of event that provides Bargh with his best profit opportunities. However, Bargh was still too shaken up by his 12% loss the day before to pull the trigger on that trade. The market had the big move Bargh anticipated, but he was not in the trade. The lesson is that the cost of a trading mistake often substantially exceeds the direct loss on the trade taken—all the more reason to avoid trading mistakes (losses due to traders breaking their own rules).

30. Don't Exit the Entire Position at the Profit Target

Frequently, market price moves will continue to extend well beyond a trader's profit target. Therefore, instead of liquidating an entire position at a profit target, traders should consider holding onto a minor portion of the position with raised protective stops. In this way, they maintain the opportunity to profit significantly further if there is a longer-term move in the direction of the trade, while risking only a small surrender of profits if the market reverses.

For example, Bargh will take profits when the market reaches his price target. However, after locking in his profits in the trade, he will routinely maintain 5%–10% of the position, which he may hold for a longer-term price move. In this way, he can add a few percent profit to a trade with minimal risk.

31. If You Are on the Right Side of Euphoria or Panic, Liquidate or Lighten Up

Parabolic price moves in either direction tend to end abruptly and sharply. If you are on the right side of such a trade, consider taking partial or total profits, while the market is moving near-vertically in your favor. Neumann's exit of his Spongetech trade provides a perfect illustration of this principle.

32. Guard Against Complacency and Sloppy Trading after Big Winning Streaks

Traders often experience their worst performance after periods when they have done exceptionally well. Why? Because winning streaks lead to complacency, and complacency leads to sloppy trading. When their accounts are sailing to new highs almost daily, and virtually all their trades are working, traders will tend to become less diligent in executing their methodology and laxer in their risk management. Several of the traders interviewed had this precise experience of worst performance following best performance:

⚡ Brandt's first losing year after becoming a full-time trader occurred immediately following his best trading year ever.

⚡ After a great first six months of trading, Sall fell into the complacency trap. In his own words: "I got cocky and relaxed with my discipline." During this time, he placed limit positions in three highly correlated markets on a marginal trade—an action that could have resulted in a huge loss were it not for the firm's risk manager's quick intervention.

⚡ When I asked Bargh about his underperformance during the first half of 2018, he explained, "I had a very good 2017 and came into 2018 with the mindset that I could push it. I was taking too much risk."

The moral is: If everything is going great, watch out!

33. The Flexibility to Change Your Opinion Is an Attribute, Not a Flaw

I find it ironic that some of Brandt's Twitter followers criticize him for changing his market opinion—something he frequently does. That is such a wrong-headed perspective. The flexibility to change your market view is essential to succeeding as a trader. If you are rigid in your market stance, you only need to be wrong once to decimate your account. Brandt's motto is: "strong opinions, weakly held." The implication is that you should have firm conviction when you enter a trade, but you should be quick to abandon that position if the trade moves against you.

34. Missed Trades Can Be More Painful—and More Expensive—than Trading Losses

Missing a large profit opportunity can impact your trading profitability as much as multiple trading losses. And such a missed opportunity can be even more painful than a trading loss. Bargh missed a massive profit opportunity because he ran a bank errand during trading hours. One primary cause of missed trades is the destabilizing impact of bad trades (see #29).

35. What to Do When You Are Out of Sync with the Markets

When you are in a losing streak, and everything you do seems wrong, the best action may be to stop trading temporarily. Losses beget losses. Taking a break can act as a circuit breaker. Bargh says that when he feels destabilized by a trading experience, he will "take some time off, exercise, go out in nature, have fun."

Brandt has another answer about what to do when you are out of sync with the markets. He cuts his trading size—an action that will mitigate the drawdown during a negative period.

Dhaliwal's method of handling losing periods combines both the above approaches. If he is in a drawdown that exceeds 5%, he will cut his position in half. If the drawdown exceeds 8%, he will cut the position in half again. If the drawdown reaches 15%, he will take a complete break from trading.

The underlying concept in all the above approaches is that if you are in a losing streak, you need to cut risk—either by stopping trading altogether or by reducing position size.

36. Counter-to-Expected Market Reactions to News

A counter-to-expected market response to news can be a very valuable trade signal. This concept came up repeatedly in the trader interviews. Some examples:

⚡ Dhaliwal recounted a short Australian dollar trade where his fundamental view coincided with a downside chart breakout. An unemployment report was released that day, and all the statistics were extremely bullish. Initially, the market rallied as expected. But then the rally fizzled, and prices moved below the low of a long-term trading range. The combination of a highly bullish report and a very bearish market response convinced Dhaliwal that the market would move sharply lower, which it did.

⚡ Brandt's worst loss occurred in one of the most extreme examples of a counter-to-expected market response. Brandt was long crude oil at the start of the First Gulf War with the news of the war's beginning hitting after the market close. Crude traded $2–$3 higher that night on the Kerb (an after-hours market in London). But the next morning, crude oil opened $7 below the New York close—a $10 swing from its nighttime levels. This extreme bearish response to bullish news served as a longer-term bearish signal.

⚡ Netto's repeated losses in selling the S&P 500 on the day President Bush issued an ultimatum to Saddam Hussein to step down (detailed in #28) were a consequence of his failure to recognize the significance of the market's counter-to-expected response to the news.

⚡ Kean ignored classic counter-to-expected price action in his largest holding, JD.com. After an announcement of a deal with Google, JD.com initially rallied but then reversed, closing sharply lower. Kean held onto his position despite this ominous price action, and the stock lost more than half its value in the ensuing months. Commenting on this experience, Kean said, "The worst mistake was ignoring that day's price action. As someone who trades for a living, I should have known better."

⚡ On election night 2016, as the returns started indicating a surprise Trump victory, stock indexes sold off, as was anticipated in such an event. But then, even though a Trump win became increasingly likely, the market reversed sharply to the upside. This counter-to-expected price action marked the start of a 14-month steady climb in stock prices.

37. Being Profitable Versus Being Right

Ego and the need to be right are detrimental to effective trading. Many traders are more invested in their market theories and prognostications being right than they are in being profitable, which is all that matters. As Dhaliwal succinctly put it, "it's not about being right; it's about making money."

38. Aiming for Consistent Profitability Can Be Counterproductive

Consistent profitability may sound like a worthwhile goal, but it can actually be counterproductive. Trade opportunities are sporadic, and aiming for consistent profitability in low-opportunity periods can lead to taking marginal trades that end up being net losers. Although Bargh was urged by his bosses to strive for consistency, he resisted this advice, sensing it was incompatible with the way he traded. "I never really thought that is how trading worked," he said. "It's more like you make nothing for a while, then you have a spurt." As a strikingly ironic observation, Sall noted that a common trait he observed among traders who failed is that they had a goal of making money every month.

39. Be Observant and Highly Attuned to New Behavioral Trends

Spotting emerging trends, both in your everyday life and in social media, can be a source for uncovering trading opportunities. Detecting consumer and cultural trends early is a critical component of the strategy employed by two of the traders in this book: Camillo and Neumann. For example, Camillo identified trades such as Cheesecake Factory and P. F. Chang's by observing Middle America's reaction to these chains—a response he knew Wall Street would be blind to. Many of Neumann's best trades involved catching trends, such as 3D printing and CBD products, early.

40. Trading Systems Sometimes Stop Working

As Parker repeatedly experienced during his career, systems can work for a time but then entirely lose their edge, or even become consistent net losers. This inconvenient fact implies that the ability to terminate or radically change systems is essential to longer-term success as a systematic trader. Parker now employs a system stop. He uses trend-following applied to a system's equity curve to signal when a system should be deactivated. Specifically, Parker will stop trading a system if its equity curve falls below its 200-day moving average.

41. Trading for a Living Is Hard

As Brandt notes, "The markets are not an annuity." As one indication of how difficult trading for a living is, Parker almost quit trading in early 2016, only eight months after having set new highs in cumulative profits and despite still being more than $5 million ahead. Aspirants to trading for a living need to keep in mind that it is not sufficient for cumulative profits to continue rising. Cumulative profits need to continually increase by more than the sum of taxes and cumulative withdrawals for living expenses. Another complicating factor is that trading profitability is inherently sporadic, while living expenses are continual. In recognition of these real-life considerations, Parker advises those seeking to trade for a living to keep their day job as long as feasible.

42. Work Commitment

Although many people are drawn to trading because they think it is an easy way to make a lot of money, ironically, traders who excel tend to have a very strong work commitment. Krejčí provides a good example of this strong work ethic. To develop his trading methodology, Krejčí had to put in 16-hour days between his day job and market research. Krejčí's methodology results in virtually no trading opportunities in five months of the year. Although he could just take those five months off, he will still devote full-time to the markets in those months, using the trading downtime to continue his market research. As another example (but by no means the only other one), Sall believes his work ethic was essential to his success. He recalls putting in 15- to 18-hour days in his early years. "I am willing to outwork everyone else," he says.

43. Take Responsibility for Your Own Results

Krejčí chose trading as a career path because he sought an endeavor in which he would be responsible for his success or failure. This innate perspective is a characteristic of winning traders. Successful traders take responsibility for their own mistakes and losses. Losing traders invariably will blame their outcome on someone or something else.

44. The Two Sides of Patience

Markets will tend to reward traits that are difficult to maintain. Patience is hard. It requires overcoming our natural instincts and desires. It is a trait I have repeatedly found in great traders. There are two aspects of patience that are critical to market success.

⚡ **Patience to wait for the right trade**—Trading opportunities are sporadic. Most traders will find it difficult to wait for trades that fit their criteria for attractive opportunities and will give in to the temptation of taking marginal trades in between. Taking such suboptimal trades will have two negative consequences. First, they will tend to result in losses on balance. Second, they will dilute attention away from true trade opportunities. Even worse, the destabilizing impact of a suboptimal trade that results in a large loss could cause a trader to miss a major profit opportunity. See, for example, Bargh's missed trade described in #29.

Sall is the epitome of a trader who has the patience to wait for the right trade as is succinctly reflected by his self-description: "My style has often been referred to that of a sniper. I am in a constant state of readiness waiting for that perfect shot." Sall maintains that executing his most profitable trades was the easy part. The difficult part was waiting for the optimal profit opportunities and avoiding marginal trades that, in his words, "waste mental and financial capital."

⚡ **Patience to stay with a good trade**—Patience is also required to stay with good trades. When a trade is profitable, it is tempting to liquidate the position prematurely out of fear that the market might take those open profits away. Shapiro learned the power of patience in staying with a good trade when circumstances involuntarily forced him into this favorable trait. At the time, he was taking a multi-week vacation in Africa, and he knew the unavailability of communication facilities would make it impossible to check on or trade the markets. Shapiro provided his broker with stop-loss instructions and didn't see his account again until he returned. He discovered that he made far more money by being away on vacation than he ever made actively trading his account. This lesson stuck, as the methodology he eventually developed allowed for staying with positions for months if warranted by the relevant conditions.

45. The Internal Game of Trading

Sall believes, "Your state of mind is the most critical factor to trading success once you have your methodology down." For Sall, the right mindset requires being calm and focused. He will mentally prepare for an anticipated trading event by using breathwork and meditation to achieve what he calls a "deep now" state. Through keeping a journal and charting the connection between emotions and losses, Sall has learned the importance of shifting any negative mindset and identifying emotions that could cause him to self-sabotage trades.

Bargh credits Sall with helping him appreciate that having a good mindset was critical to trading well. Similar to Sall, Bargh seeks to trade from a calm state free of any inner conflict. He maintains a daily spreadsheet that monitors a variety of emotional factors (e.g., ego, fear of missing out, happiness rating, etc.) alongside with trading actions. Bargh uses his feelings as an input to his trading. If Bargh feels his emotional state is not conducive to good trading, he will take a break until his mindset is back in the right place. Bargh says, "Mental capital is the most critical aspect of trading. What matters most is how you respond when you make a mistake, miss a trade, or take a significant loss. If you respond poorly, you will just make more mistakes."

46. Successful Traders Love What They Do

Reading these interviews, you should have been struck by how many of the traders talked about their love of trading. Some examples:

⚡ Dhaliwal used a gamelike analogy to describe trading: "To me, playing the markets is like a never-ending chess game. It's the most exciting game you can play."

⚡ Camillo described the joy he finds in identifying trade ideas: "The four hours I spend every night doing my analysis is something that I love. I never know when I'm going to hit on that thing that will take me down the path to my next big trade. It's the same feeling I had as a kid going to garage sales."

⚡ Netto explained his success, saying, "I am successful because Monday is my favorite day of the week. When you love what you do, you're going to be successful."

⚡ Shapiro went through depression during a period when he stopped trading, even though everything in his personal life seemed to be going well. When I asked Shapiro how he finally figured out what was causing his depression, he replied, "It was obvious. I loved trading."

⚡ Sall recalled the origin of his passion for trading: "[The University of Reading] had a simulated trading room, which was my first exposure to markets and trading, and I fell in love with it."

⚡ Kean explained why a love of trading is an essential trait for a trader: "You need to love trading so that you can get through the tough times."

⚡ Brandt's reaction upon first seeing the traders in the commodity pits was, "Whoa! I want to do this." Brandt's passion for trading also comes across in his description of his early days when he had a virtual compulsion to trade—an enthusiasm that lasted for well over a decade. His love of trading eventually faded, and after 14 years, he abandoned his trading career. Speaking of that time, he says, "The fun of trading had left me at that point. Trading had become drudgery." After an 11-year hiatus, the compulsion to trade returned, leading to a second successful trading career, 13 years and counting.

If you want to trade, your odds for success will be significantly enhanced if you are motivated by a genuine love of the endeavor.

EPILOGUE

To recast an old joke, two congregants at a synagogue have had the same running argument for years. Dave contends that markets are efficient and that it is impossible for anyone to beat the markets other than by chance. Sam asserts that trading opportunities exist, and market outperformance is achievable. Finally, after years of fruitless bickering, they agree to let the rabbi decide who is right.

They arrange to meet with the rabbi, explaining they would like him to settle a dispute. When they arrive at the rabbi's home, he tells them he will speak with them one at a time in his office. Dave enters the rabbi's office first.

"I hope you don't mind my wife being here," the rabbi says, "but she takes notes for me."

Dave assures the rabbi that is fine and begins to explain his side of the argument. "I believe that the markets are efficient—a contention supported by thousands of academic papers. And it is not just a theoretical argument. Empirical studies repeatedly demonstrate that individual investors who make timing decisions do significantly worse than passive index funds. Even professional managers, on average, consistently do worse than the market. In light of all this evidence, trading is a fool's game. People would be much better off just putting their money in index funds."

The rabbi, who has been listening intently, simply says, "You're right."

Dave smiles smugly, quite content with the conversation outcome, and leaves the rabbi's office.

Sam walks in next. After the same preliminary formalities, he presents his side of the argument. He begins with a lengthy explanation of the myriad flaws in the efficient market hypothesis.* He then says, "Also, rabbi, you know that I earn my living as a trader. I have a nice home. My family is well cared for. My generous annual contributions to the synagogue come from my trading profits. Clearly, it is entirely possible to profit handsomely from trading."

The rabbi, who has paid close attention, replies, "You're right."

Sam smiles with satisfaction and walks out of the rabbi's office.

Once they are alone, the rabbi's wife turns to him and says, "Dearest husband, I know you are a wise man, but how can they possibly both be right?"

"You're right," replies the rabbi.

Except, the rabbi's wife is not right. Both Dave and Sam are right but in different contexts. The world of traders (or investors) can be divided into two categories: those who possess a methodology with an edge and those who do not. The second category is far larger than the first. Market participants who do not have any special skill in trading or investing—a group that includes most people—would be better off investing in index funds than in trying to make their own market decisions. So, ironically, although I do not believe the efficient market hypothesis is valid, I think most people would be best off behaving as if the theory were entirely accurate—a conclusion that would support the idea of index investing. This is the context in which Dave is right.

---

* An adequate discussion of the deficiencies in the efficient market hypothesis is far too long to present here. Interested readers should refer to Chapter 2 in my book *Market Sense and Nonsense*.

However, there is a big difference between difficult and impossible. The magnitude by which the traders in this book outperformed market benchmarks over long periods (typically, decade-plus) cannot simply be explained away as "luck." This is the context in which Sam is right.

If there is one message in this book about the possibility of trading success, it is: It can be done! However, it is not a goal within reach of most people. Succeeding as a trader requires some combination of hard work, innate skill, and beneficial psychological traits (e.g., patience, discipline, etc.). For the small minority of market participants who can develop a methodology with a demonstrated market edge and combine it with rigorous risk management, trading success is an achievable, albeit challenging, goal.

APPENDIX 1

*Understanding the Futures Markets**

WHAT ARE FUTURES?

THE essence of a futures market is in its name: Trading involves a commodity or financial instrument for a future delivery date, as opposed to the present time. Thus, if a cotton farmer wished to make a current sale, he would sell his crop in the local cash market. However, if the same farmer wanted to lock in a price for an anticipated future sale (e.g., the marketing of a still unharvested crop), he would have two options. He could locate an interested buyer and negotiate a contract specifying the price and other details (quantity, quality, delivery time, location, etc.). Alternatively, he could sell futures, which provide multiple attributes.

---

* Sections of this appendix have been adapted from Jack D. Schwager, *A Complete Guide to the Futures Market* (New Jersey, John Wiley and Sons, Inc., 2017) and Jack D. Schwager, *Market Wizards* (New Jersey, John Wiley and Sons, Inc., 2012).

ADVANTAGES OF FUTURES

Some of the major advantages of futures markets for the hedger are:

1. The futures contract is standardized; hence, the farmer does not have to find a specific buyer.

2. The transaction can be executed virtually instantaneously online.

3. The cost of the trade (commissions) is minimal compared with the cost of an individualized forward contract.

4. The farmer can offset his sale at any time between the original transaction date and the final trading day of the contract.

5. The futures contract is guaranteed by the exchange.

While hedgers, such as the aforementioned cotton farmer, participate in futures markets to reduce the risk of an adverse price move, traders participate in an effort to profit from anticipated price changes. In fact, most traders will prefer the futures markets over their cash counterparts for a variety of reasons (a number of which are analogous to the advantages just listed for hedgers):

1. **Standardized contracts**—Futures contracts are standardized (in terms of quantity and quality); thus, the trader does not have to find a specific buyer or seller in order to initiate or liquidate a position.

2. **Liquidity**—All of the major futures markets provide excellent liquidity.

3. **Ease of going short**—The futures markets allow equal ease of going short as well as long. For example, the short seller in the stock market needs to first borrow the stock, which is not always possible, and must wait for an uptick before initiating a position. No such impediments exist in the futures markets.

4. **Leverage**—The futures markets offer tremendous leverage. Roughly speaking, initial margin requirements are usually equal to 5%–10% of the contract value. (The use of the term margin in the futures market is unfortunate because it leads to tremendous confusion with the concept of margins in stocks. In the futures markets, margins do not imply

partial payments, since no actual physical transaction occurs until the expiration date; rather, margins are basically good-faith deposits.) Although high leverage is one of the attributes of futures markets for traders, it should be emphasized that leverage is a two-edged sword. The undisciplined use of leverage is the single most important reason why most traders lose money in the futures markets. In general, futures prices are no more volatile than the underlying cash prices or, for that matter, most stocks. The high-risk reputation of futures is largely a consequence of the leverage factor.

5. **Low transaction costs**—Futures markets provide very low transaction costs. For example, it is far less expensive for a stock portfolio manager to reduce market exposure by selling the equivalent dollar amount of stock index futures contracts than by selling individual stocks.

6. **Ease of offset**—A futures position can be offset at any time during market hours, providing prices are not locked at limit-up or limit-down. (Some futures markets specify daily maximum price changes. In cases in which free market forces would normally seek an equilibrium price outside the range of boundaries implied by price limits, the market will simply move to the limit and virtually cease to trade.)

7. **Guaranteed by exchange**—The futures trader does not have to be concerned about the financial stability of the person on the other side of the trade. The exchange clearing house guarantees all futures transactions.

TRADING FUTURES

The trader seeks to profit by anticipating price changes. For example, if the price of December gold is \$1,550/oz, a trader who expects the price to rise above \$1,650/oz will go long. The trader has no intention of actually taking delivery of the gold in December. Right or wrong, the trader will offset the position sometime before expiration. For example, if the price rises to \$1,675 and the trader decides to take profits, the gain on the trade will be \$12,500 per contract (100 oz × \$125/oz). If, on the other hand, the trader's forecast is wrong and prices decline to \$1,475/oz, with the expiration date drawing near, the trader has little choice but to liquidate. In this situation, the loss would be equal to \$7,500 per contract. Note the trader would not take delivery even given a desire to maintain the long gold position. In this case, the trader would liquidate the December contract and simultaneously go long in a more forward contract. (This type of transaction is called a *rollover* and would be implemented with a *spread* order.) Traders should always avoid taking delivery, since it can result in substantial extra costs without any compensating benefits.

Novice traders should caution against the securities-based bias of trading only from the long side. In futures trading, there is no distinction between going short and going long.* Since prices can go down as well as up, the trader who takes only long positions will eliminate approximately half the potential trading opportunities. Also, it should be noted that futures often command a premium to current prices; consequently, the inflation argument for a long-side bias is frequently erroneous.

The successful trader must employ some method for forecasting prices. The two basic analytical approaches are:

1. **Technical Analysis.** The technical analyst bases projections on non-economic data. Price data are by far the most important—and often only—input in technical analysis. The basic assumption of technical analysis is that prices exhibit repetitive patterns and that the recognition of these patterns can be used to identify trading opportunities. Technical analysis can also include other data, such as volume, open interest, and sentiment measures.

---

* Some beginners are confused about how it is possible for a trader to sell a commodity he does not own. The key to the answer lies in the fact that the trader is selling a *futures* contract, not the cash commodity. Even though the trader who stays short past the last trading day must acquire the actual commodity to fulfill his contractual obligation, there is no need for him to own the commodity before that time. The short sale is simply a bet that prices will go down before the last trading day. Right or wrong, the trader will offset his short position before the last trading day, eliminating any need for actual ownership of the commodity.

2. **Fundamental Analysis.** The fundamental analyst uses economic data (e.g., production, consumption, exports) to forecast prices. In essence, the fundamentalist seeks to uncover trading opportunities by identifying potential transitions to significantly more ample or tighter supply-demand balances. For financial futures, fundamental inputs will include items such as central bank policy, inflation statistics, employment data, etc.

Technical and fundamental analysis are not mutually exclusive approaches. Many traders use both in the decision-making process or as components of automated trading systems.

DELIVERY

Shorts who maintain their positions in deliverable future contracts after the last trading day are obligated to deliver the given commodity or financial instrument against the contract. Similarly, longs who maintain their positions after the last trading day must accept delivery. In futures markets, the number of open long contracts is always equal to the number of open short contracts. Most traders have no intention of making or accepting delivery, and hence will offset their positions before the last trading day. It has been estimated that fewer than 3% of open contracts actually result in delivery. Some futures contracts (e.g., stock indexes, Eurodollar) use a *cash settlement* process whereby outstanding long and short positions are offset at the prevailing price level at expiration instead of being physically delivered.

THE SCOPE OF FUTURES MARKETS

Until the early 1970s, futures markets were restricted to commodities (e.g., wheat, sugar, copper, cattle). Since that time, the futures area has expanded to incorporate additional market sectors, most significantly stock indexes, interest rates, and currencies (foreign exchange). The same basic principles apply to these financial futures markets. Trading quotes represent prices for a future expiration date rather than current market prices. For example, the quote for December 10-year T-notes implies a specific price for a $100,000, 10-year US Treasury Note to be delivered in December. Financial markets have experienced spectacular growth since their introduction, and today trading volume in these contracts dwarfs that in commodities. Nevertheless, futures markets are still commonly, albeit erroneously, referred to as commodity markets, and these terms are synonymous.

Since by their very structure futures are closely tied to their underlying markets (the activity of arbitrageurs assures that deviations are relatively minor and short-lived), price moves in futures will very closely parallel those in the corresponding cash markets. Keeping in mind that the majority of futures trading activity is concentrated in financial instruments, many futures traders are, in reality, traders in stocks, bonds, and currencies. In this context, the comments of futures traders interviewed in this book have direct relevance even to investors who have never ventured beyond stocks and bonds.

APPENDIX 2

Performance Metrics

MANY traders and investors make the mistake of focusing almost exclusively on returns. This emphasis is a mistake because return levels only have meaning in context of the risk undertaken to achieve those returns. Do you want to double your returns? Easy—just double the size of all your trades. Does this make you a better trader? Of course not—because you will also be doubling the risk. Focusing on returns only is as absurd as assuming that higher returns due solely to larger position sizing is indicative of better performance. For this reason, I focus on return/risk rather than return in evaluating and comparing traders and managers. The return level is still relevant, though, because it doesn't make sense to consider a low return track record as being superior even if the return/risk is very high.

The following metrics are referenced in the trader chapters in this book.

AVERAGE ANNUAL COMPOUNDED RETURN

This value is the return level that, when compounded annually, will yield the cumulative return. Although I pay more attention to the return/risk metrics than return, a performance record can have superior return/risk values and an unacceptably low return level. Therefore, it is still necessary to check return alone.

THE SHARPE RATIO

The Sharpe ratio is the most widely used risk-adjusted return measure. The Sharpe ratio is defined as the average *excess return* divided by the standard deviation. Excess return is the return above the risk-free return (e.g., T-bill rate). For example, if the average return is 8% per year and the T-bill rate is 3%, the excess return would be 5%. The standard deviation is a measure of the variability of return. In essence, the Sharpe ratio is the average excess return normalized by the volatility of returns.

There are two basic problems with the Sharpe ratio:

1. **The return measure is based on average rather than compounded return.** The return an investor realizes is the compounded return, not the average return. The more volatile the return series, the more the average return will deviate from the actual (i.e., compounded) return. For example, a two-year period with a 50% gain in one year and a 50% loss in the other would represent a 0% average return, but the investor would actually realize a 25% loss (150% × 50% = 75%). The average annual compounded return of -13.4%, however, would reflect the reality (86.6% × 86.6% = 75%).

2. **The Sharpe ratio does not distinguish between upside and downside volatility.** The risk measure inherent in the Sharpe ratio—the standard deviation—does not reflect the way most investors perceive risk. Traders and investors care about loss, not volatility. They are averse to downside volatility but actually like upside volatility. I have yet to meet an investor who complained because his manager made too

much money in a month. The standard deviation, and by inference the Sharpe ratio, however, is indifferent between upside and downside volatility. This characteristic of the Sharpe ratio can result in rankings that would contradict most people's perceptions and preferences.*

SORTINO RATIO

The Sortino ratio addresses both the problems cited for the Sharpe ratio. First, it uses the compounded return, which represents the actual realized return over any period, instead of the arithmetic return. Second, and most importantly, the Sortino ratio focuses on defining risk in terms of the downside deviation, which is calculated using only returns below a specified Minimum Acceptable Return (MAR). In contrast, the standard deviation, used in the Sharpe ratio, includes all deviations, upside as well as downside. The Sortino ratio is defined as the compounded return in excess of the MAR divided by the downside deviation. The MAR in the Sortino ratio can be set to any level, but one of the following three definitions are typically used for the MAR:

1. **Zero**—Deviations are calculated for all negative returns (the definition assumed in this book).

2. **Risk-free Return**—Deviations are calculated for all returns below the risk-free return.

3. **Average Return**—Deviations are calculated for all returns below the average of the series being analyzed. This formulation is closest to the standard deviation, but only considers deviations for the lower half of returns.

Because it distinguishes between upside and downside deviations, the Sortino ratio comes closer to reflecting most people's performance

---

* In some cases, high upside volatility can be indicative of a greater potential for downside volatility. In these instances, the Sharpe ratio will be an appropriate measure. The Sharpe ratio, however, will be particularly misleading in evaluating strategies designed to achieve sporadic large gains, while strictly controlling downside risk (that is, right-skewed strategies).

preferences than does the Sharpe ratio, and, in this sense, it is a better tool for comparing traders. But the Sortino ratio cannot be directly compared with the Sharpe ratio for reasons explained in the next section.

ADJUSTED SORTINO RATIO

Frequently, the fact that a manager has a higher Sortino ratio than Sharpe ratio is cited as evidence that returns are positively skewed—a tendency for larger deviations on the upside than on the downside. This type of comparison and inference is incorrect. The Sortino and Sharpe ratios cannot be directly compared. As formulated, the Sortino ratio will almost invariably be higher than the Sharpe ratio, *even for managers whose worst losses tend to be larger than their best gains.* The reason for the upward bias in the Sortino ratio (as compared with the Sharpe ratio) is that it calculates deviations for only a portion of returns—those returns below the MAR—but uses a divisor based on the number of *all* returns to calculate the downside deviation.

The *adjusted* Sortino ratio is equal to the Sortino ratio/$\sqrt{2}$. The reason for dividing by $\sqrt{2}$ is explained in the technical note below. I much prefer the adjusted Sortino ratio to the Sharpe ratio because it only penalizes downside volatility, whereas the risk measure of the Sharpe ratio doesn't distinguish between upside and downside volatility.

Technical Note: Since the loss measure in the Sortino ratio is based on summing a smaller number of deviations (i.e., only the deviations of losing returns), the Sortino ratio will invariably be higher than the Sharpe ratio. To allow for comparing the Sortino ratio to the Sharpe ratio, we multiply the risk measure of the Sortino ratio by the square root of 2 (which is equivalent to dividing the Sortino ratio by the square root of 2). Multiplying the risk measure of the Sortino ratio by the square root of 2 will equalize the risk measures of the Sharpe and Sortino ratios when upside and downside deviations are equal, which seems appropriate. The adjusted version of the Sortino ratio allows for direct comparisons of the Sharpe and Sortino ratios. Generally speaking, a higher adjusted Sortino ratio implies that the distribution of returns is right-skewed (a greater tendency for large gains than large losses). And, similarly, a lower adjusted Sortino ratio implies returns are left-skewed (a greater propensity for large losses than large gains).

GAIN TO PAIN RATIO

The Gain to Pain ratio (GPR) is the sum of all monthly returns divided by the absolute value of the sum of all monthly losses.* This performance measure indicates the ratio of cumulative *net* gain to the cumulative loss realized to achieve that gain. For example, a GPR of 1.0 would imply that, on average, an investor has to experience an equal amount of monthly losses to the net amount gained. If the average return per year is 12% (arithmetic not compounded), the average amount of monthly losses per year would also sum to 12%. The GPR penalizes all losses in proportion to their size, and upside volatility is beneficial since it impacts only the return portion of the ratio.

A key difference between the GPR and measures such as the Sharpe ratio and the Sortino ratio is that the GPR will be indifferent between five 2% losses and one 10% loss, whereas the other ratios discussed so far will be impacted far more by the single larger loss. This difference results because the standard deviation and downside deviation calculations used for the other ratios involve squaring the deviation between the reference return level (e.g., average, zero, risk-free) and the loss. For example, if the reference return is 0%, the squared deviation for one 10% loss would be five times greater than the squared deviation for five 2% losses ($10^2 = 100$; 5

---

* The Gain to Pain Ratio (GPR) is a performance statistic I have been using for many years. I am not aware of any prior use of this statistic, although the term is sometimes used as a generic reference for return/risk measures or a return/drawdown measure. The GPR is similar to the "profit factor," which is a commonly used statistic in evaluating trading systems. The profit factor is defined as the sum of all profitable trades divided by the absolute value of the sum of all losing trades. The profit factor is applied to trades, whereas the GPR is applied to interval (e.g., monthly) returns. Algebraically, it can easily be shown that if the profit factor calculation were applied to monthly returns, the profit factor would equal GPR+1 and would provide the same performance ordering as the GPR. For quantitatively oriented readers familiar with the Omega function, note that the Omega function evaluated at zero is also equal to GPR+1.

$\times 2^2 = 20$). In contrast, in the GPR calculation, both cases will add 10% to the denominator. I believe there is value in using both the adjusted Sortino ratio and the GPR in performance evaluation.

Although the GPR would typically be applied to monthly data, it can also be calculated for other time intervals. If daily data is available, the GPR can provide a statistically very significant measure because of the large amount of sample data. The longer the time frame, the higher the GPR, because many of the losses visible on a shorter time interval will be smoothed out over a longer period. In my experience, on average, monthly GPR values tend to be about six to seven times as large as the daily GPR for the same trader, although this multiple can vary widely among traders. For monthly data, roughly speaking, GPRs greater than 1.0 are very good, and those above 2.0 are excellent. For daily data, the corresponding numbers would be approximately 0.15 and 0.30.